THE NOBODY

VERTIGO

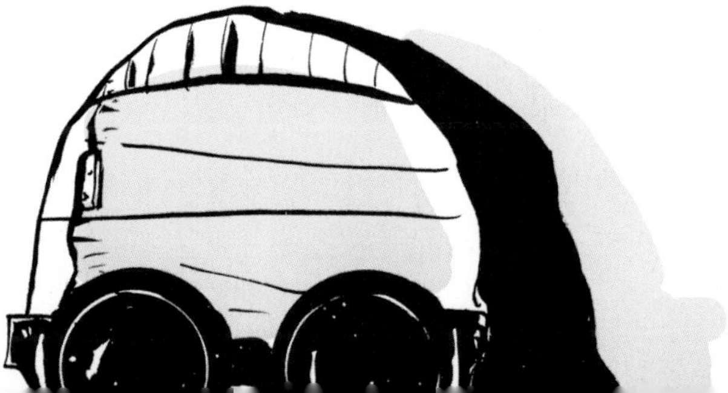

Written and Illustrated by JEFF LEMIRE

Letterers by SEAN KONOT

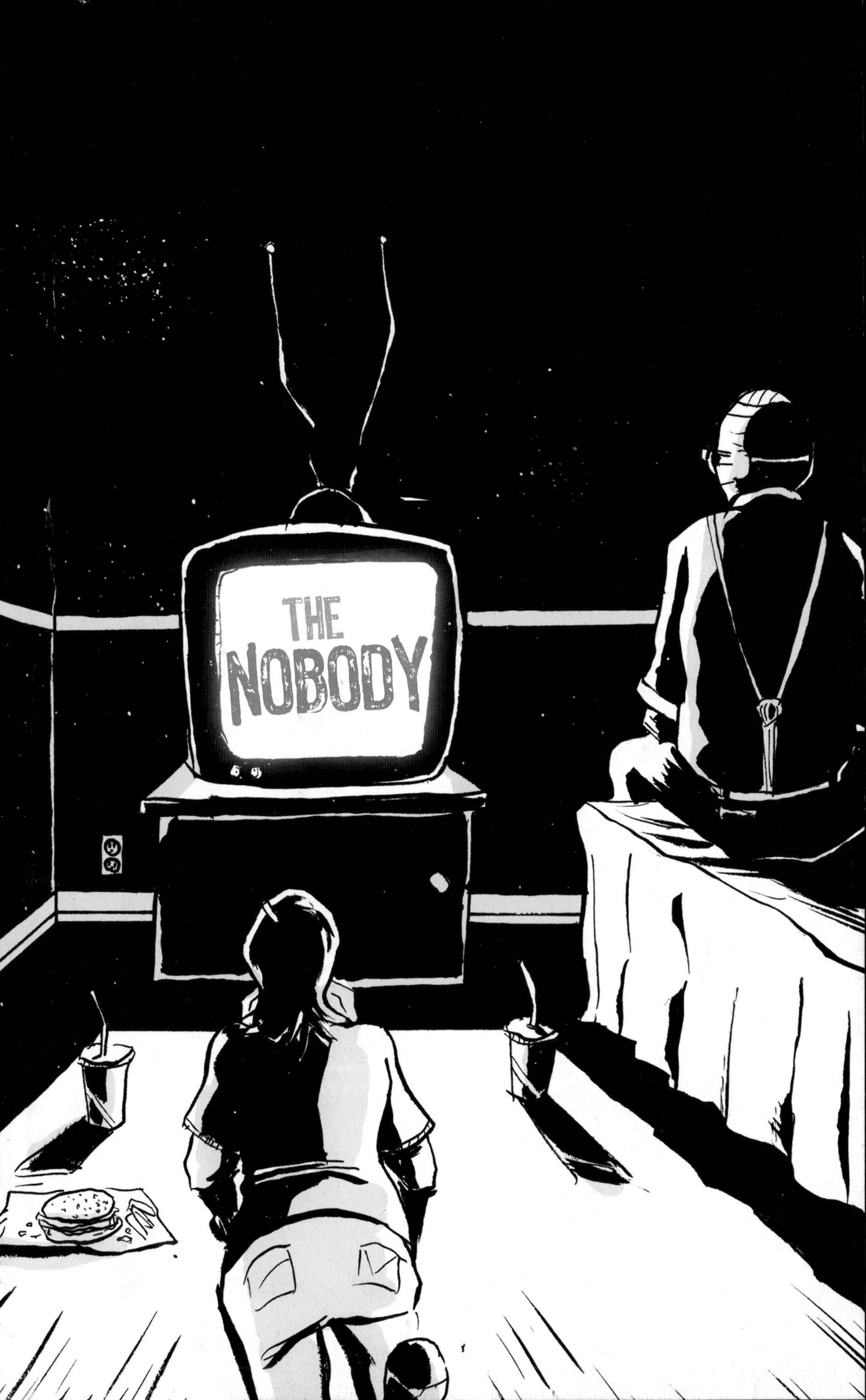
THE
NOBODY

Dedicated to Gus
Love, Dad.

Karen Berger Senior VP-Executive Editor   Bob Schreck Editor   Brandon Montclare Assistant Editor   Louis Prandi Art Director   Robbin Brosterman Design Director-Books
Paul Levitz President & Publisher   Georg Brewer VP-Design & DC Direct Creative   Richard Bruning Senior VP-Creative Director   Patrick Caldon Executive VP-Finance & Operations
Chris Caramalis VP-Finance   John Cunningham VP-Marketing   Terri Cunningham VP-Managing Editor   Amy Genkins Senior VP-Business & Legal Affairs   Alison Gill VP-Manufacturing
David Hyde VP-Publicity   Hank Kanalz VP-General Manager, WildStorm   Jim Lee Editorial Director-WildStorm   Gregory Noveck Senior VP-Creative Affairs   Sue Pohja VP-Book Trade Sales
Steve Rotterdam Senior VP-Sales & Marketing   Cheryl Rubin Senior VP-Brand Management   Alysse Soll VP-Advertising & Custom Publishing
Jeff Trojan VP-Business Development, DC Direct   Bob Wayne VP-Sales

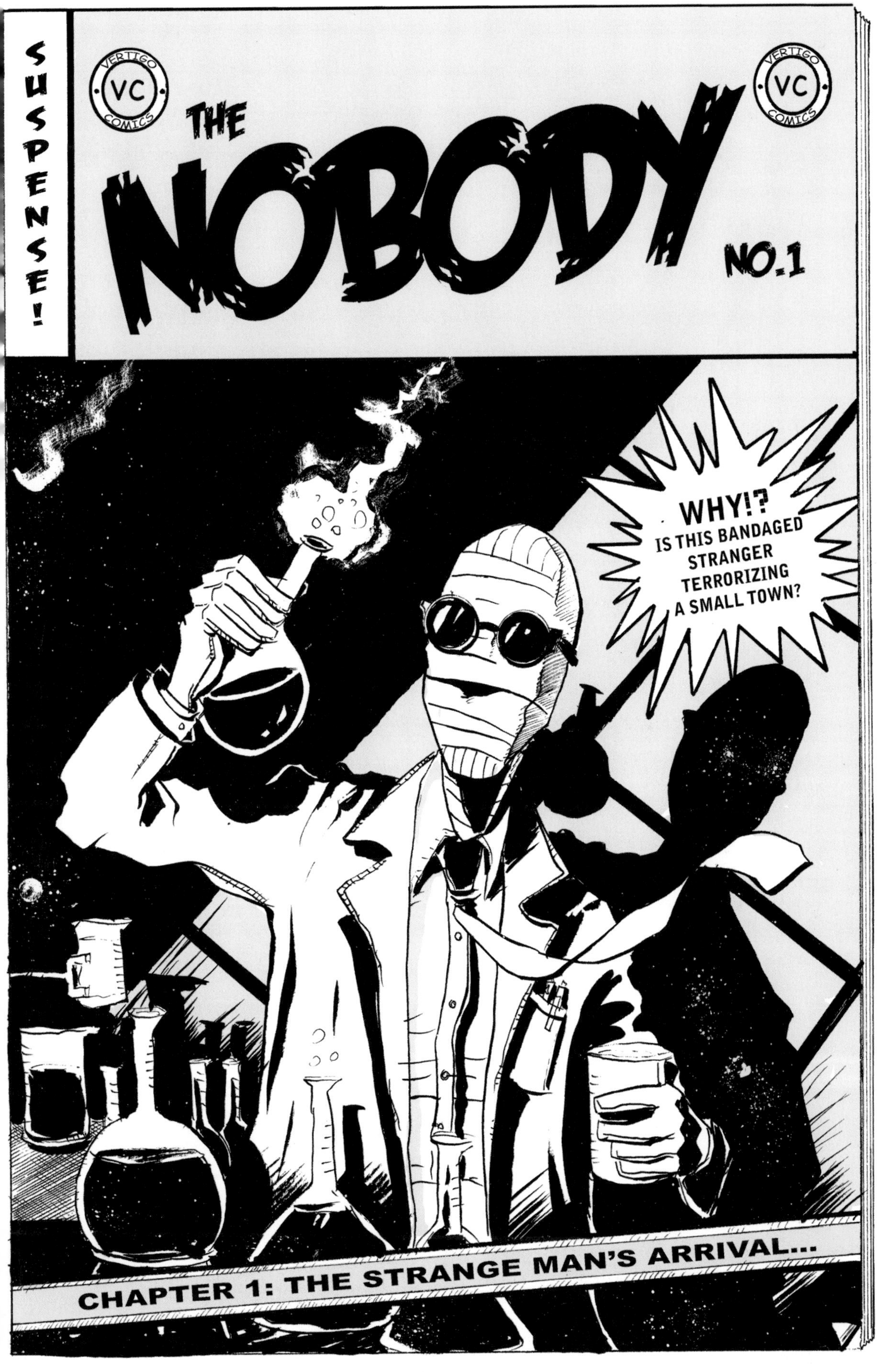
SUSPENSE!
VERTIGO VC COMICS
THE NOBODY
NO.1
WHY!? IS THIS BANDAGED STRANGER TERRORIZING A SMALL TOWN?
CHAPTER 1: THE STRANGE MAN'S ARRIVAL...

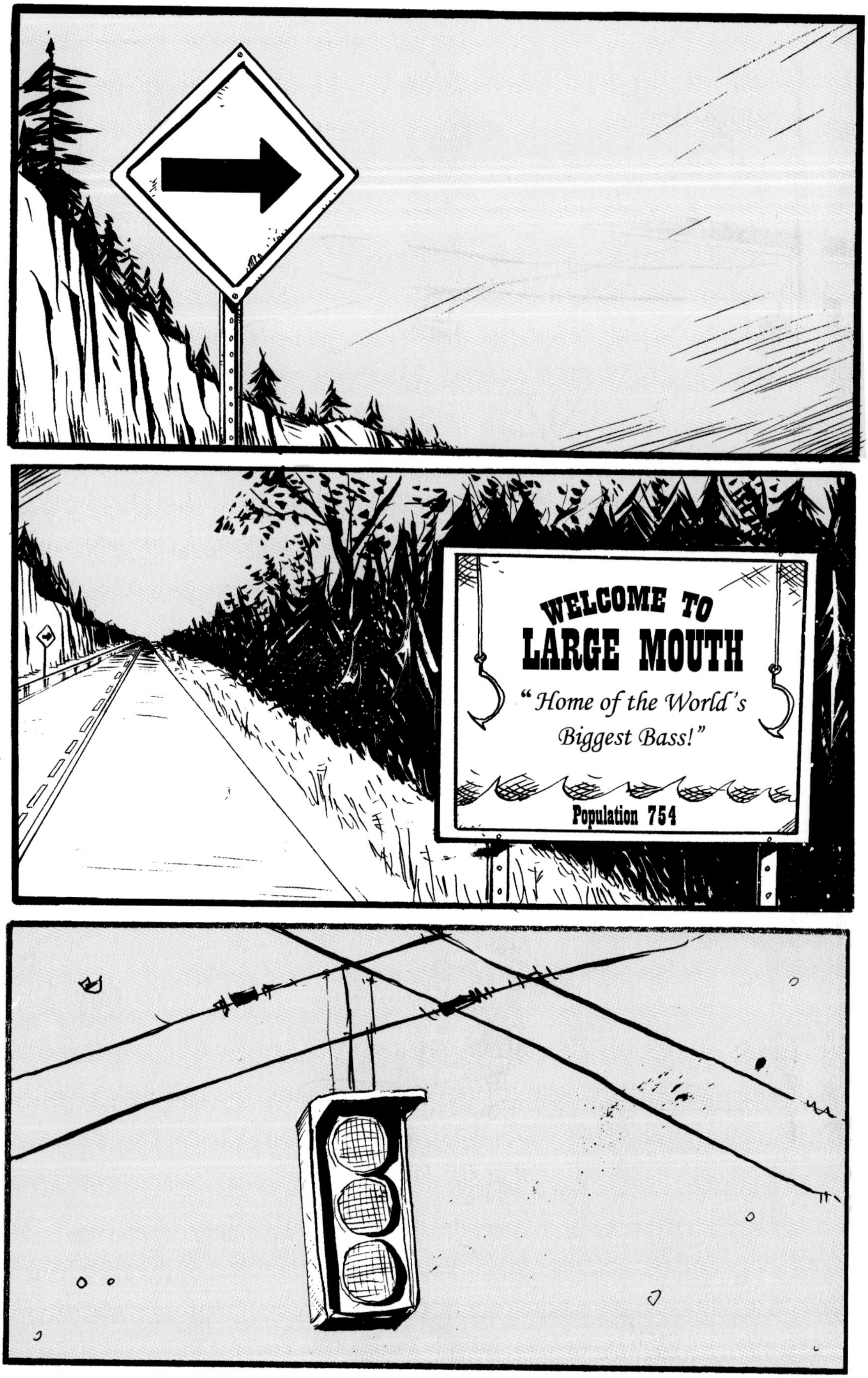
WELCOME TO
LARGE MOUTH
"Home of the World's
Biggest Bass!"
Population 754

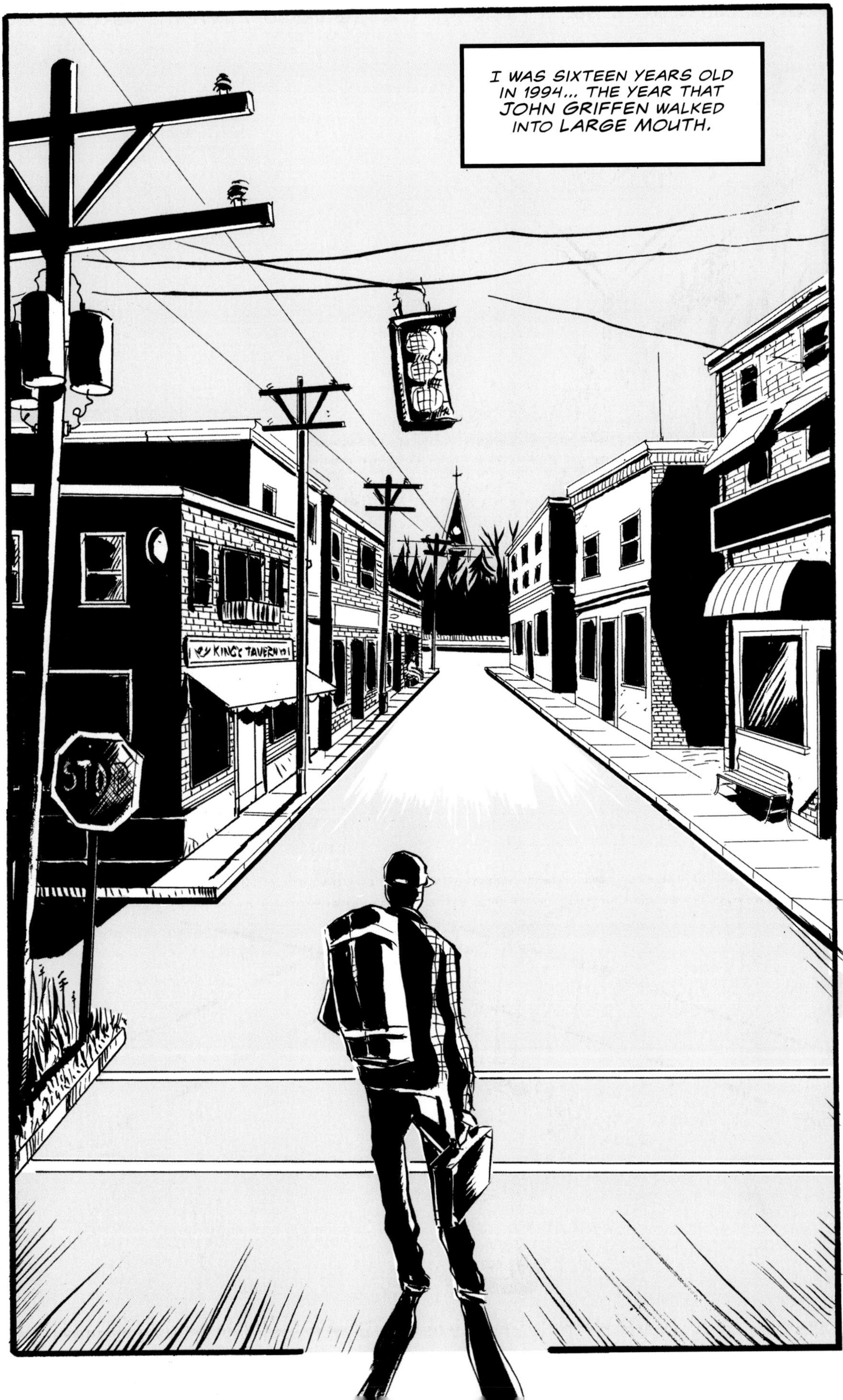
I WAS SIXTEEN YEARS OLD IN 1994... THE YEAR THAT JOHN GRIFFEN WALKED INTO LARGE MOUTH.
KING'S TAVERN
STOP

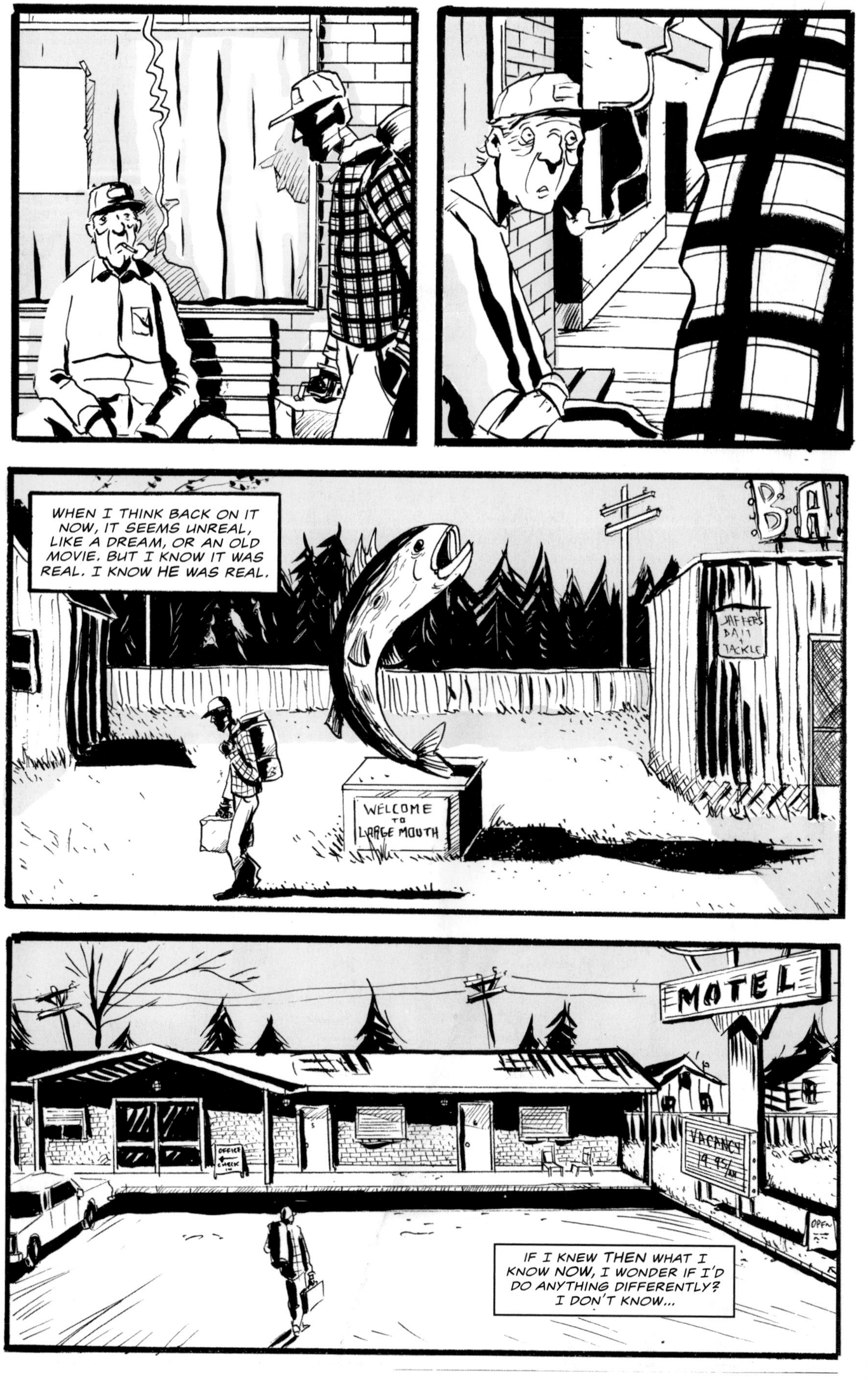
WHEN I THINK BACK ON IT NOW, IT SEEMS UNREAL, LIKE A DREAM, OR AN OLD MOVIE. BUT I KNOW IT WAS REAL. I KNOW HE WAS REAL.
JAFFER'S BAIT + TACKLE
WELCOME TO LARGE MOUTH
MOTEL
VACANCY
IF I KNEW THEN WHAT I KNOW NOW, I WONDER IF I'D DO ANYTHING DIFFERENTLY? I DON'T KNOW...

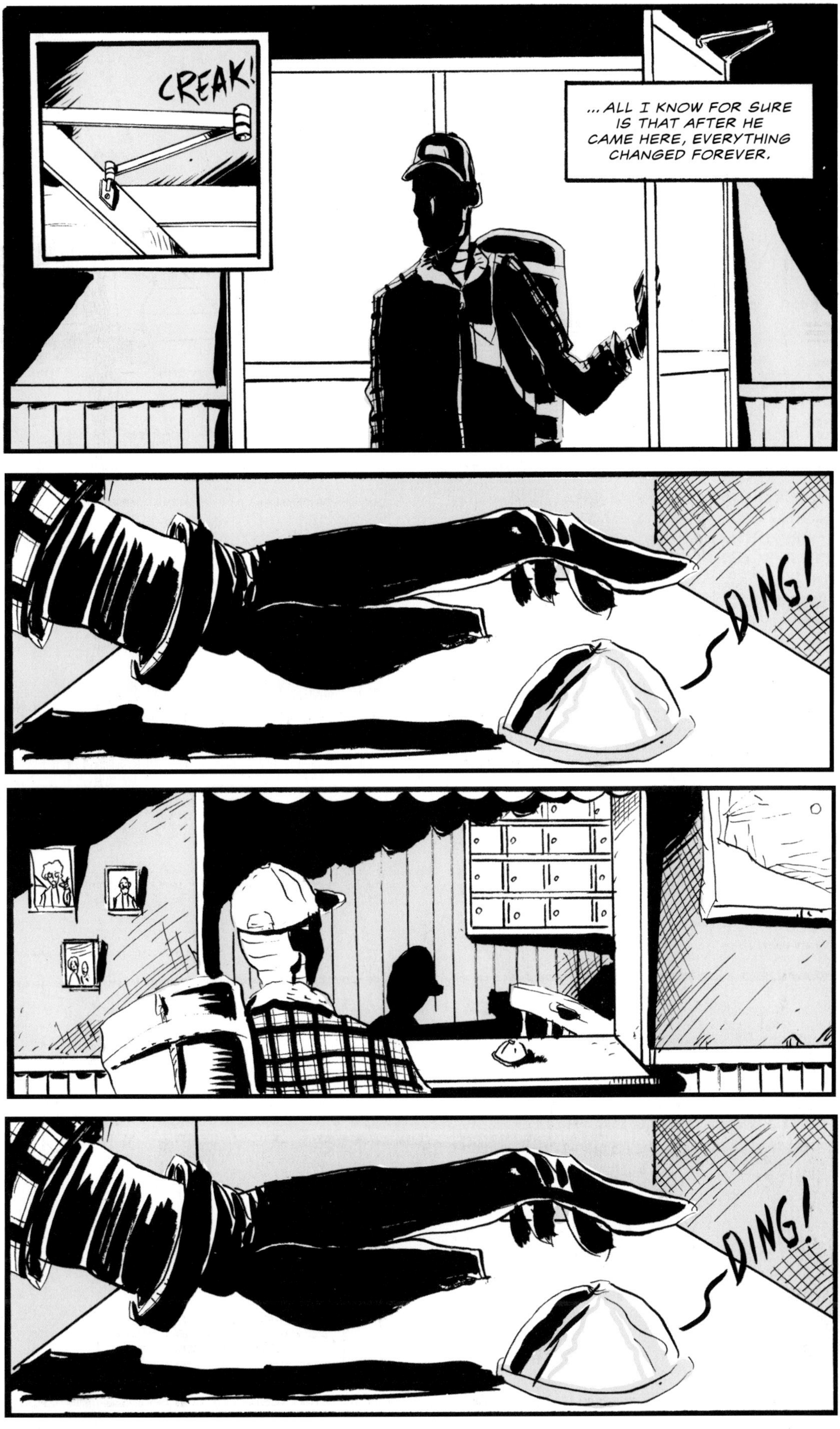
CREAK!
...ALL I KNOW FOR SURE IS THAT AFTER HE CAME HERE, EVERYTHING CHANGED FOREVER.
DING!
DING!

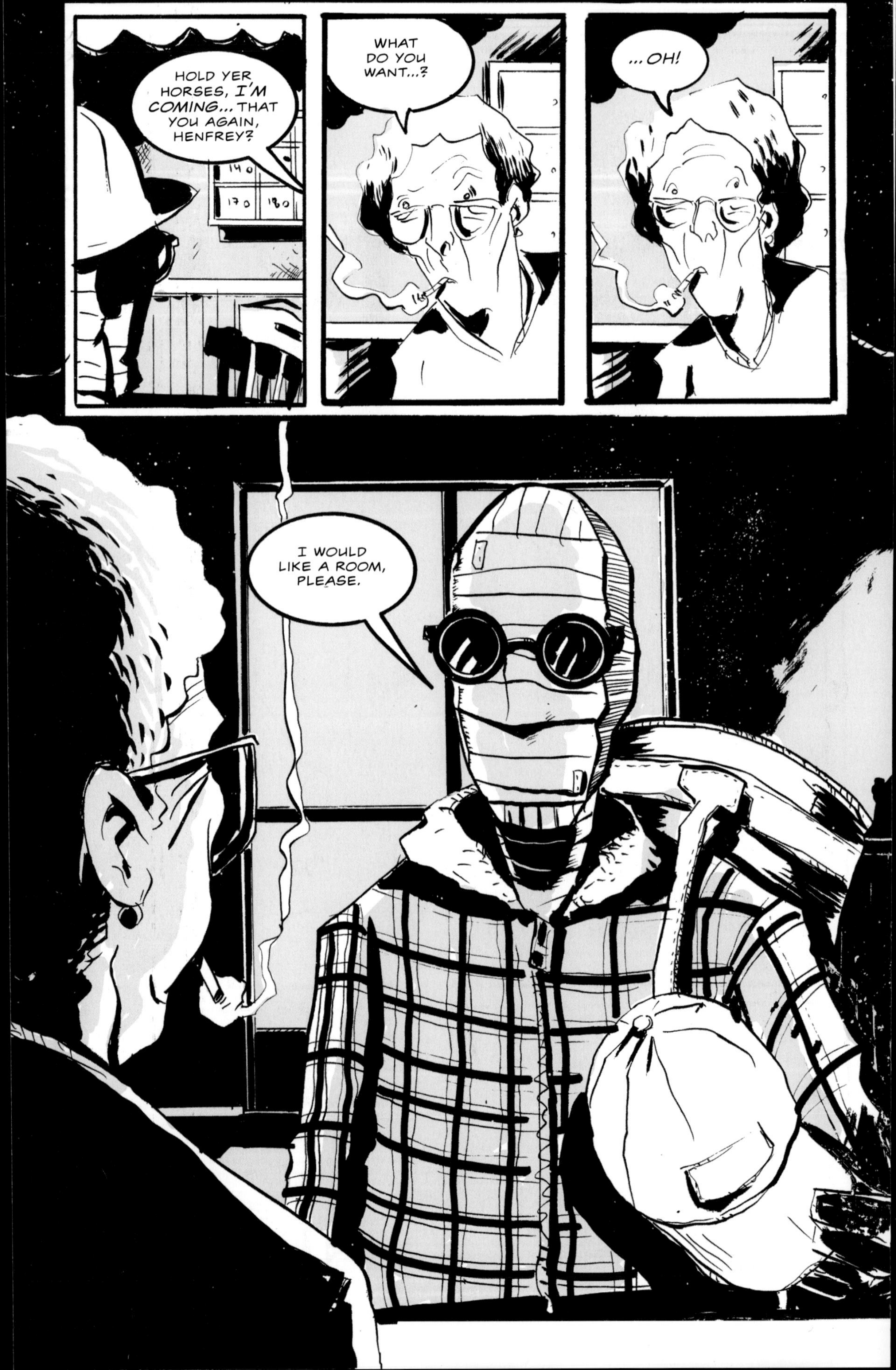
HOLD YER HORSES, I'M COMING... THAT YOU AGAIN, HENFREY?
WHAT DO YOU WANT...?
...OH!
I WOULD LIKE A ROOM, PLEASE.

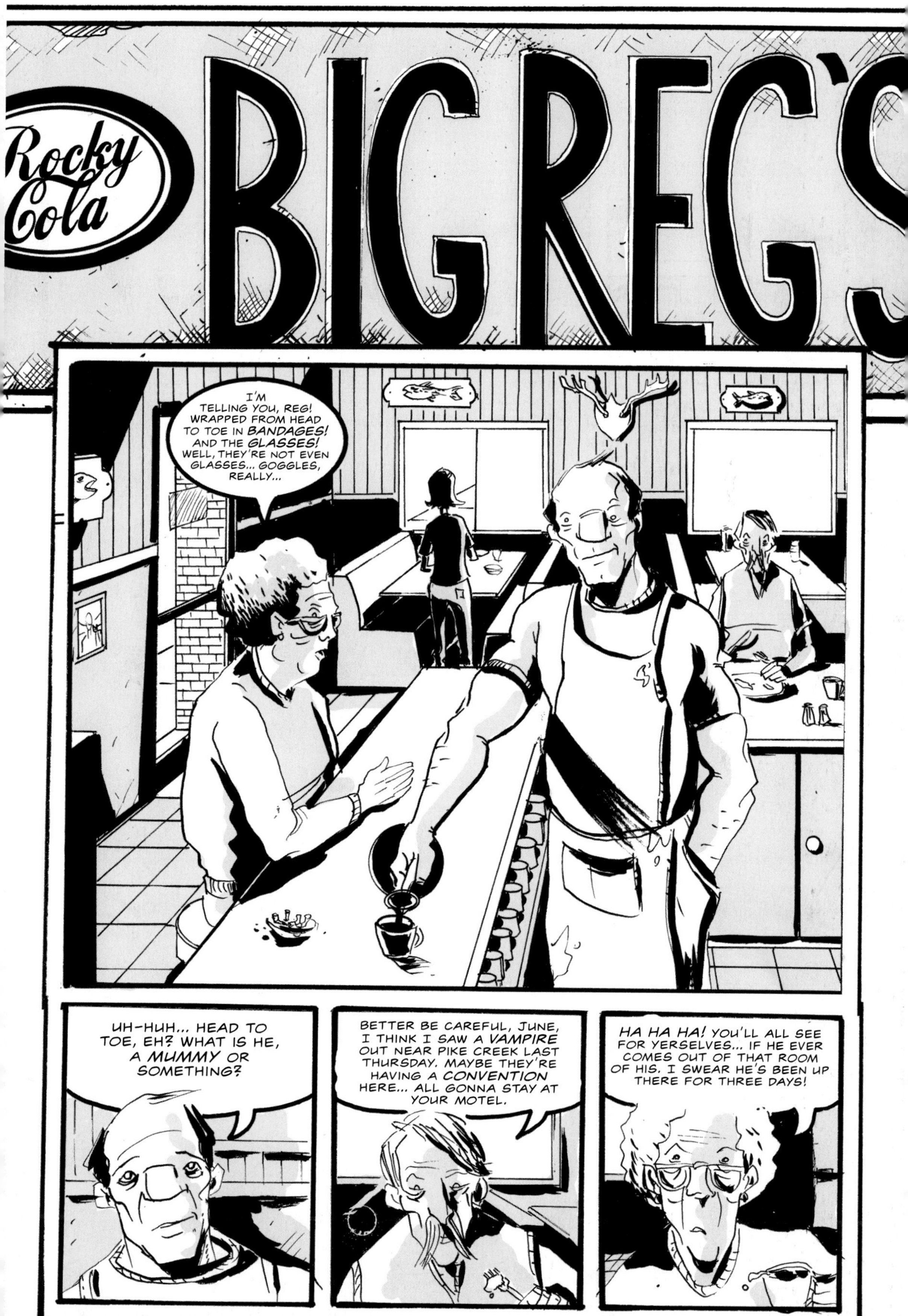
Rocky Cola
BIG REG'S
I'M TELLING YOU, REG! WRAPPED FROM HEAD TO TOE IN BANDAGES! AND THE GLASSES! WELL, THEY'RE NOT EVEN GLASSES... GOGGLES, REALLY...
UH-HUH... HEAD TO TOE, EH? WHAT IS HE, A MUMMY OR SOMETHING?
BETTER BE CAREFUL, JUNE, I THINK I SAW A VAMPIRE OUT NEAR PIKE CREEK LAST THURSDAY. MAYBE THEY'RE HAVING A CONVENTION HERE... ALL GONNA STAY AT YOUR MOTEL.
HA HA HA! YOU'LL ALL SEE FOR YERSELVES... IF HE EVER COMES OUT OF THAT ROOM OF HIS. I SWEAR HE'S BEEN UP THERE FOR THREE DAYS!

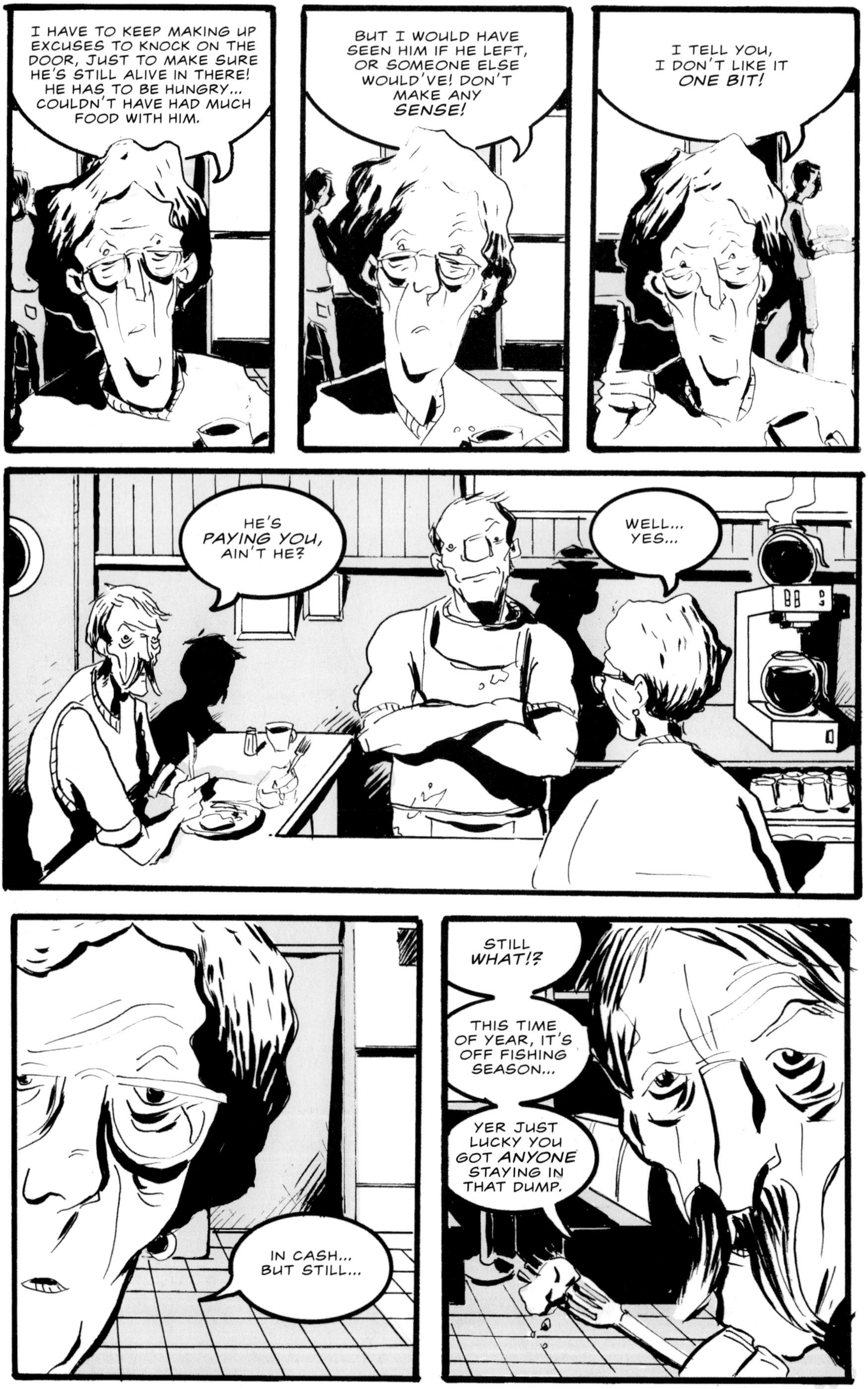
I HAVE TO KEEP MAKING UP EXCUSES TO KNOCK ON THE DOOR, JUST TO MAKE SURE HE'S STILL ALIVE IN THERE! HE HAS TO BE HUNGRY... COULDN'T HAVE HAD MUCH FOOD WITH HIM.
BUT I WOULD HAVE SEEN HIM IF HE LEFT, OR SOMEONE ELSE WOULD'VE! DON'T MAKE ANY *SENSE!*
I TELL YOU, I DON'T LIKE IT *ONE BIT!*
HE'S *PAYING YOU,* AIN'T HE?
WELL... YES...
IN CASH... BUT STILL...
STILL *WHAT!?*
THIS TIME OF YEAR, IT'S OFF FISHING SEASON...
YER JUST LUCKY YOU GOT *ANYONE* STAYING IN THAT DUMP.

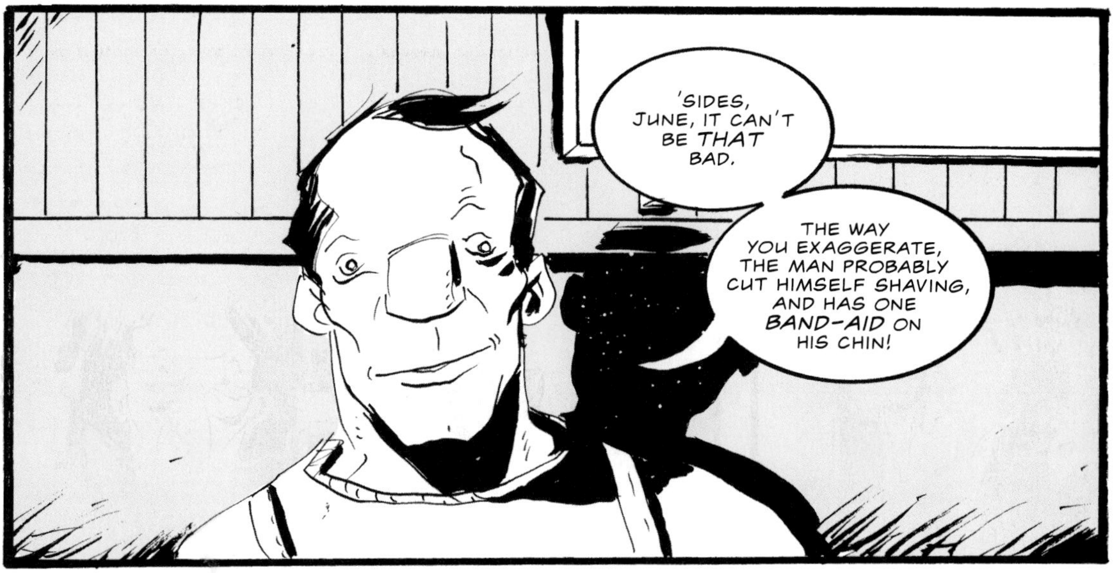
'SIDES, JUNE, IT CAN'T BE THAT BAD.
THE WAY YOU EXAGGERATE, THE MAN PROBABLY CUT HIMSELF SHAVING, AND HAS ONE BAND-AID ON HIS CHIN!

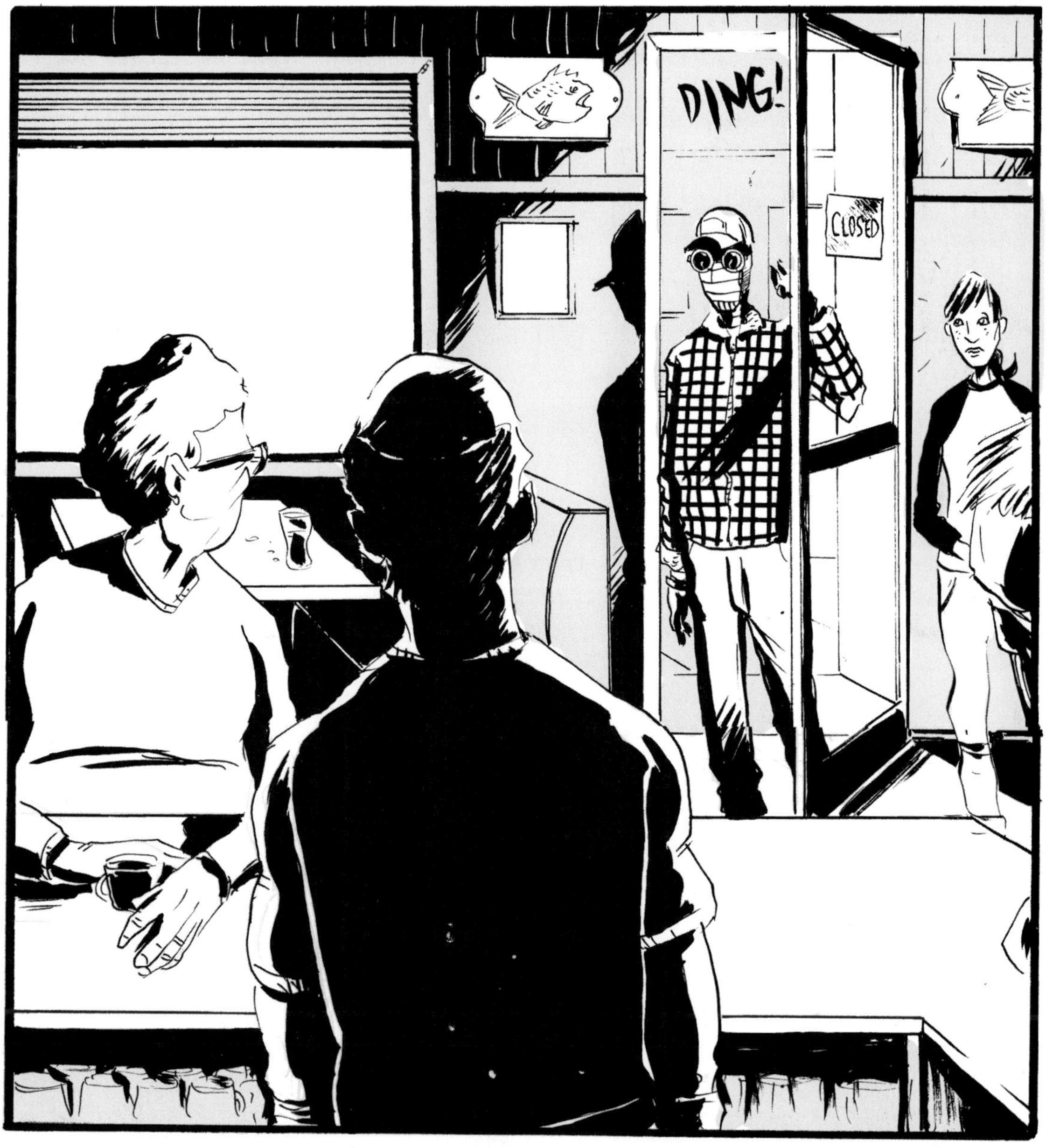
DING!
CLOSED

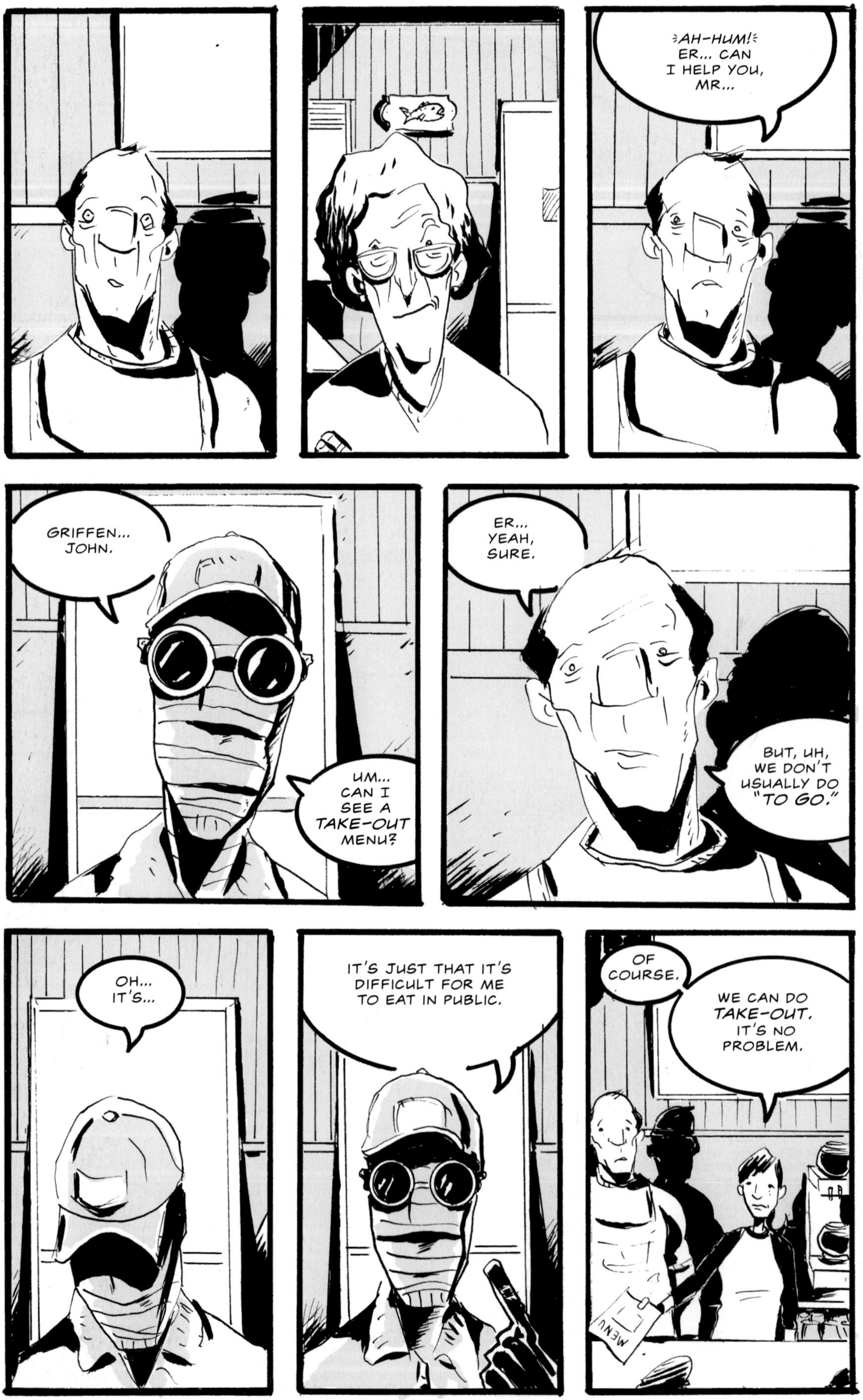
AH-HUM! ER... CAN I HELP YOU, MR...
GRIFFEN... JOHN.
UM... CAN I SEE A TAKE-OUT MENU?
ER... YEAH, SURE.
BUT, UH, WE DON'T USUALLY DO "TO GO."
OH... IT'S...
IT'S JUST THAT IT'S DIFFICULT FOR ME TO EAT IN PUBLIC.
OF COURSE.
WE CAN DO TAKE-OUT. IT'S NO PROBLEM.
MENU

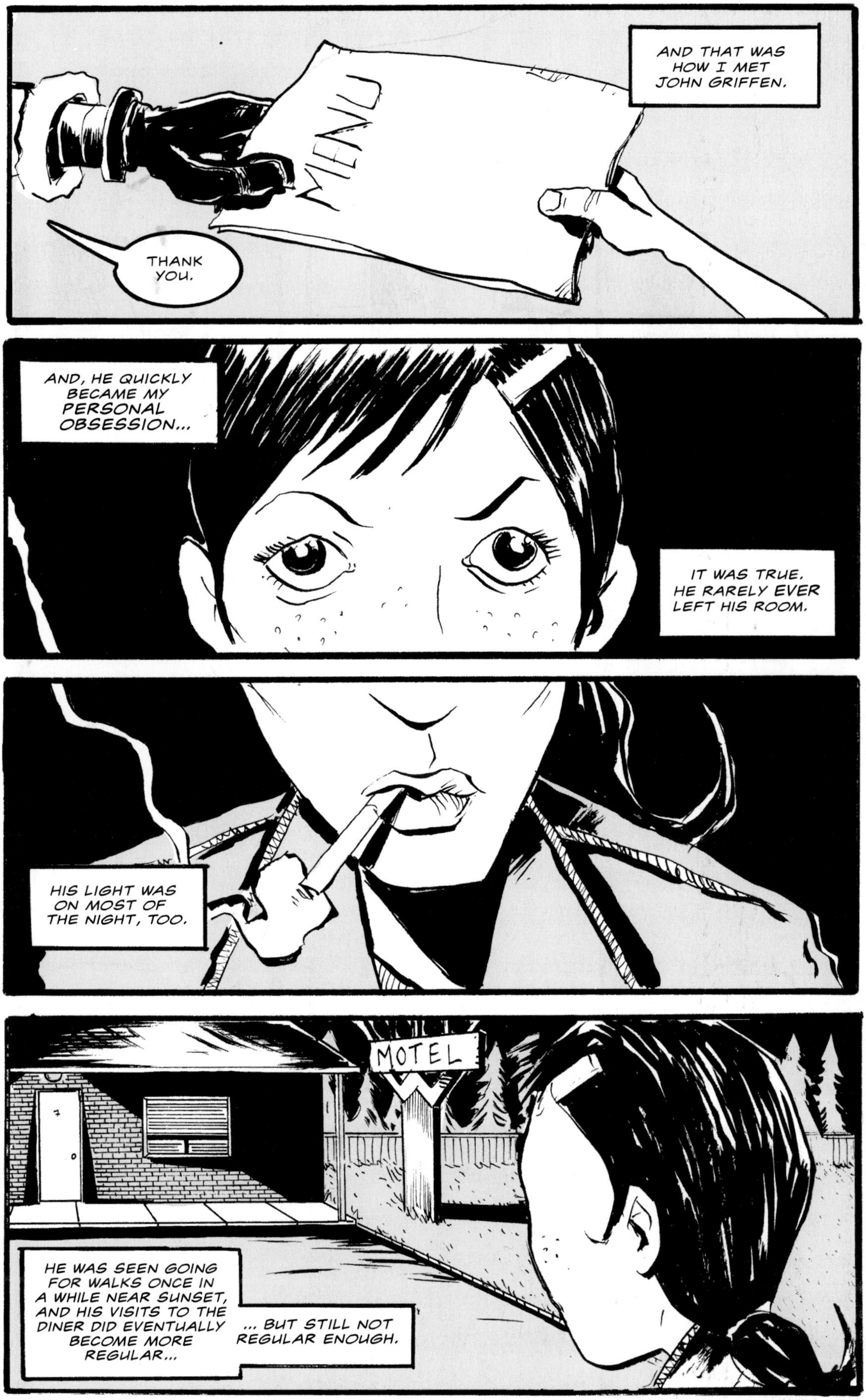
AND THAT WAS HOW I MET JOHN GRIFFEN.
MENU
THANK YOU.
AND, HE QUICKLY BECAME MY PERSONAL OBSESSION...
IT WAS TRUE. HE RARELY EVER LEFT HIS ROOM.
HIS LIGHT WAS ON MOST OF THE NIGHT, TOO.
MOTEL
HE WAS SEEN GOING FOR WALKS ONCE IN A WHILE NEAR SUNSET, AND HIS VISITS TO THE DINER DID EVENTUALLY BECOME MORE REGULAR...
... BUT STILL NOT REGULAR ENOUGH.

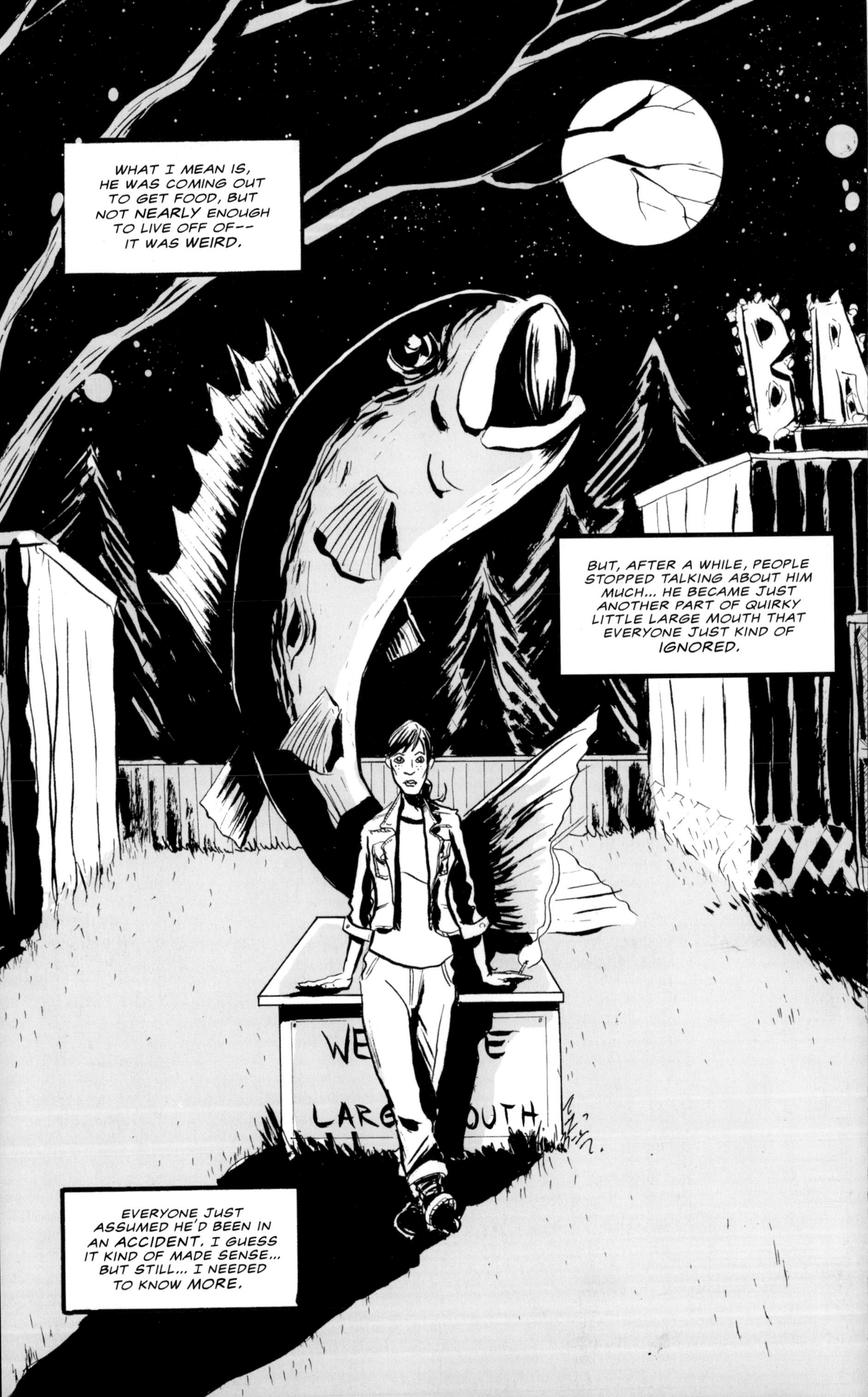
WHAT I MEAN IS, HE WAS COMING OUT TO GET FOOD, BUT NOT NEARLY ENOUGH TO LIVE OFF OF-- IT WAS WEIRD.
BUT, AFTER A WHILE, PEOPLE STOPPED TALKING ABOUT HIM MUCH... HE BECAME JUST ANOTHER PART OF QUIRKY LITTLE LARGE MOUTH THAT EVERYONE JUST KIND OF IGNORED.
EVERYONE JUST ASSUMED HE'D BEEN IN AN ACCIDENT. I GUESS IT KIND OF MADE SENSE... BUT STILL... I NEEDED TO KNOW MORE.

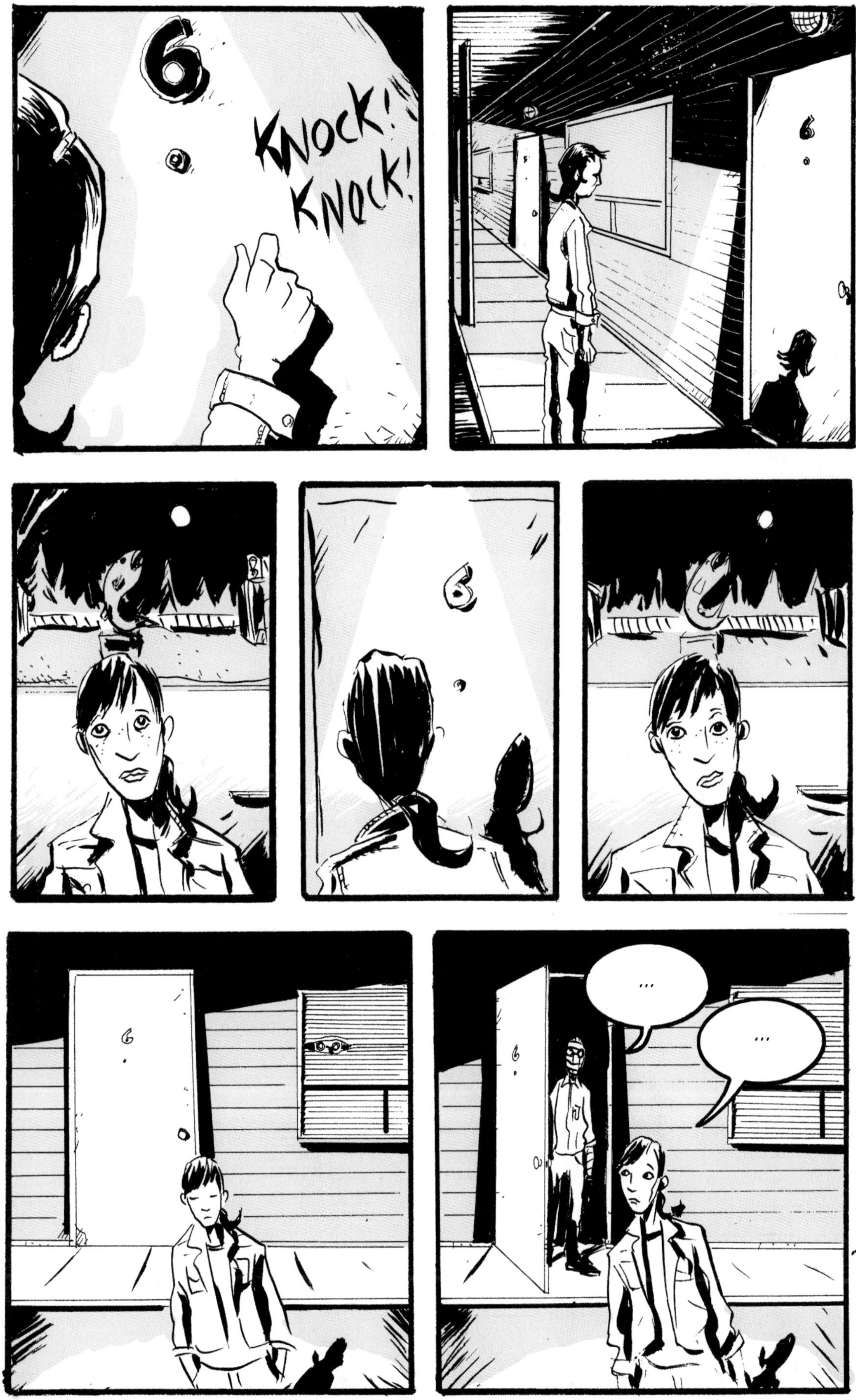
KNOCK! KNOCK!
...
...

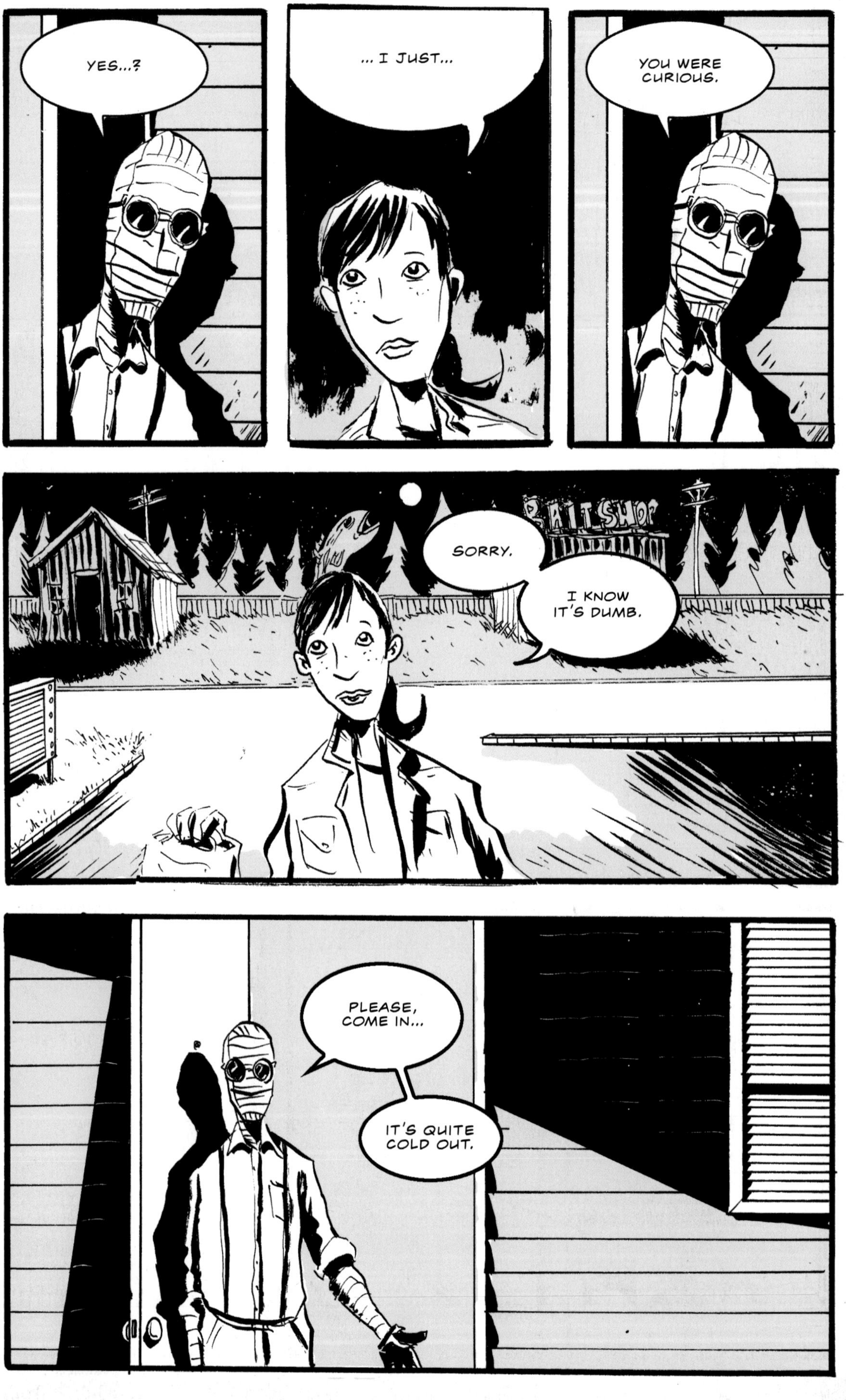
YES...?
... I JUST...
YOU WERE CURIOUS.
BAIT SHOP
SORRY.
I KNOW IT'S DUMB.
PLEASE, COME IN...
IT'S QUITE COLD OUT.

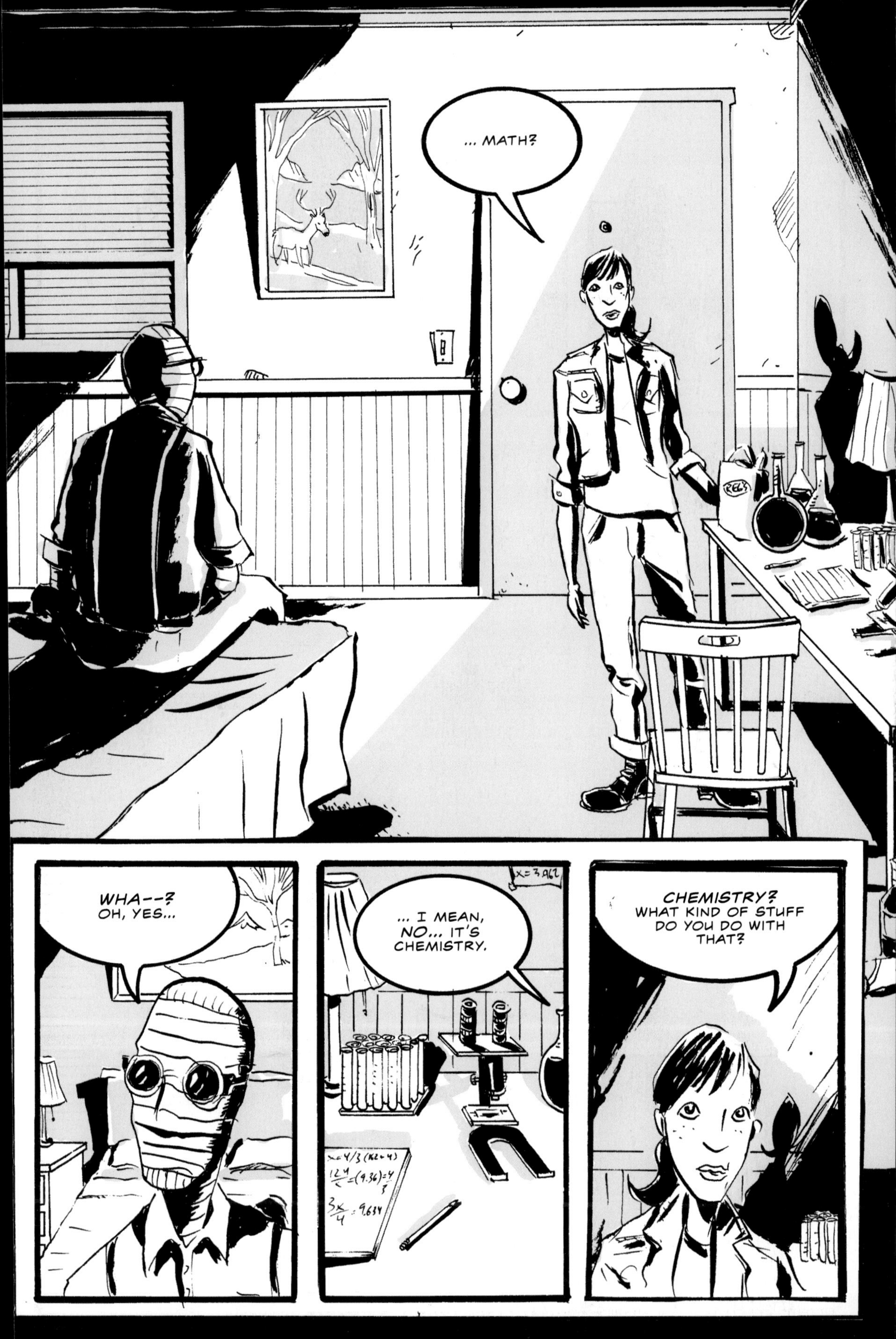
... MATH?
WHA--? OH, YES...
... I MEAN, NO... IT'S CHEMISTRY.
CHEMISTRY? WHAT KIND OF STUFF DO YOU DO WITH THAT?

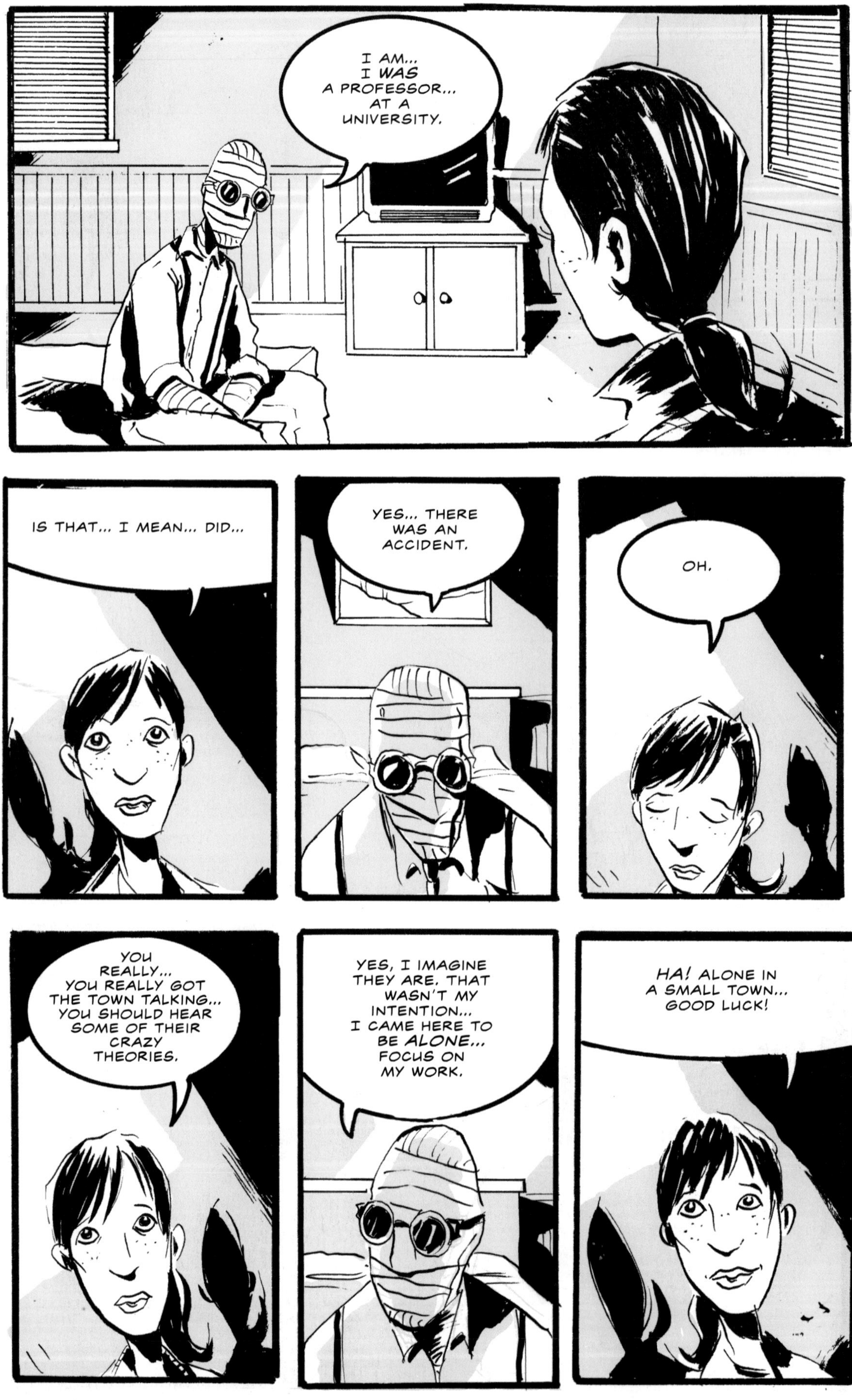
I AM... I *WAS* A PROFESSOR... AT A UNIVERSITY.
IS THAT... I MEAN... DID...
YES... THERE WAS AN ACCIDENT.
OH.
YOU REALLY... YOU REALLY GOT THE TOWN TALKING... YOU SHOULD HEAR SOME OF THEIR CRAZY THEORIES.
YES, I IMAGINE THEY ARE. THAT WASN'T MY INTENTION... I CAME HERE TO BE *ALONE*... FOCUS ON MY WORK.
HA! ALONE IN A SMALL TOWN... GOOD LUCK!

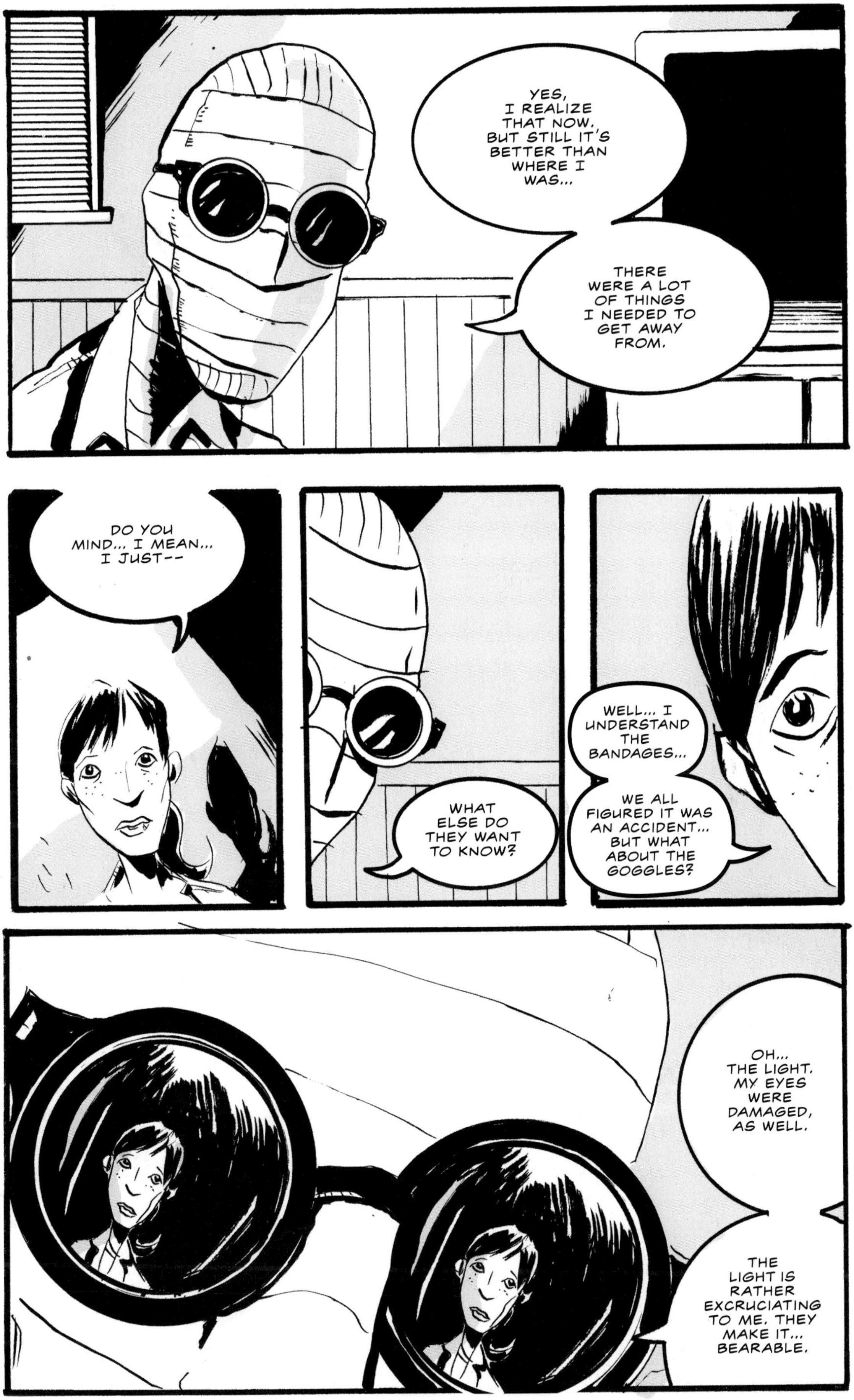
YES, I REALIZE THAT NOW. BUT STILL IT'S BETTER THAN WHERE I WAS...
THERE WERE A LOT OF THINGS I NEEDED TO GET AWAY FROM.
DO YOU MIND... I MEAN... I JUST--
WHAT ELSE DO THEY WANT TO KNOW?
WELL... I UNDERSTAND THE BANDAGES...
WE ALL FIGURED IT WAS AN ACCIDENT... BUT WHAT ABOUT THE GOGGLES?
OH... THE LIGHT. MY EYES WERE DAMAGED, AS WELL.
THE LIGHT IS RATHER EXCRUCIATING TO ME. THEY MAKE IT... BEARABLE.

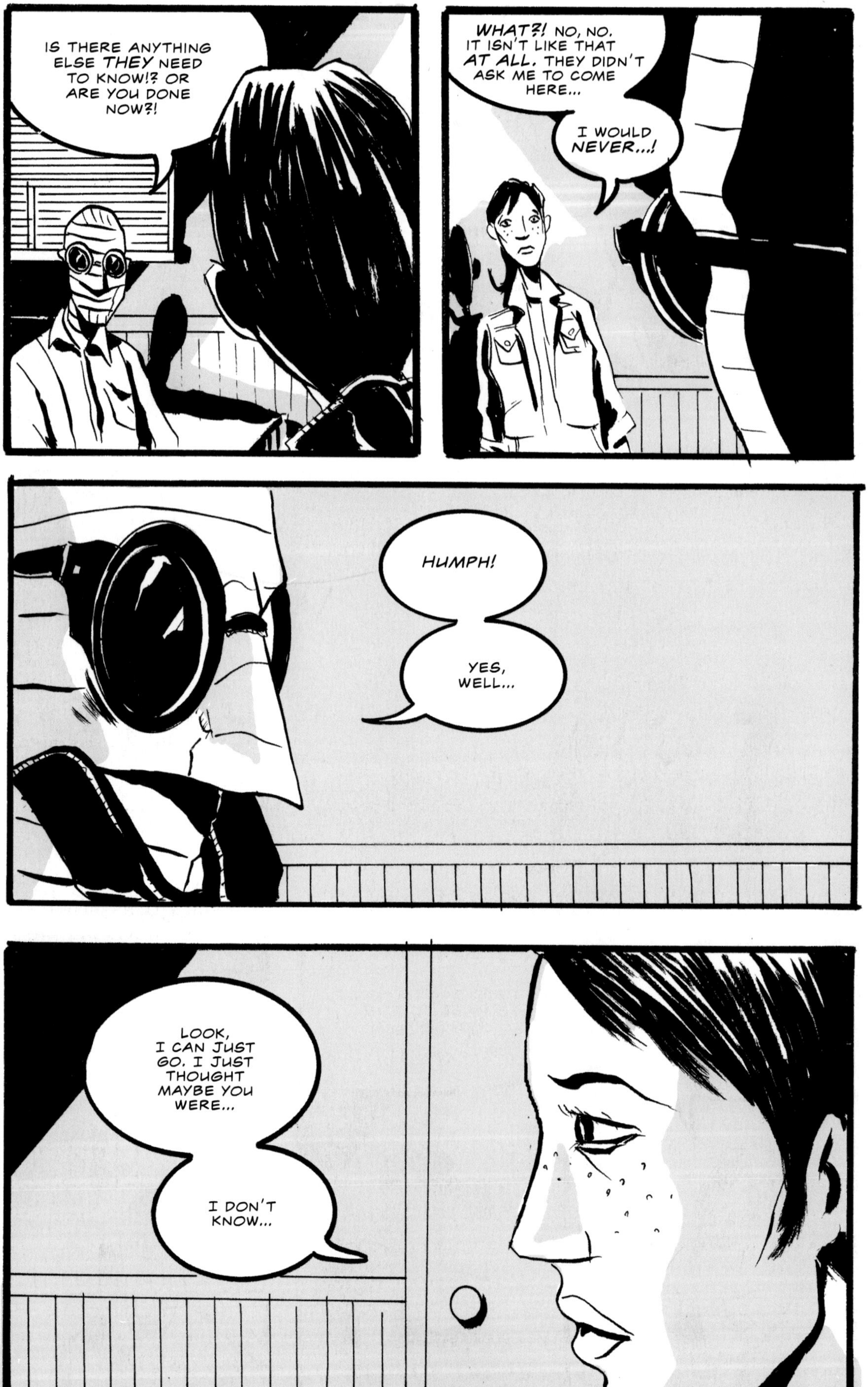
IS THERE ANYTHING ELSE THEY NEED TO KNOW!? OR ARE YOU DONE NOW?!
WHAT?! NO, NO. IT ISN'T LIKE THAT AT ALL. THEY DIDN'T ASK ME TO COME HERE...
I WOULD NEVER...!
HUMPH!
YES, WELL...
LOOK, I CAN JUST GO. I JUST THOUGHT MAYBE YOU WERE...
I DON'T KNOW...

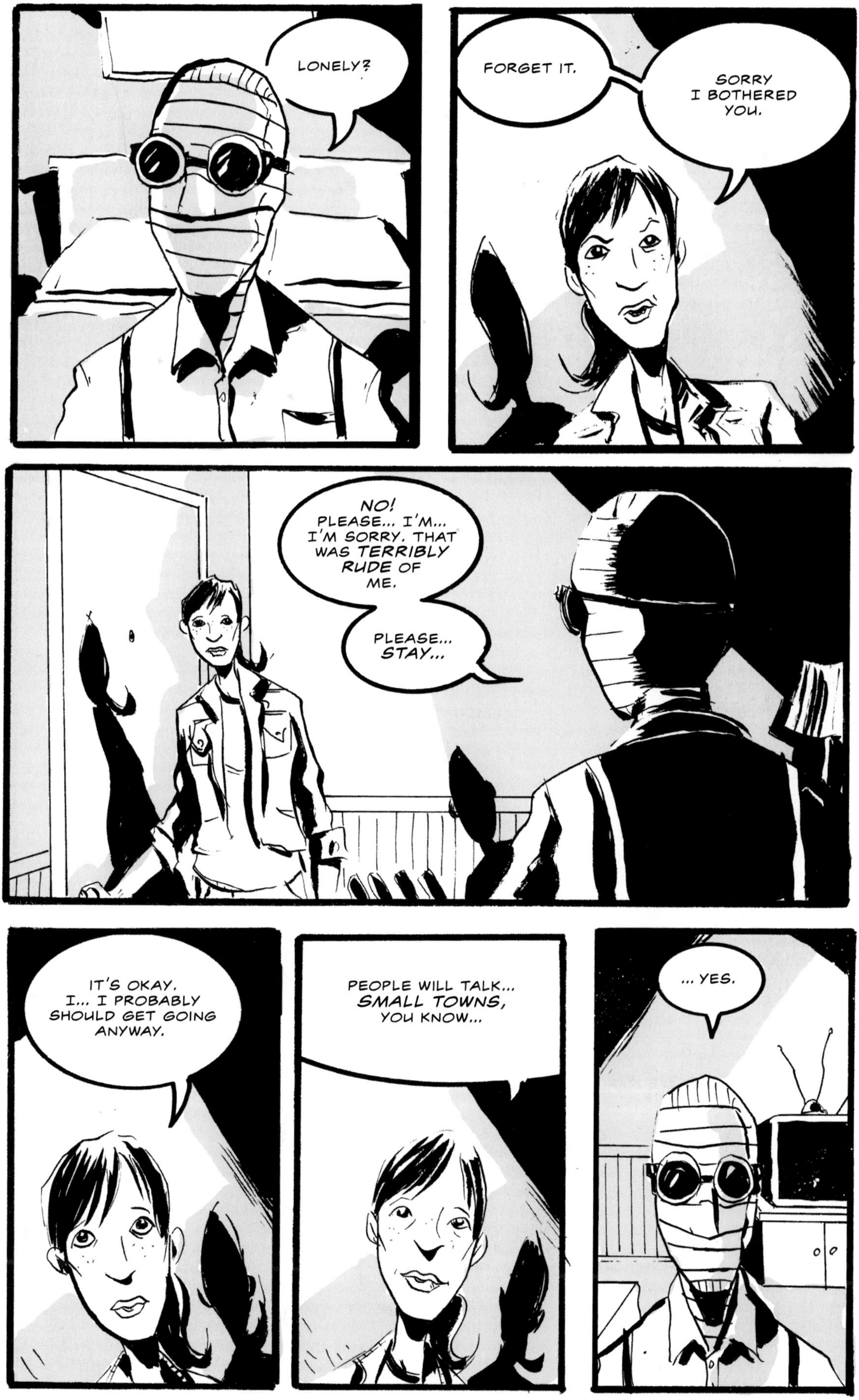
LONELY?
FORGET IT.
SORRY I BOTHERED YOU.
NO! PLEASE... I'M... I'M SORRY. THAT WAS TERRIBLY RUDE OF ME.
PLEASE... STAY...
IT'S OKAY. I... I PROBABLY SHOULD GET GOING ANYWAY.
PEOPLE WILL TALK... SMALL TOWNS, YOU KNOW...
...YES.

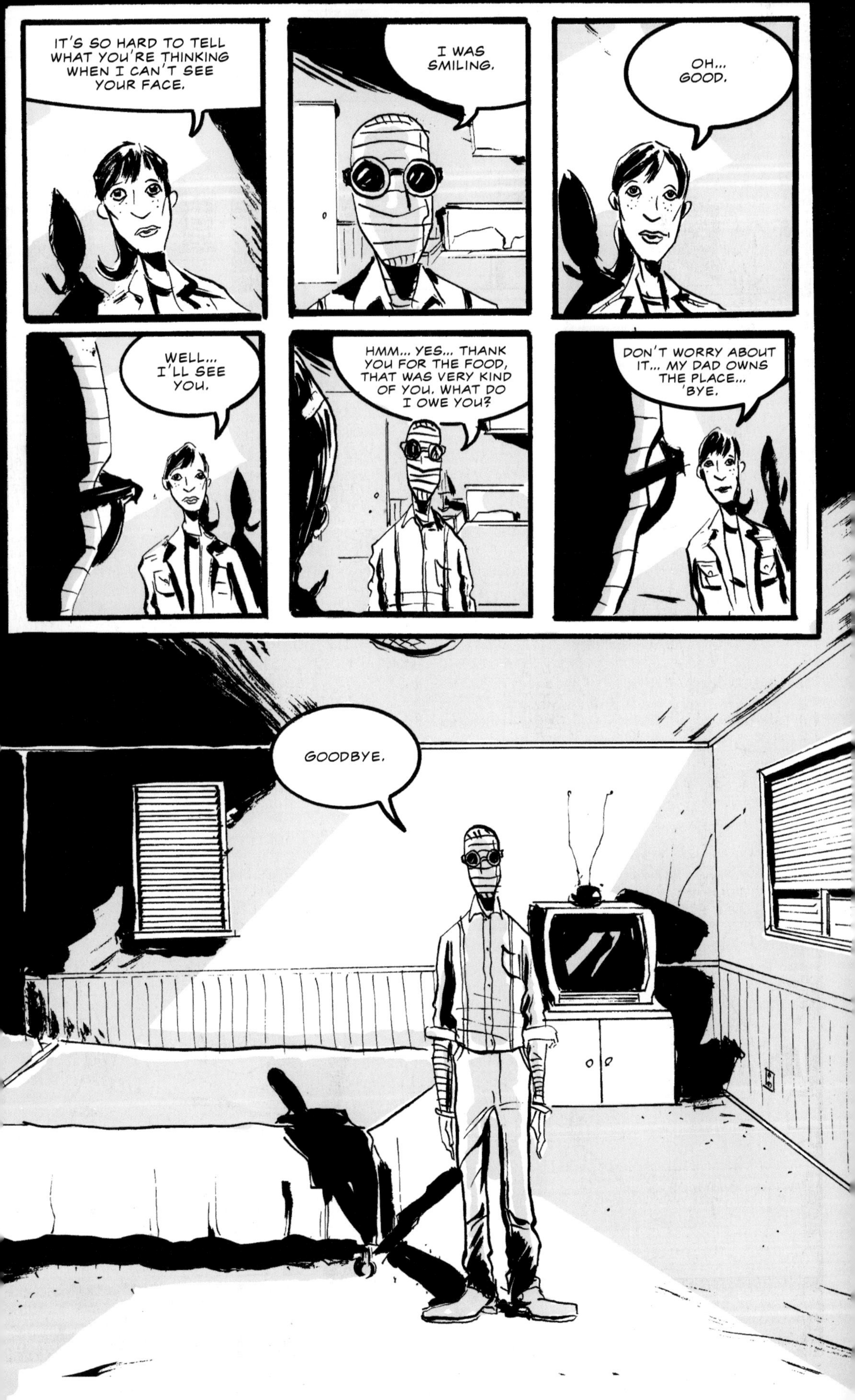
IT'S SO HARD TO TELL WHAT YOU'RE THINKING WHEN I CAN'T SEE YOUR FACE.
I WAS SMILING.
OH... GOOD.
WELL... I'LL SEE YOU.
HMM... YES... THANK YOU FOR THE FOOD, THAT WAS VERY KIND OF YOU. WHAT DO I OWE YOU?
DON'T WORRY ABOUT IT... MY DAD OWNS THE PLACE... 'BYE.
GOODBYE.

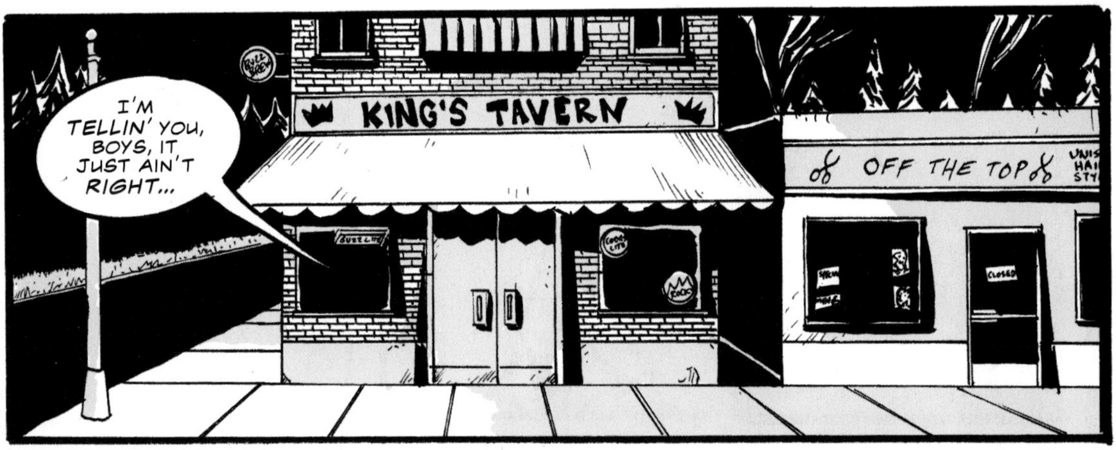
KING'S TAVERN
OFF THE TOP
I'M *TELLIN'* YOU, BOYS, IT JUST AIN'T *RIGHT*...

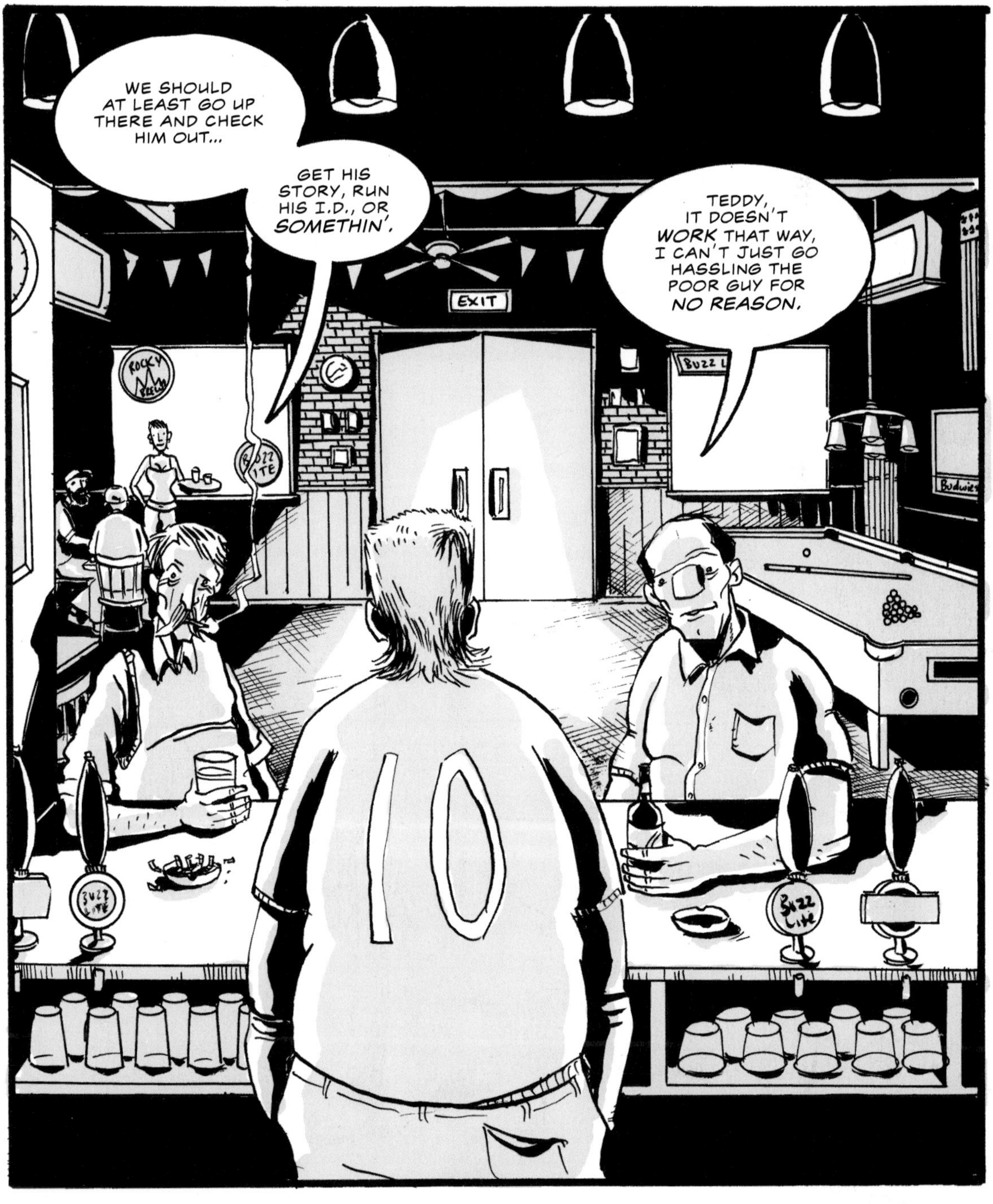
WE SHOULD AT LEAST GO UP THERE AND CHECK HIM OUT...
GET HIS STORY, RUN HIS I.D., OR *SOMETHIN'*.
EXIT
TEDDY, IT DOESN'T *WORK* THAT WAY, I CAN'T JUST GO HASSLING THE POOR GUY FOR *NO REASON*.

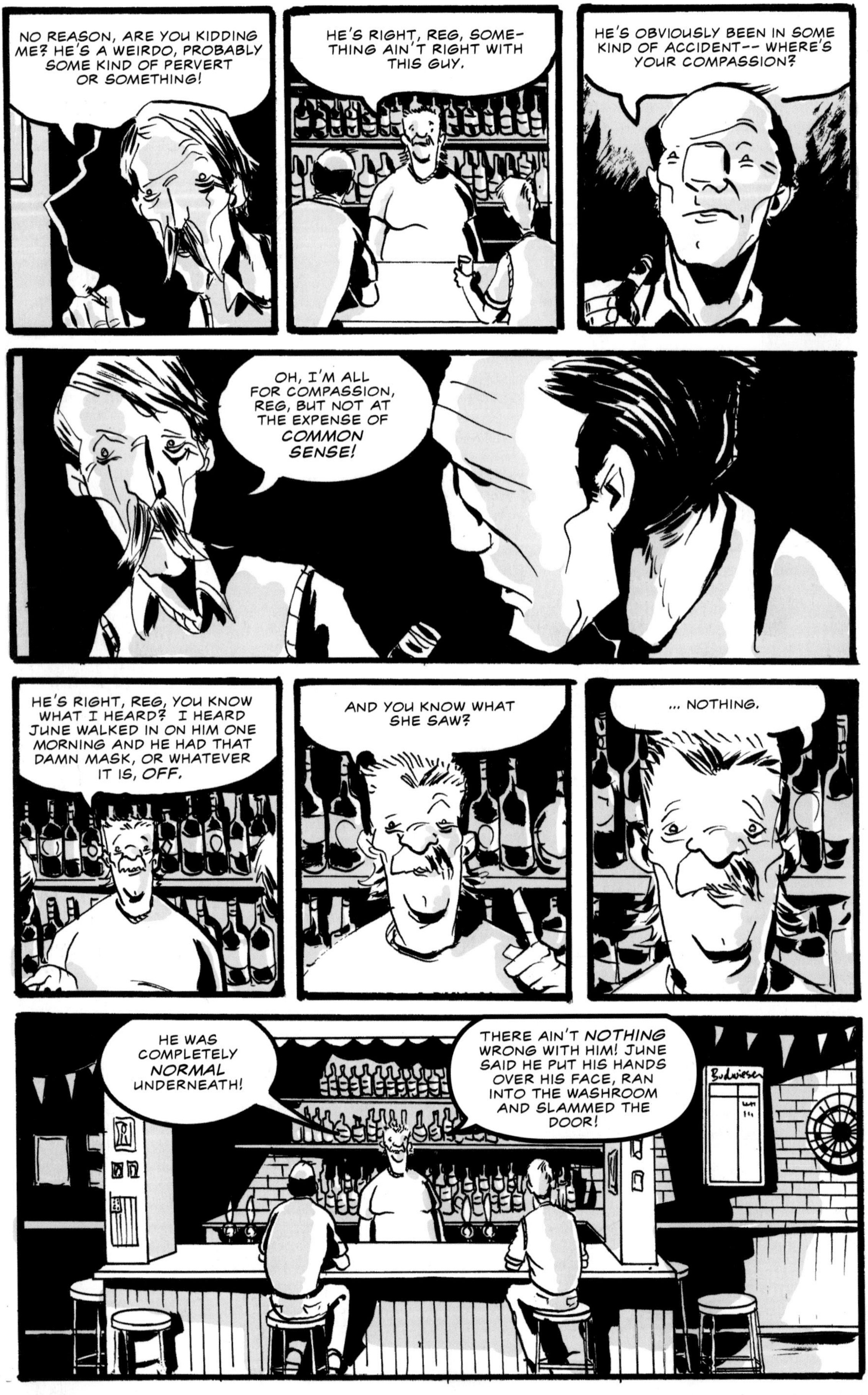
NO REASON, ARE YOU KIDDING ME? HE'S A WEIRDO, PROBABLY SOME KIND OF PERVERT OR SOMETHING!
HE'S RIGHT, REG, SOMETHING AIN'T RIGHT WITH THIS GUY.
HE'S OBVIOUSLY BEEN IN SOME KIND OF ACCIDENT-- WHERE'S YOUR COMPASSION?
OH, I'M ALL FOR COMPASSION, REG, BUT NOT AT THE EXPENSE OF COMMON SENSE!
HE'S RIGHT, REG, YOU KNOW WHAT I HEARD? I HEARD JUNE WALKED IN ON HIM ONE MORNING AND HE HAD THAT DAMN MASK, OR WHATEVER IT IS, OFF.
AND YOU KNOW WHAT SHE SAW?
... NOTHING.
HE WAS COMPLETELY NORMAL UNDERNEATH!
THERE AIN'T NOTHING WRONG WITH HIM! JUNE SAID HE PUT HIS HANDS OVER HIS FACE, RAN INTO THE WASHROOM AND SLAMMED THE DOOR!
Budweiser

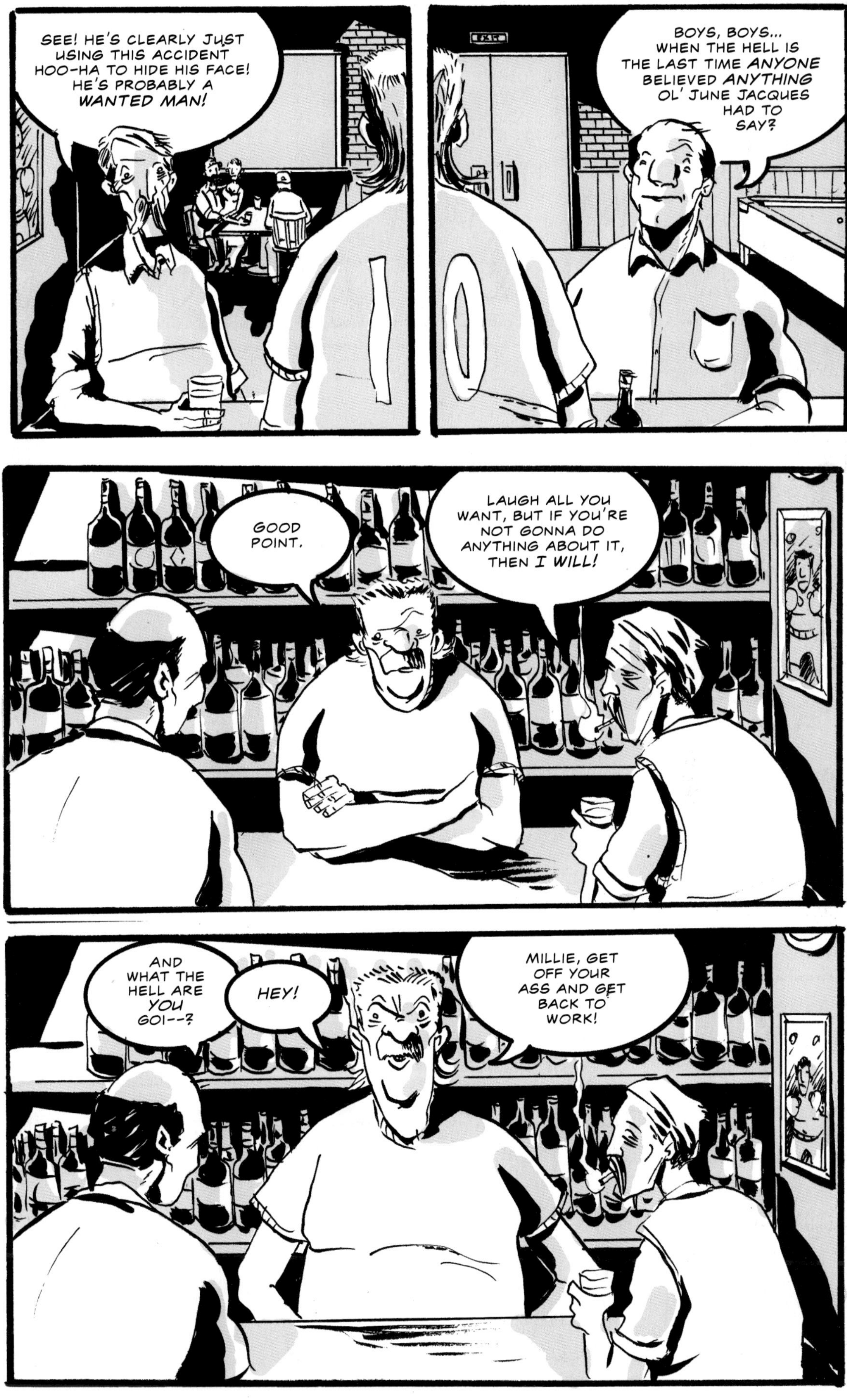
SEE! HE'S CLEARLY JUST USING THIS ACCIDENT HOO-HA TO HIDE HIS FACE! HE'S PROBABLY A WANTED MAN!
BOYS, BOYS... WHEN THE HELL IS THE LAST TIME ANYONE BELIEVED ANYTHING OL' JUNE JACQUES HAD TO SAY?
GOOD POINT.
LAUGH ALL YOU WANT, BUT IF YOU'RE NOT GONNA DO ANYTHING ABOUT IT, THEN I WILL!
AND WHAT THE HELL ARE YOU GOI--?
HEY!
MILLIE, GET OFF YOUR ASS AND GET BACK TO WORK!

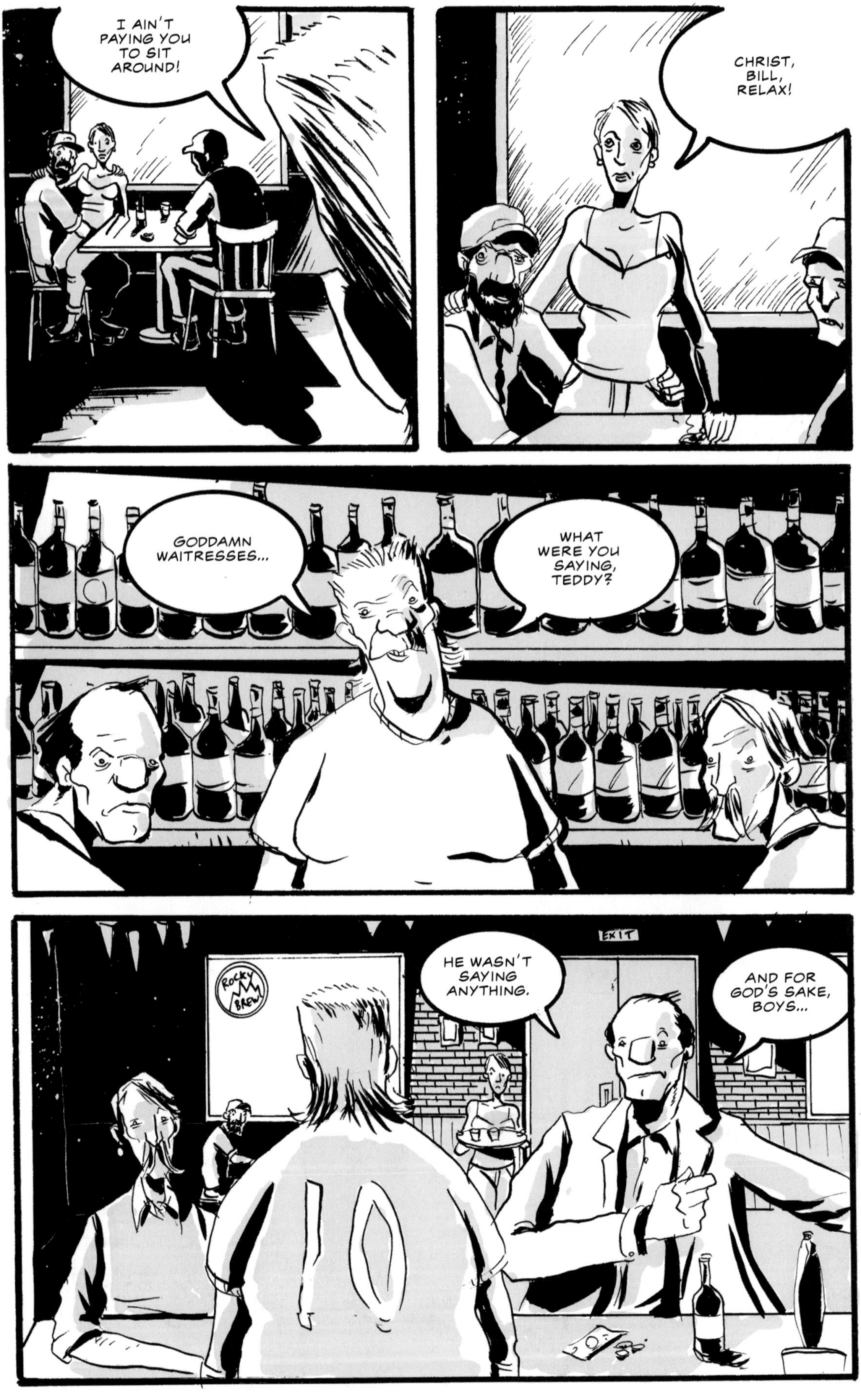
I AIN'T PAYING YOU TO SIT AROUND!
CHRIST, BILL, RELAX!
GODDAMN WAITRESSES...
WHAT WERE YOU SAYING, TEDDY?
EXIT
ROCKY BREW
HE WASN'T SAYING ANYTHING.
AND FOR GOD'S SAKE, BOYS...

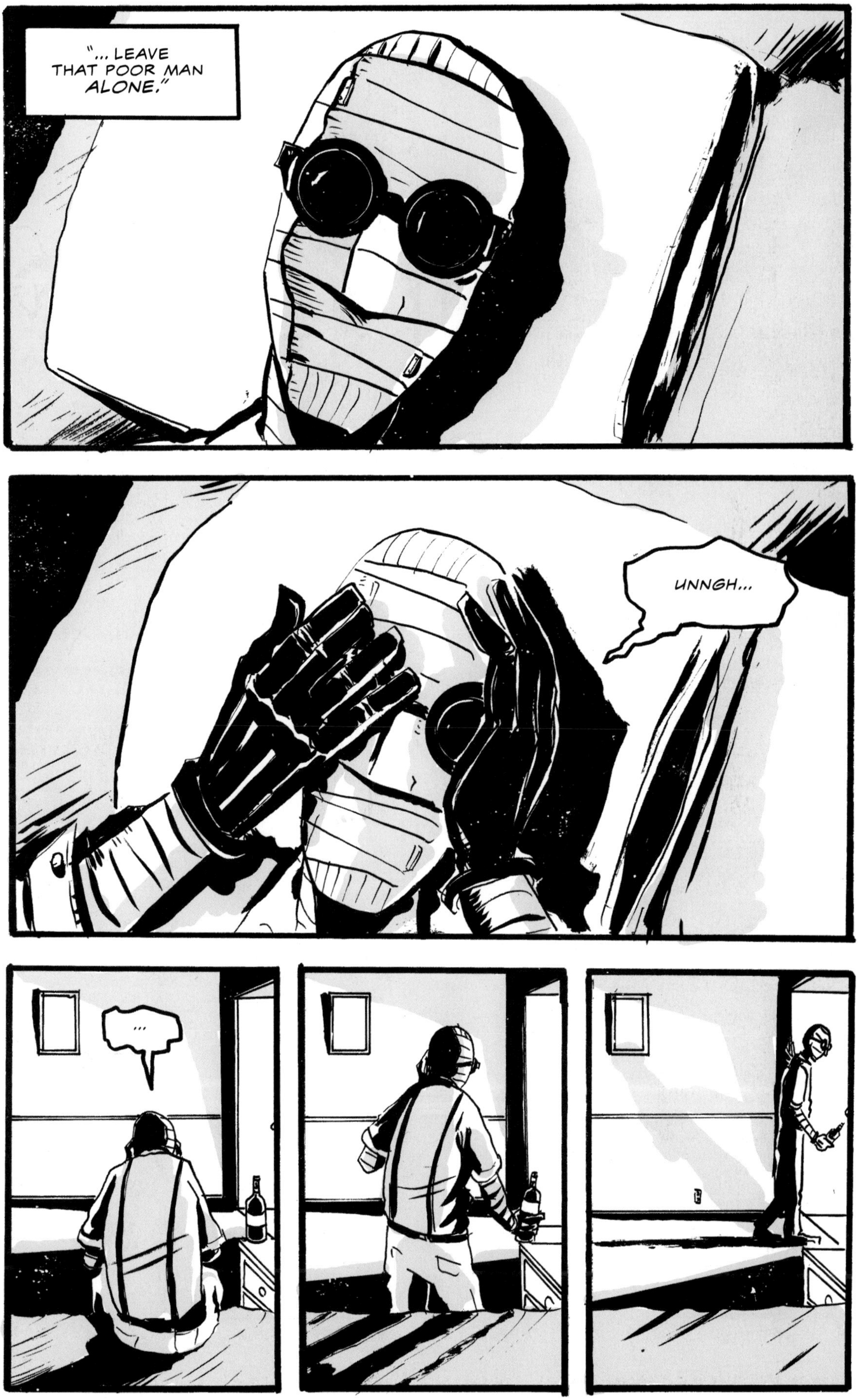
"... LEAVE THAT POOR MAN ALONE."
UNNGH...
...

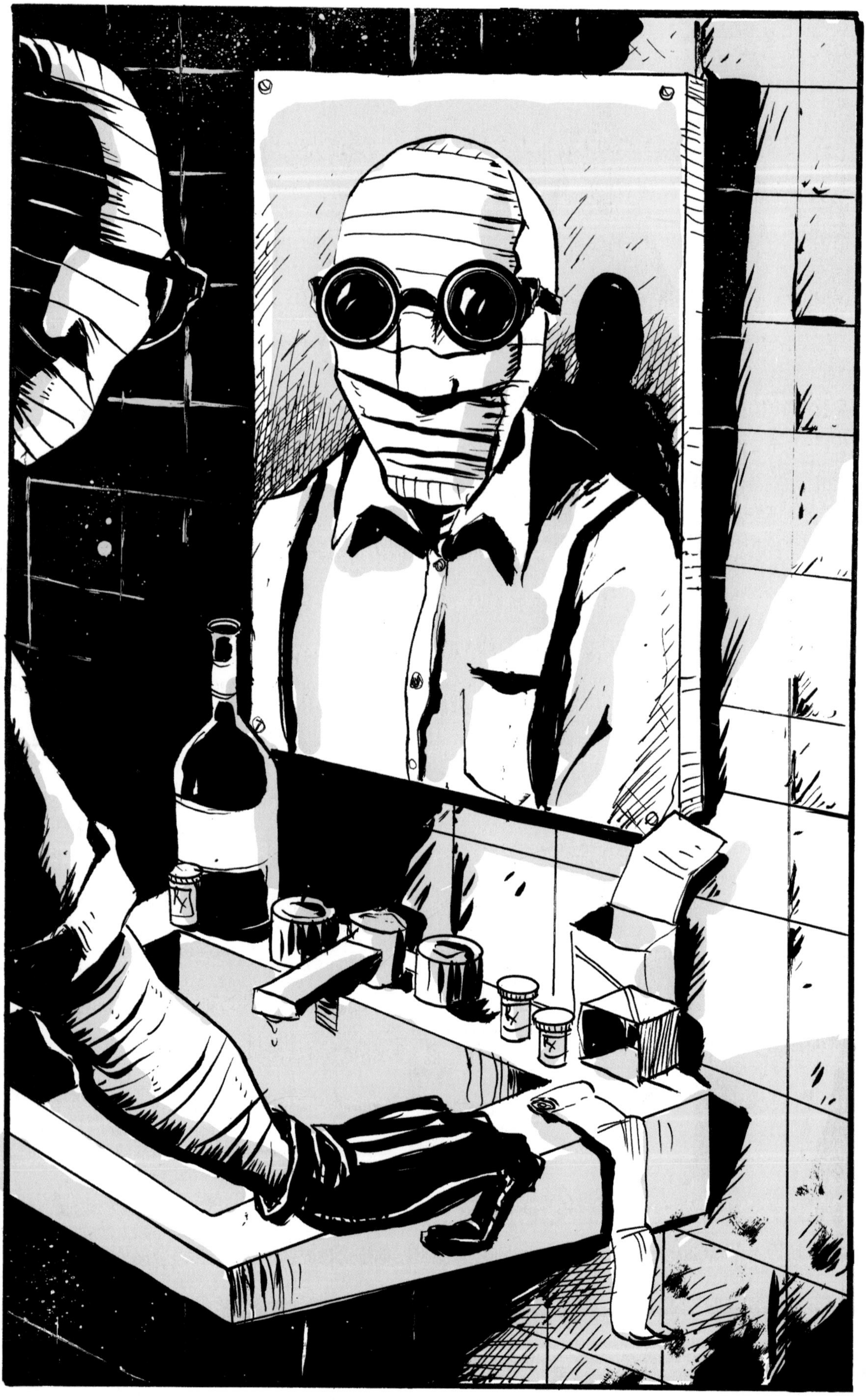

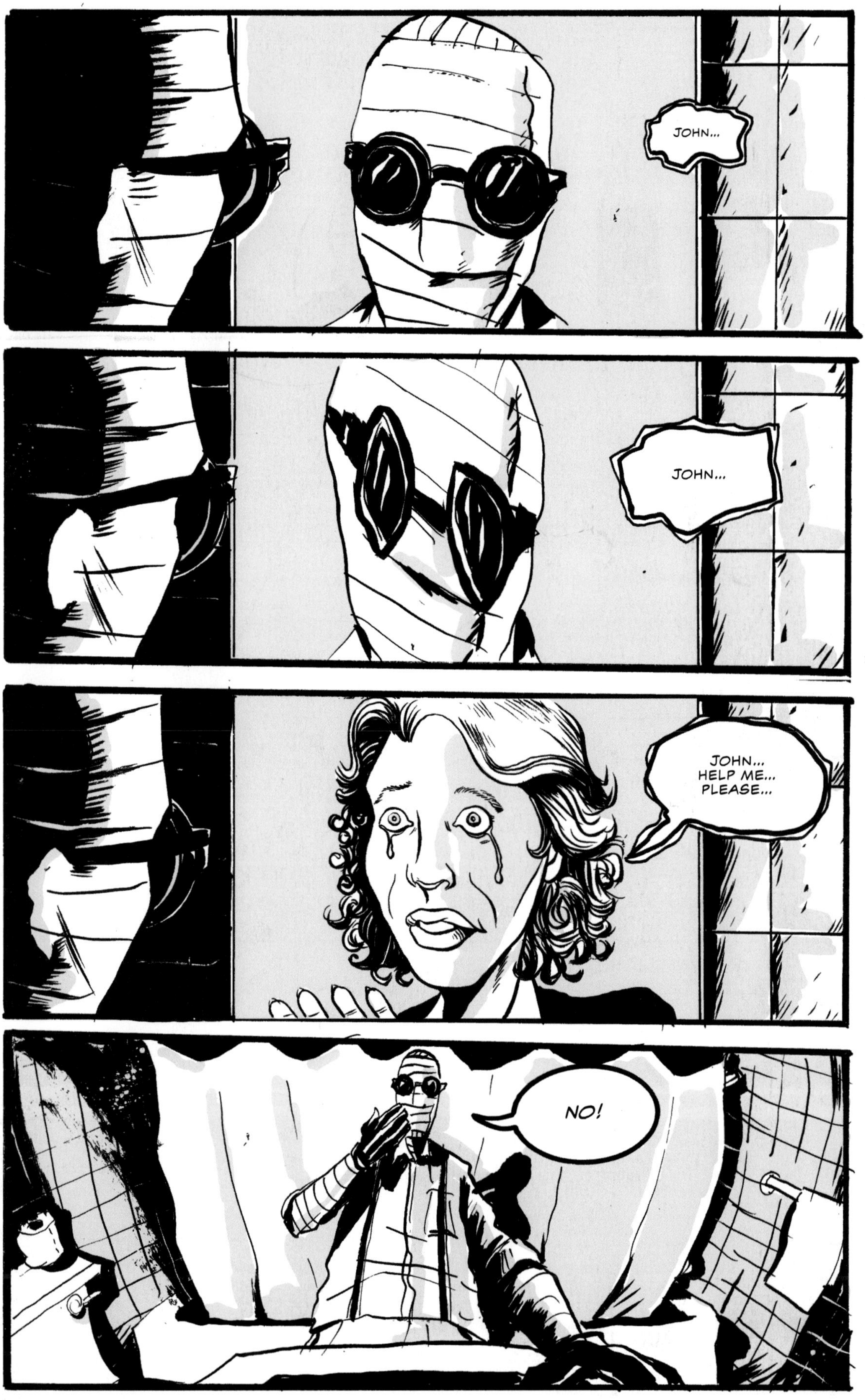
JOHN...
JOHN...
JOHN... HELP ME... PLEASE...
NO!

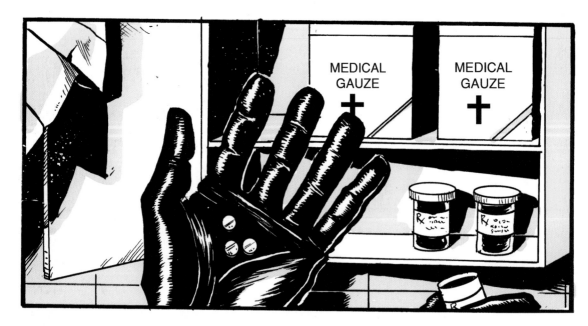

MEDICAL
GAUZE

MEDICAL
GAUZE

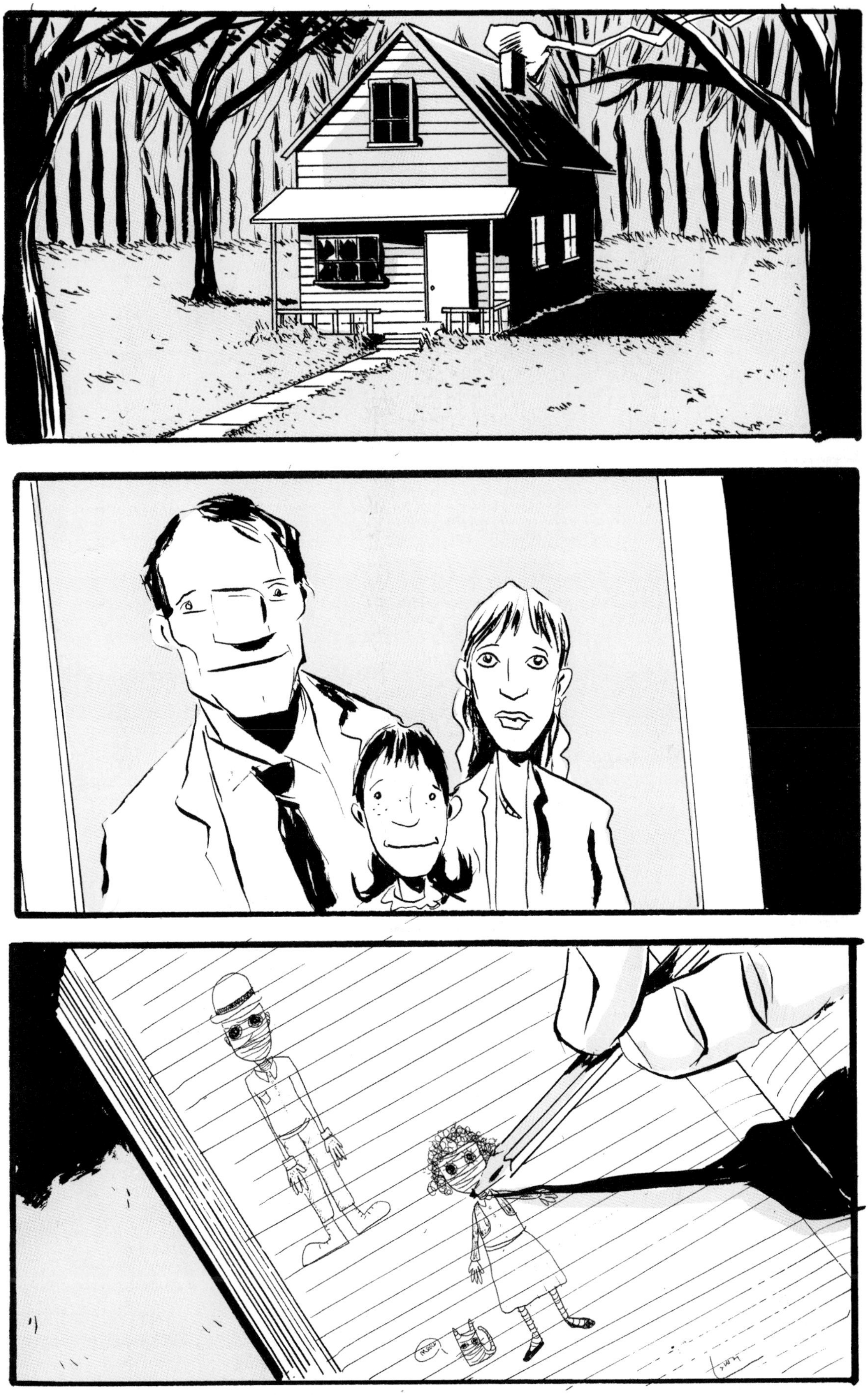

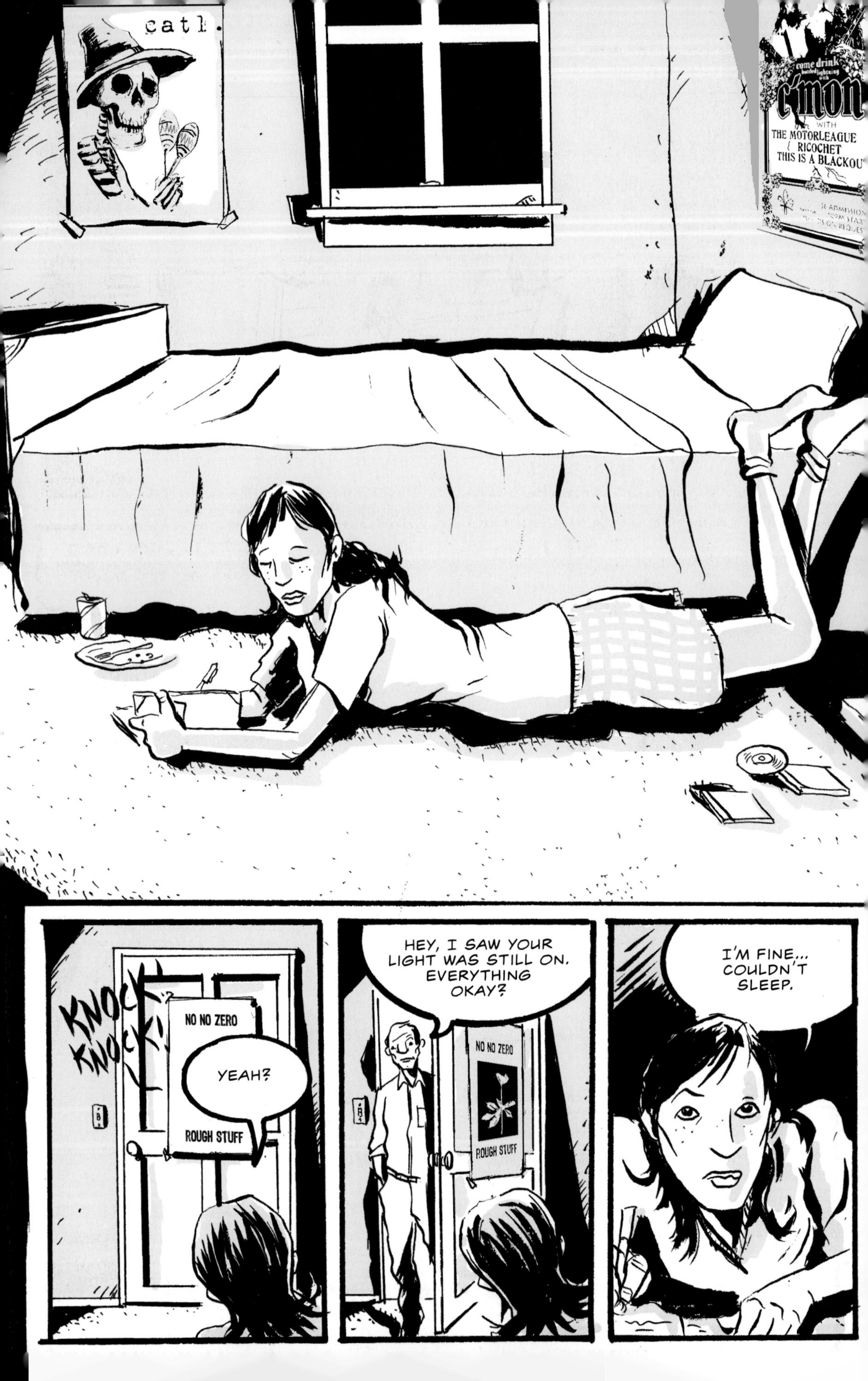
catl.
come drink
c'mon
WITH
THE MOTORLEAGUE
RICOCHET
THIS IS A BLACKOU
KNOCK KNOCK!
NO NO ZERO
ROUGH STUFF
YEAH?
HEY, I SAW YOUR LIGHT WAS STILL ON. EVERYTHING OKAY?
NO NO ZERO
ROUGH STUFF
I'M FINE... COULDN'T SLEEP.

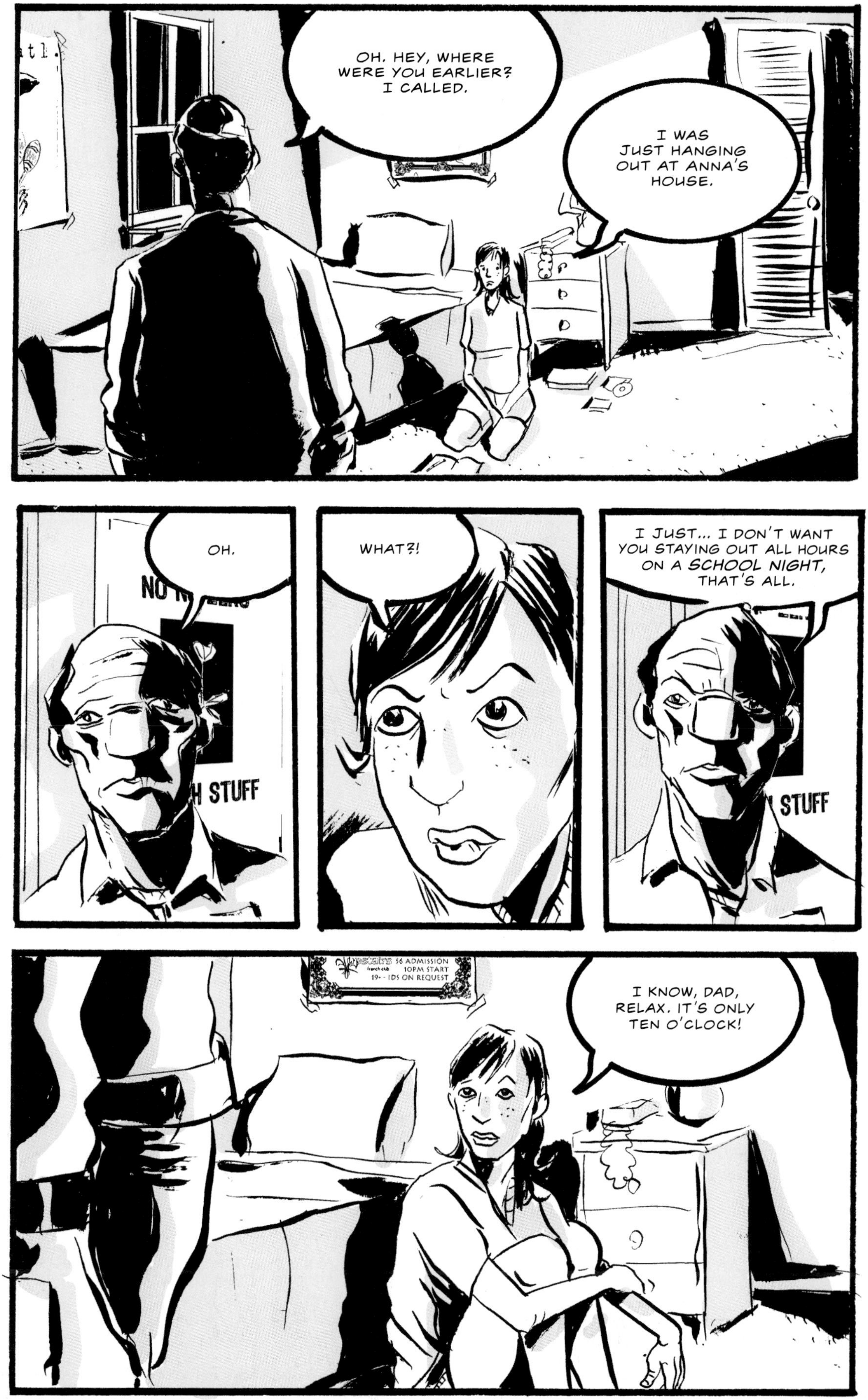

OH. HEY, WHERE WERE YOU EARLIER? I CALLED.
I WAS JUST HANGING OUT AT ANNA'S HOUSE.
OH.
WHAT?!
I JUST... I DON'T WANT YOU STAYING OUT ALL HOURS ON A *SCHOOL NIGHT*, THAT'S ALL.
$6 ADMISSION
10PM START
19+ - IDS ON REQUEST
I KNOW, DAD, RELAX. IT'S ONLY TEN O'CLOCK!

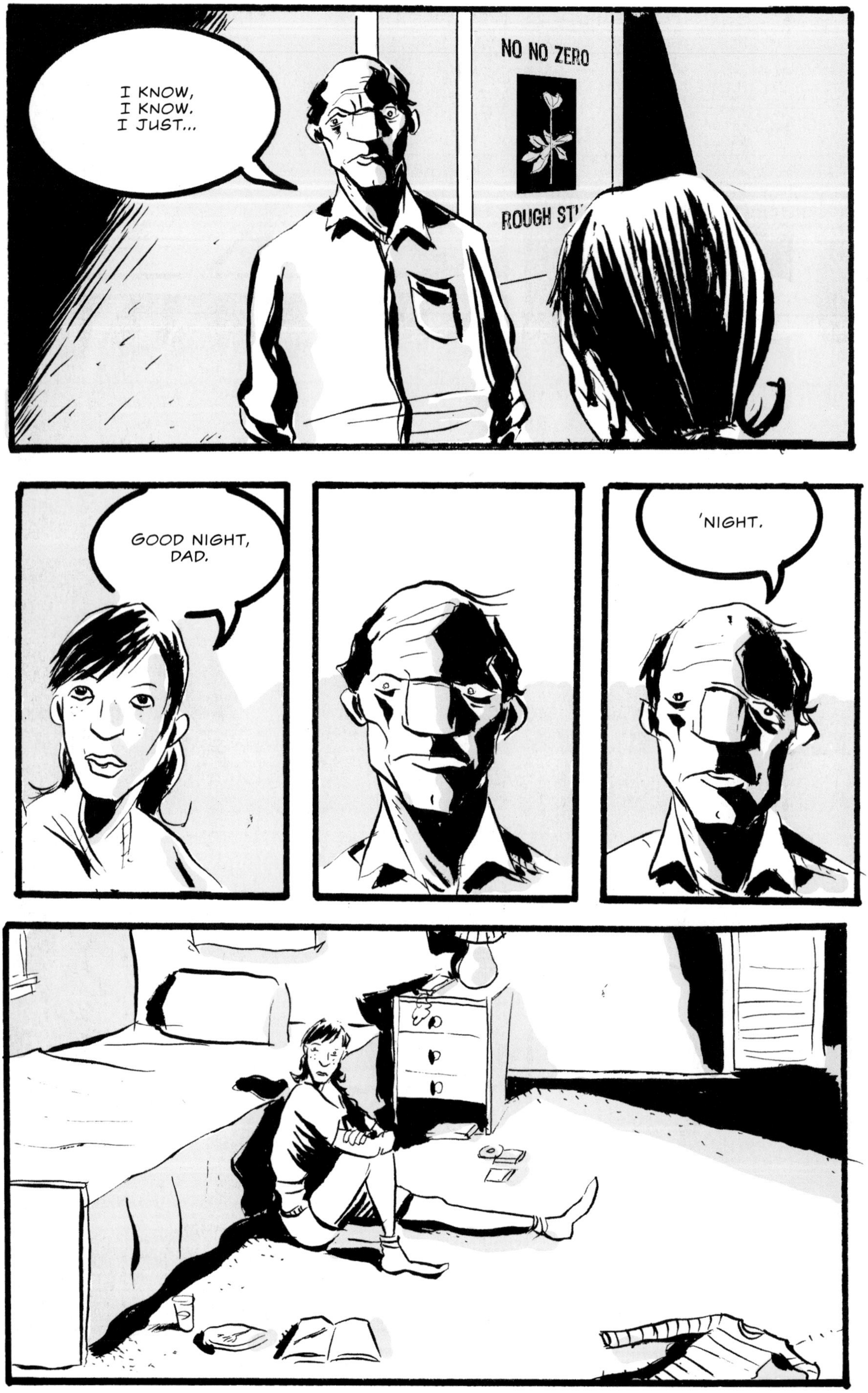
I KNOW, I KNOW. I JUST...
NO NO ZERO
ROUGH ST
GOOD NIGHT, DAD.
'NIGHT.

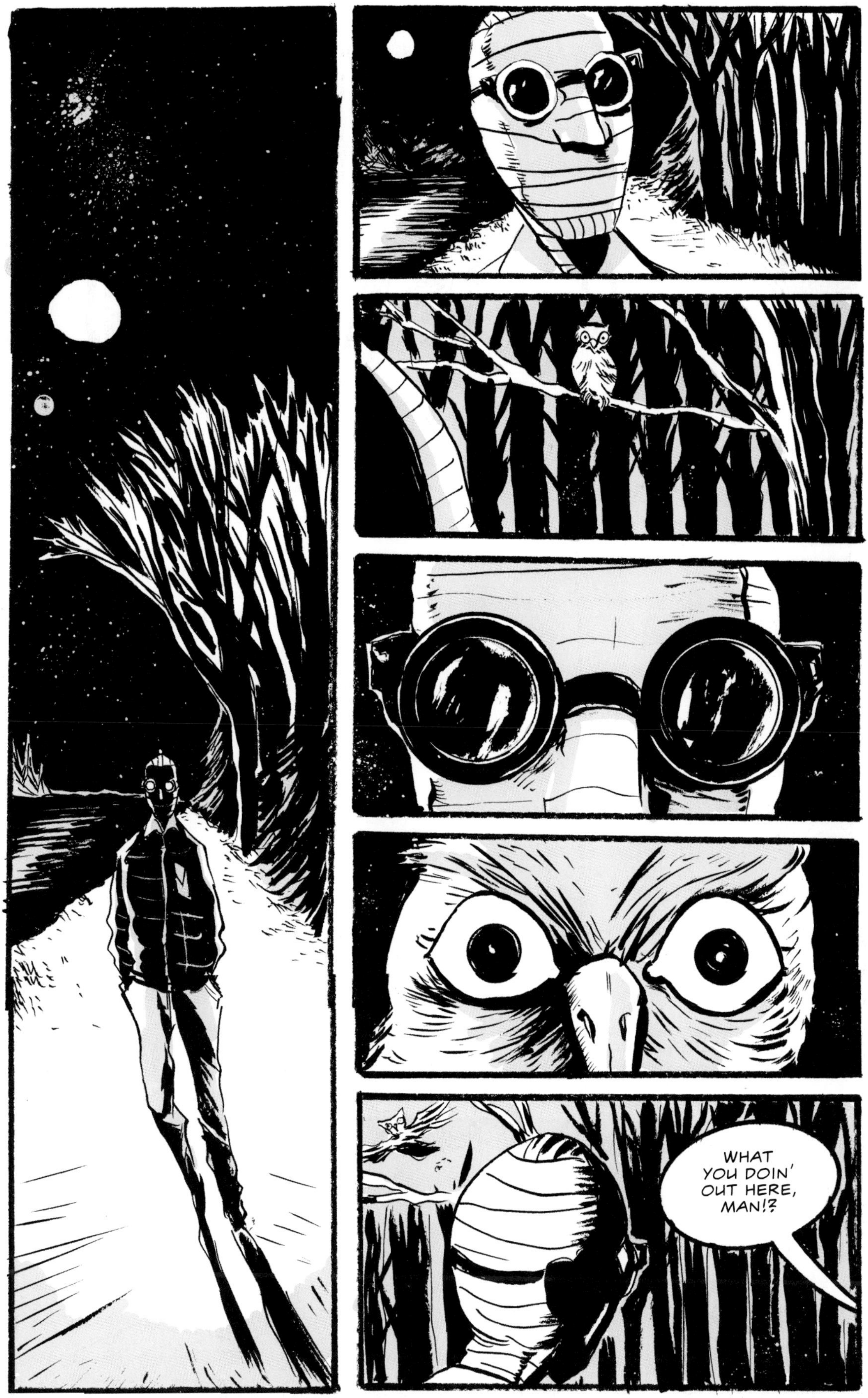
WHAT YOU DOIN' OUT HERE, MAN!?

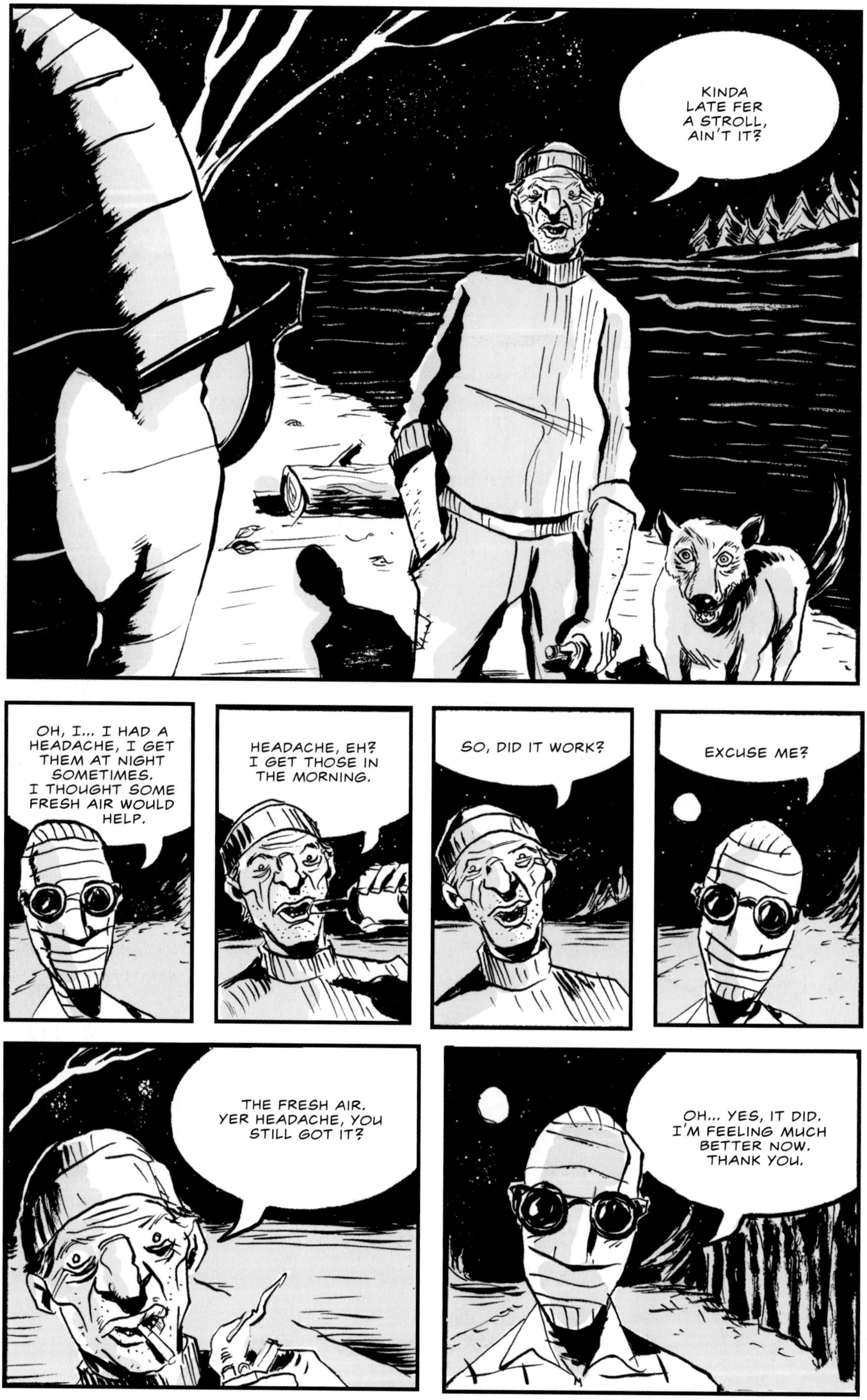
KINDA LATE FER A STROLL, AIN'T IT?
OH, I... I HAD A HEADACHE, I GET THEM AT NIGHT SOMETIMES. I THOUGHT SOME FRESH AIR WOULD HELP.
HEADACHE, EH? I GET THOSE IN THE MORNING.
SO, DID IT WORK?
EXCUSE ME?
THE FRESH AIR. YER HEADACHE, YOU STILL GOT IT?
OH... YES, IT DID. I'M FEELING MUCH BETTER NOW. THANK YOU.

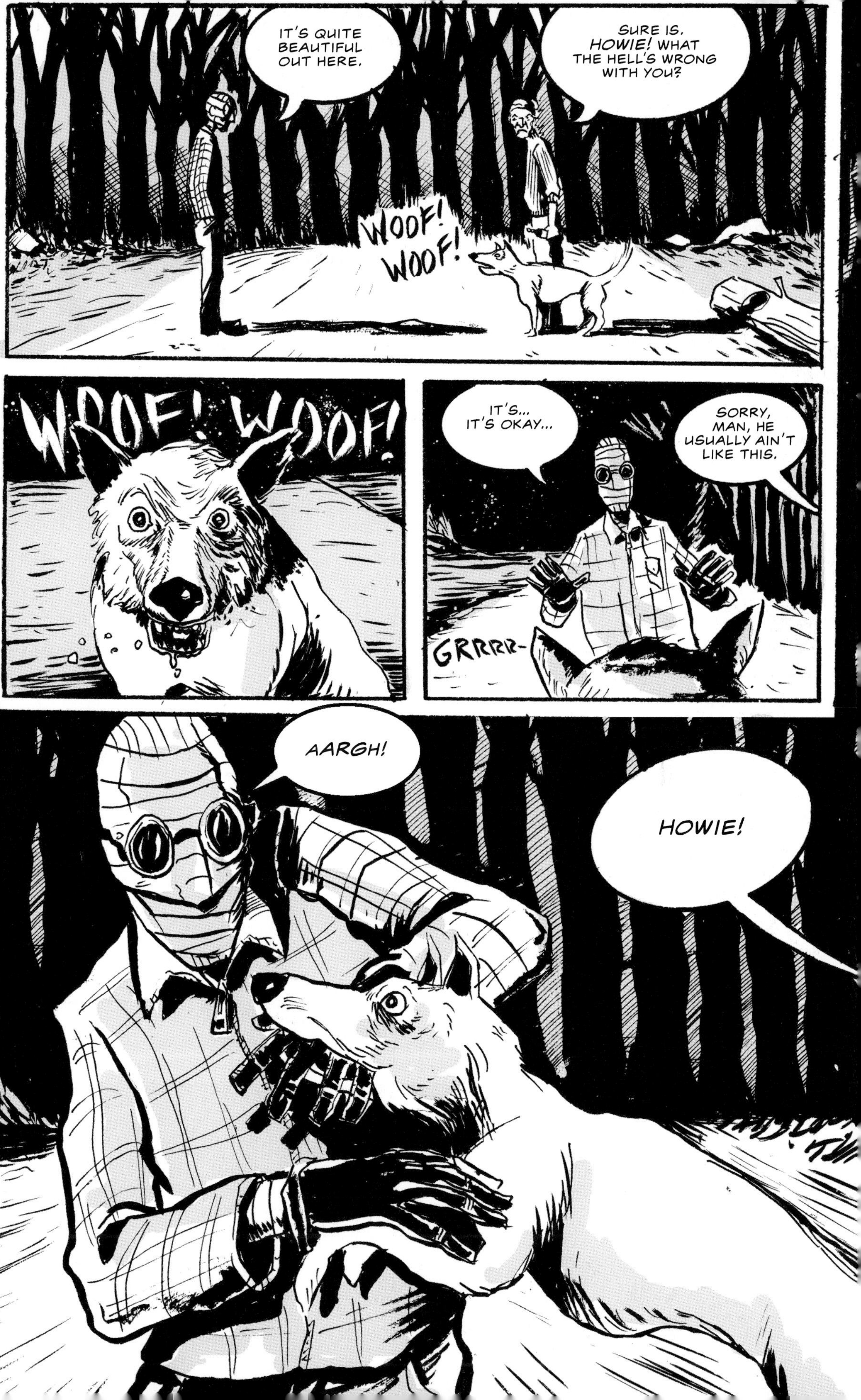
IT'S QUITE BEAUTIFUL OUT HERE.
SURE IS. HOWIE! WHAT THE HELL'S WRONG WITH YOU?
WOOF! WOOF!
WOOF! WOOF!
IT'S... IT'S OKAY...
SORRY, MAN, HE USUALLY AIN'T LIKE THIS.
GRRRR-
AARGH!
HOWIE!

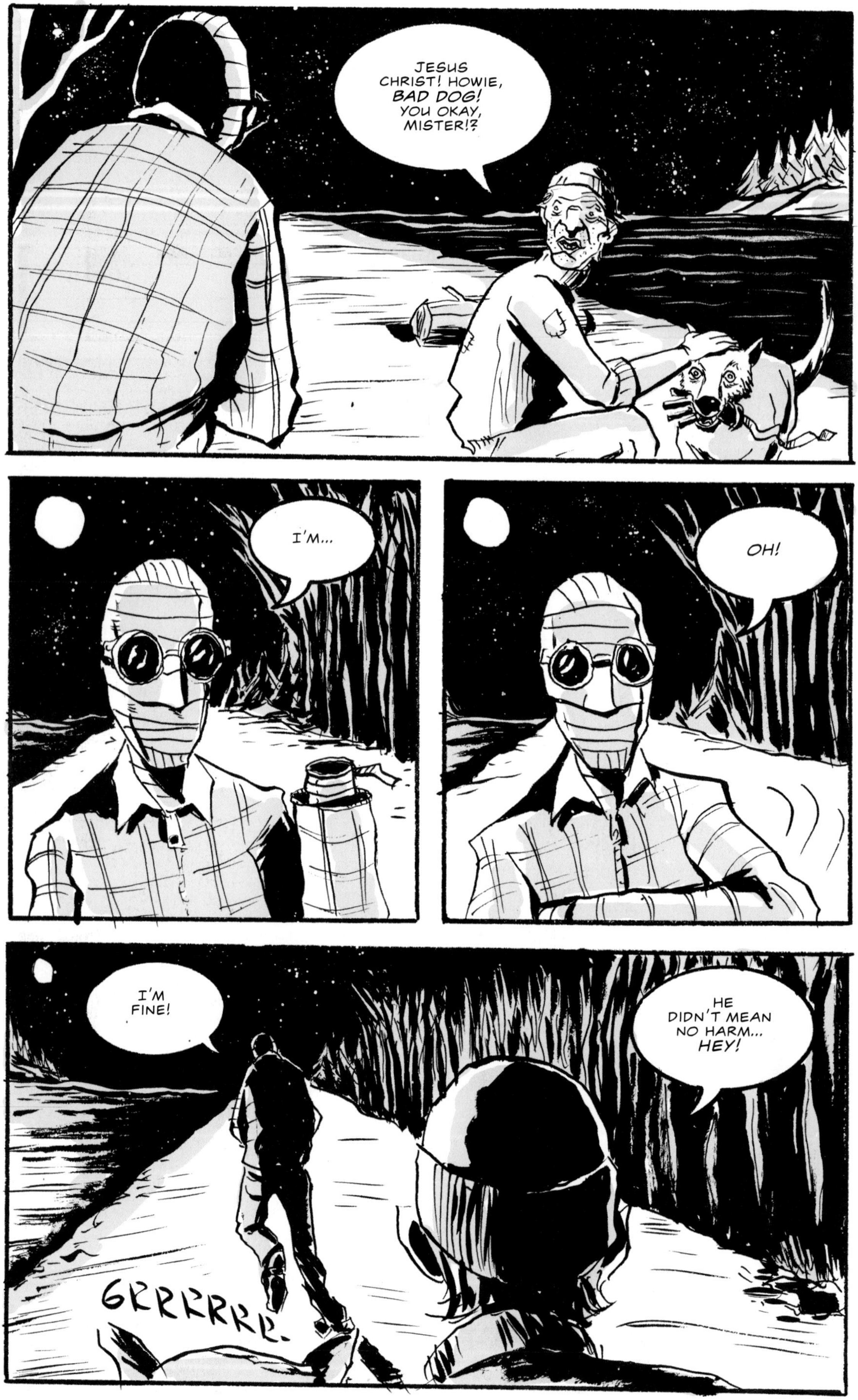
JESUS CHRIST! HOWIE, BAD DOG! YOU OKAY, MISTER!?
I'M...
OH!
I'M FINE!
HE DIDN'T MEAN NO HARM... HEY!
GRRRRRR.

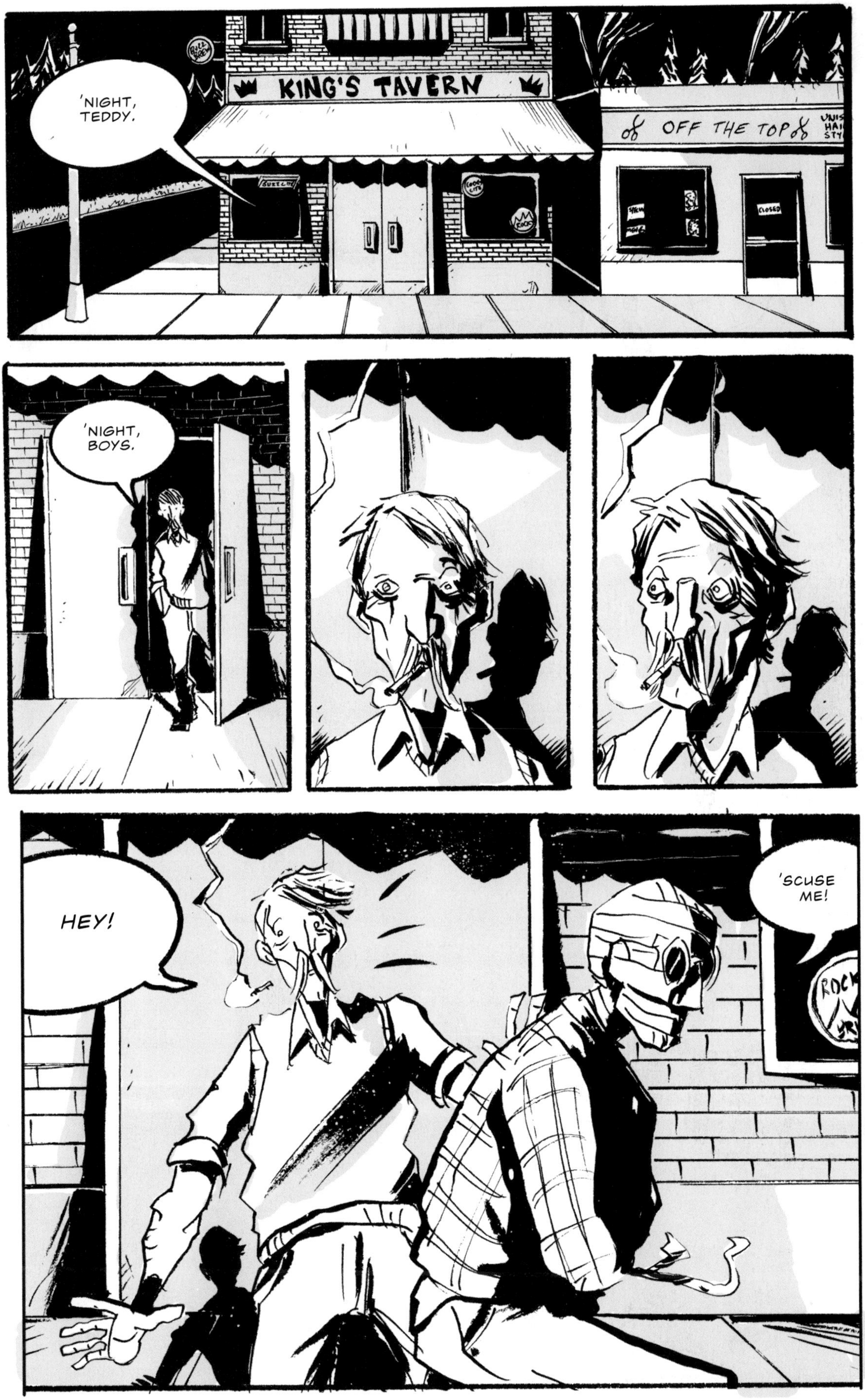
KING'S TAVERN
OFF THE TOP
CLOSED
'NIGHT, TEDDY.
'NIGHT, BOYS.
HEY!
'SCUSE ME!

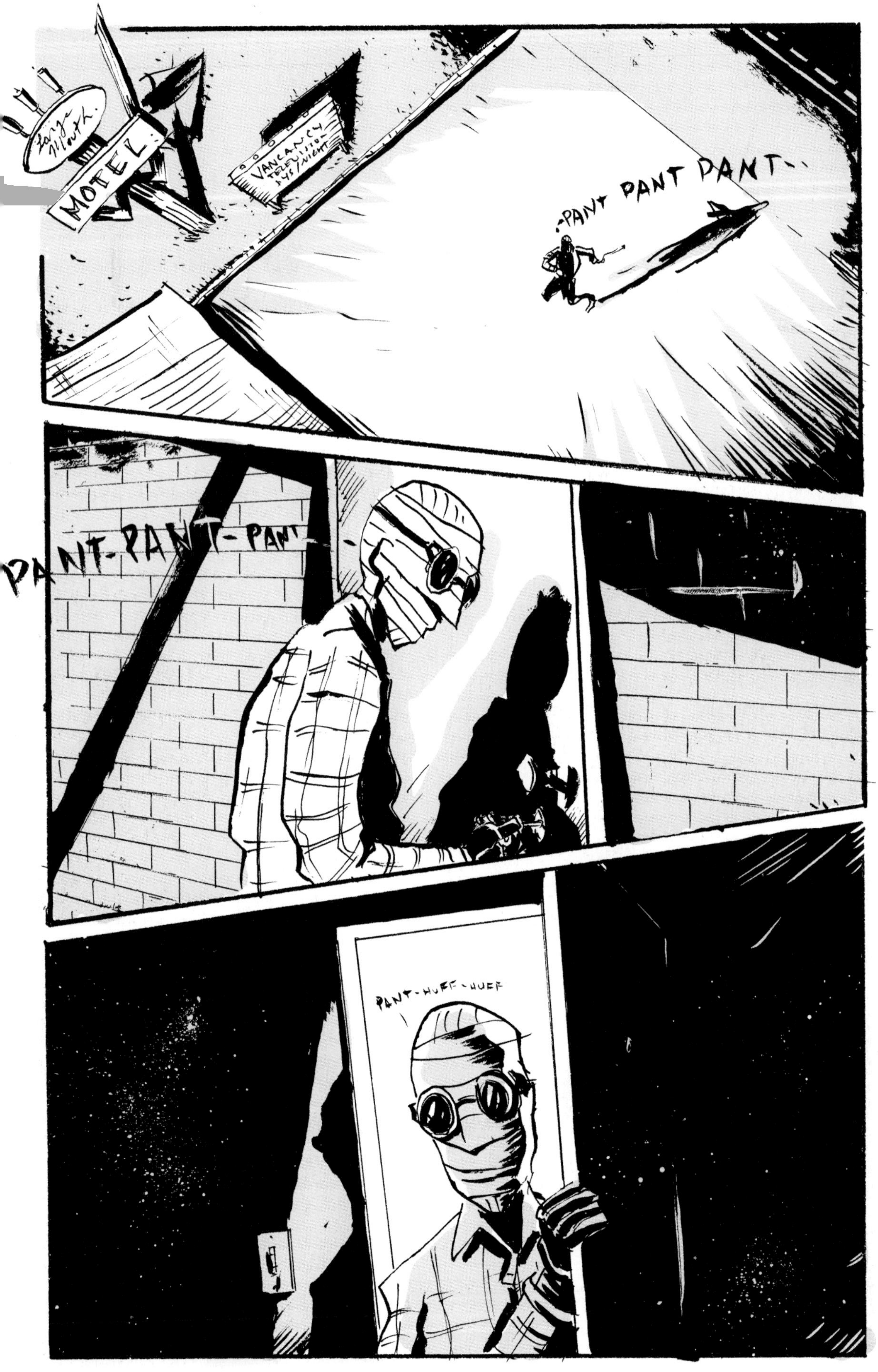
Large Mouth
MOTEL
VANCANCY
TELEVISION
$45/NIGHT
-PANT PANT PANT-
PANT-PANT-PAN'-
PANT-HUFF-HUFF

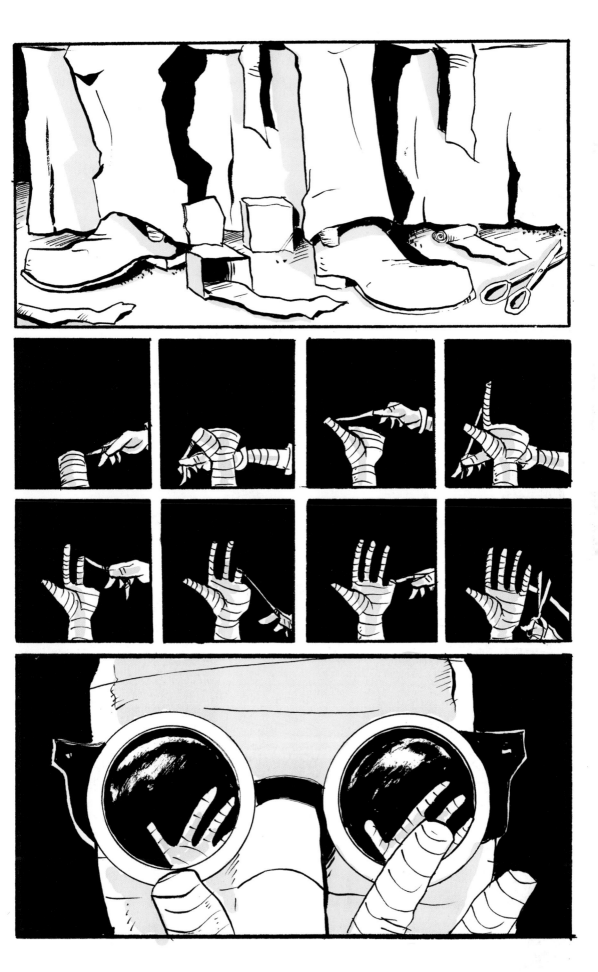

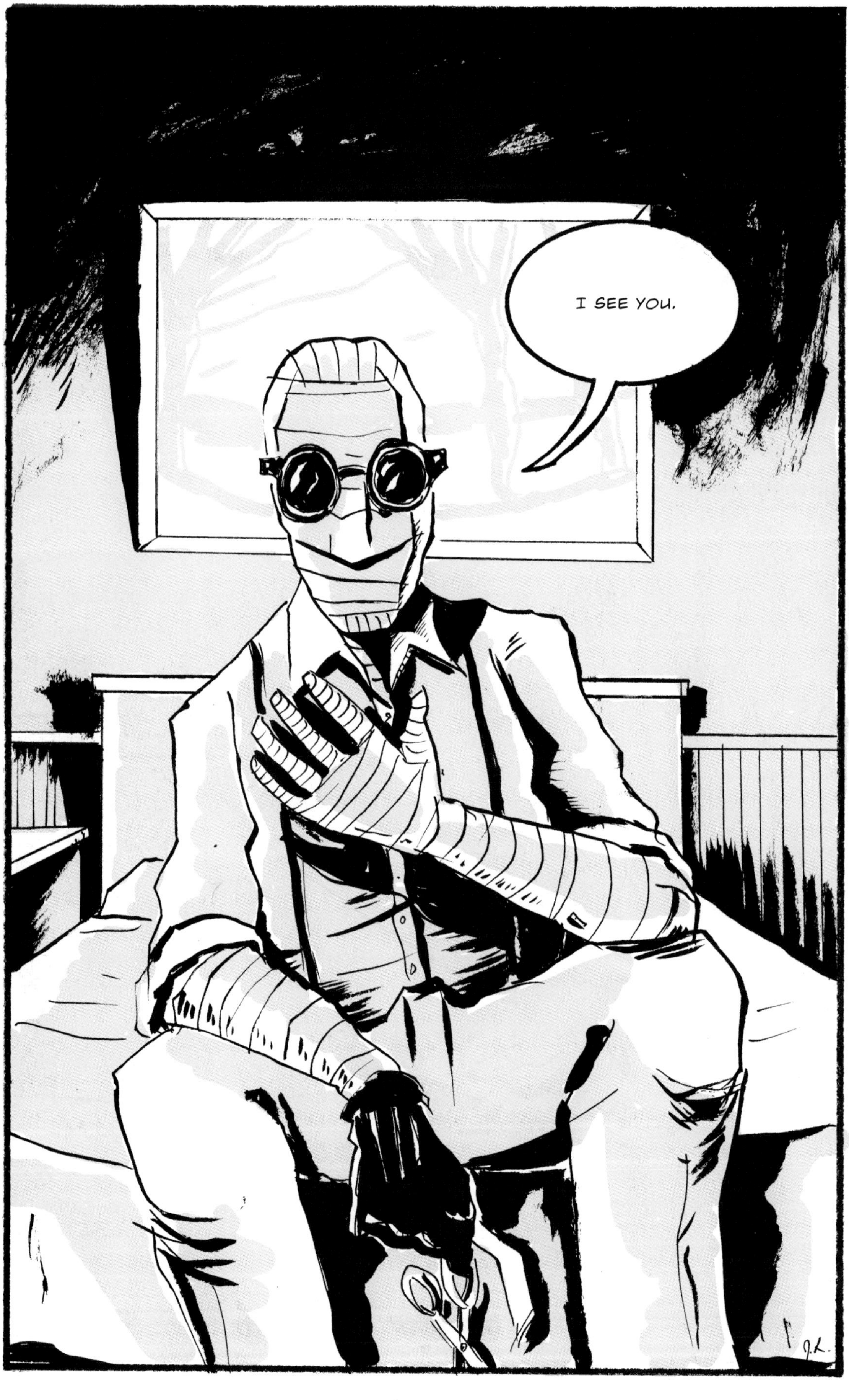
I SEE YOU.

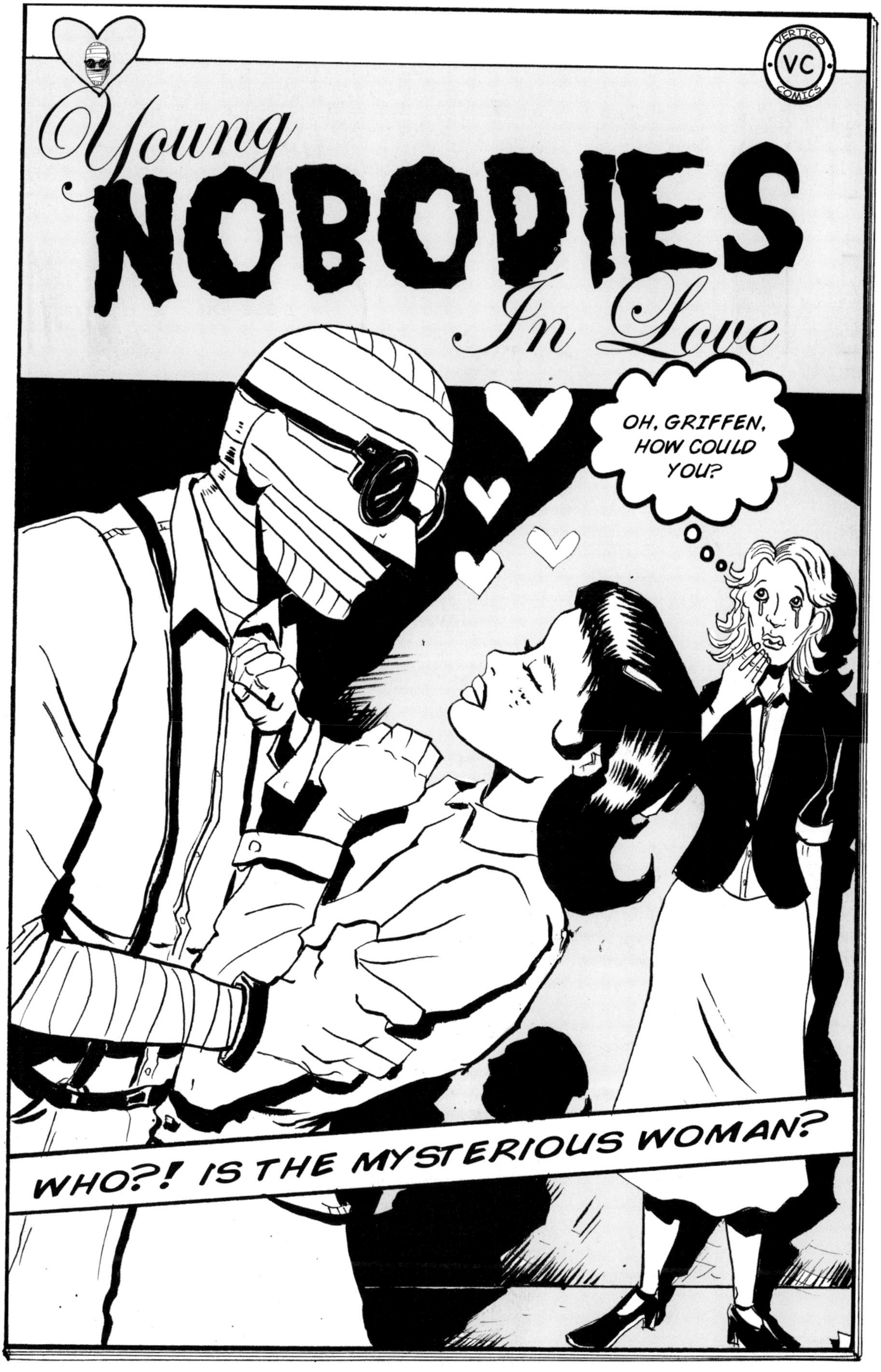
VERTIGO VC COMICS
Young NOBODIES In Love
OH, GRIFFEN, HOW COULD YOU?
WHO?! IS THE MYSTERIOUS WOMAN?

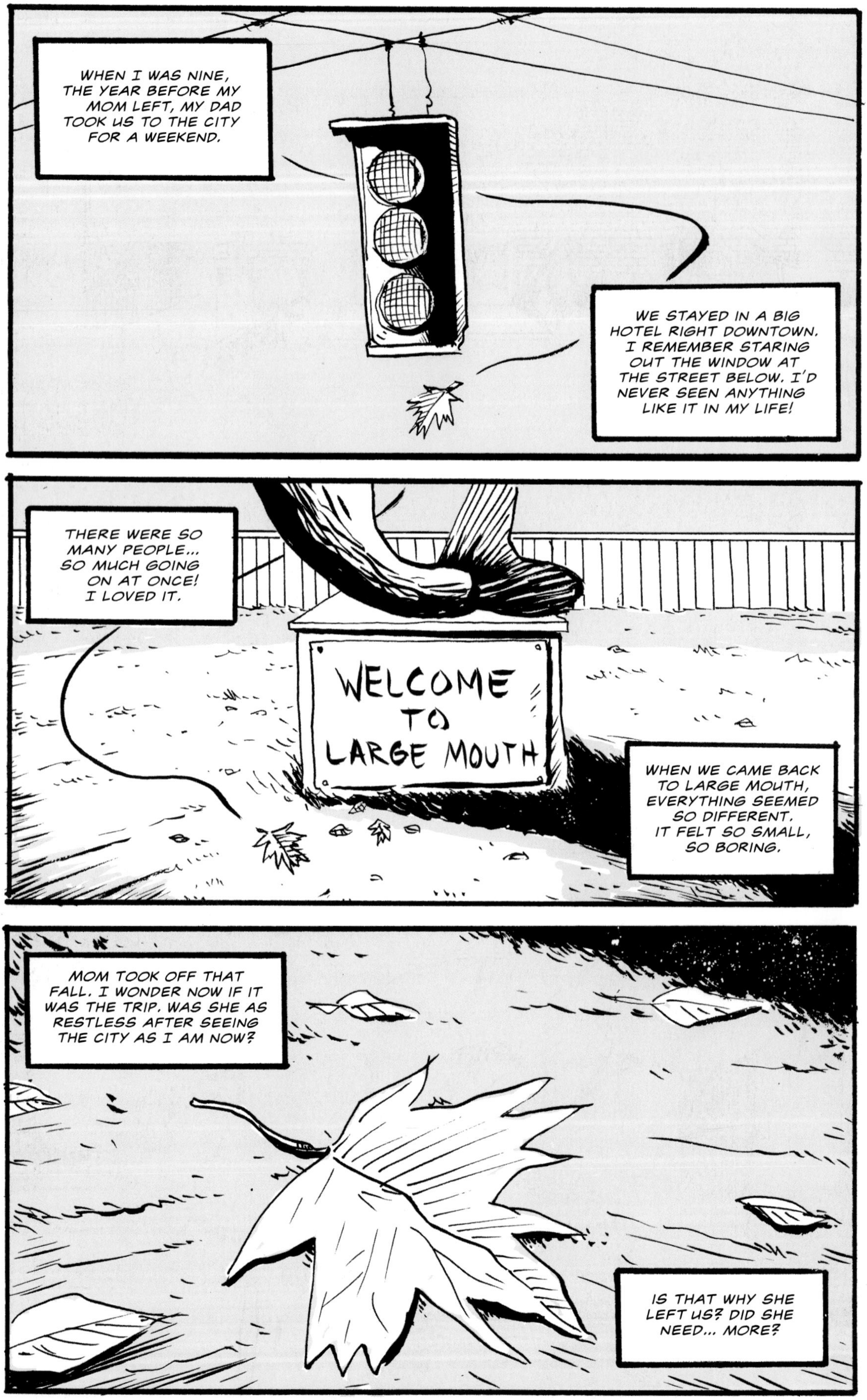

WHEN I WAS NINE, THE YEAR BEFORE MY MOM LEFT, MY DAD TOOK US TO THE CITY FOR A WEEKEND.
WE STAYED IN A BIG HOTEL RIGHT DOWNTOWN. I REMEMBER STARING OUT THE WINDOW AT THE STREET BELOW. I'D NEVER SEEN ANYTHING LIKE IT IN MY LIFE!
THERE WERE SO MANY PEOPLE... SO MUCH GOING ON AT ONCE! I LOVED IT.
WELCOME TO LARGE MOUTH
WHEN WE CAME BACK TO LARGE MOUTH, EVERYTHING SEEMED SO DIFFERENT. IT FELT SO SMALL, SO BORING.
MOM TOOK OFF THAT FALL. I WONDER NOW IF IT WAS THE TRIP. WAS SHE AS RESTLESS AFTER SEEING THE CITY AS I AM NOW?
IS THAT WHY SHE LEFT US? DID SHE NEED... MORE?

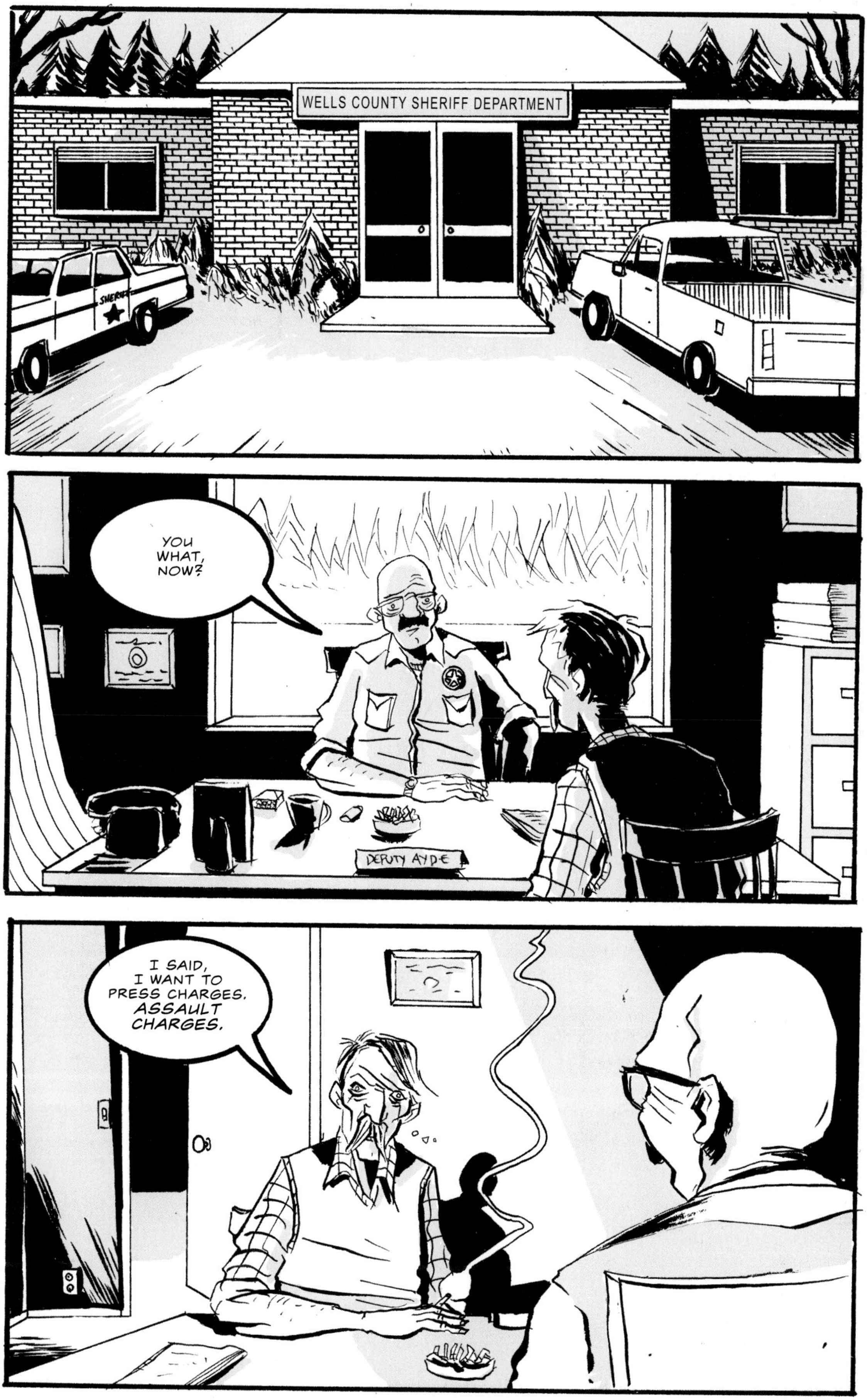
WELLS COUNTY SHERIFF DEPARTMENT
SHERIFF
YOU WHAT, NOW?
DEPUTY AYDE
I SAID, I WANT TO PRESS CHARGES. ASSAULT CHARGES.

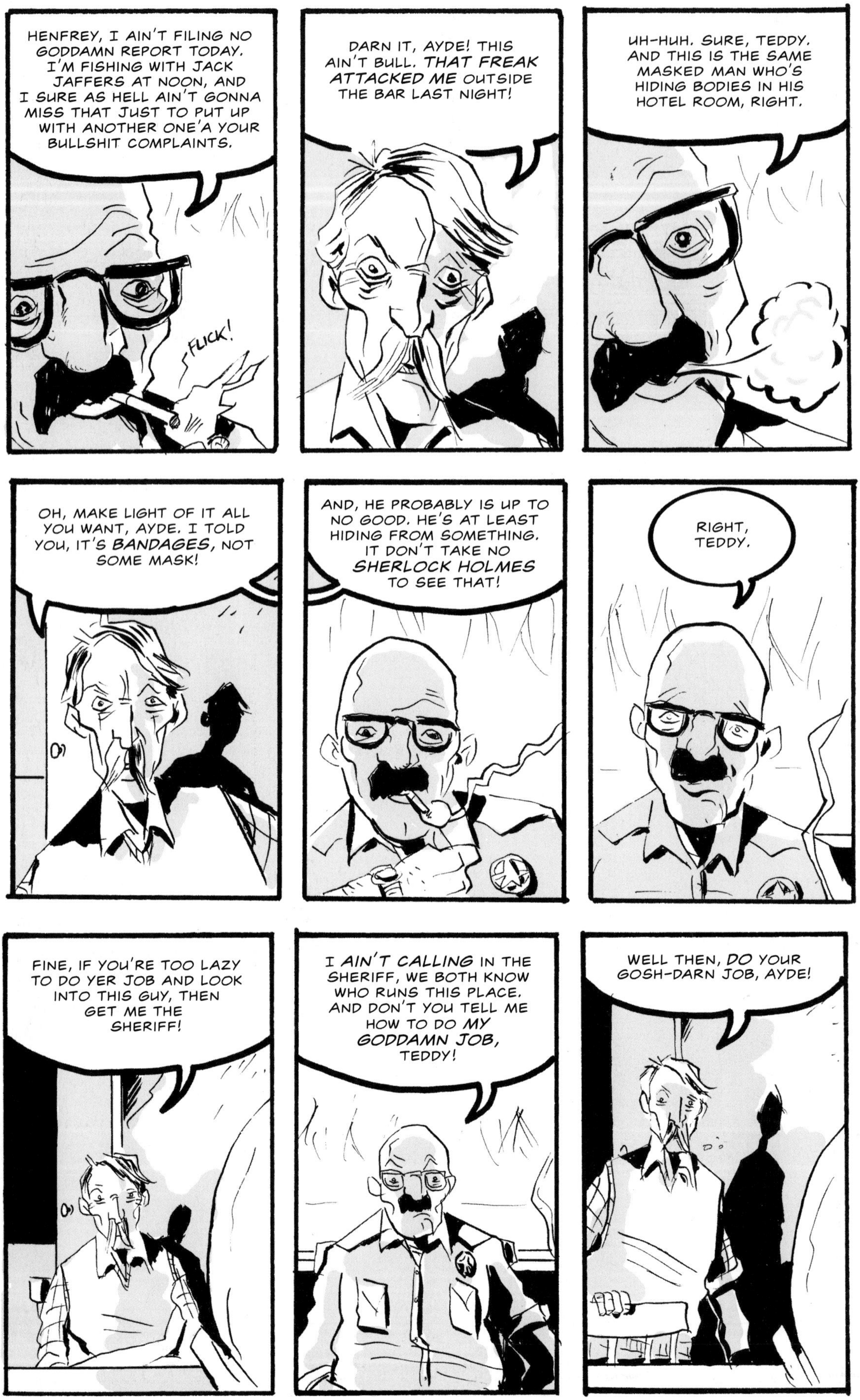
HENFREY, I AIN'T FILING NO GODDAMN REPORT TODAY. I'M FISHING WITH JACK JAFFERS AT NOON, AND I SURE AS HELL AIN'T GONNA MISS THAT JUST TO PUT UP WITH ANOTHER ONE'A YOUR BULLSHIT COMPLAINTS.
FLICK!
DARN IT, AYDE! THIS AIN'T BULL. THAT FREAK ATTACKED ME OUTSIDE THE BAR LAST NIGHT!
UH-HUH. SURE, TEDDY. AND THIS IS THE SAME MASKED MAN WHO'S HIDING BODIES IN HIS HOTEL ROOM, RIGHT.
OH, MAKE LIGHT OF IT ALL YOU WANT, AYDE. I TOLD YOU, IT'S BANDAGES, NOT SOME MASK!
AND, HE PROBABLY IS UP TO NO GOOD. HE'S AT LEAST HIDING FROM SOMETHING. IT DON'T TAKE NO SHERLOCK HOLMES TO SEE THAT!
RIGHT, TEDDY.
FINE, IF YOU'RE TOO LAZY TO DO YER JOB AND LOOK INTO THIS GUY, THEN GET ME THE SHERIFF!
I AIN'T CALLING IN THE SHERIFF, WE BOTH KNOW WHO RUNS THIS PLACE. AND DON'T YOU TELL ME HOW TO DO MY GODDAMN JOB, TEDDY!
WELL THEN, DO YOUR GOSH-DARN JOB, AYDE!

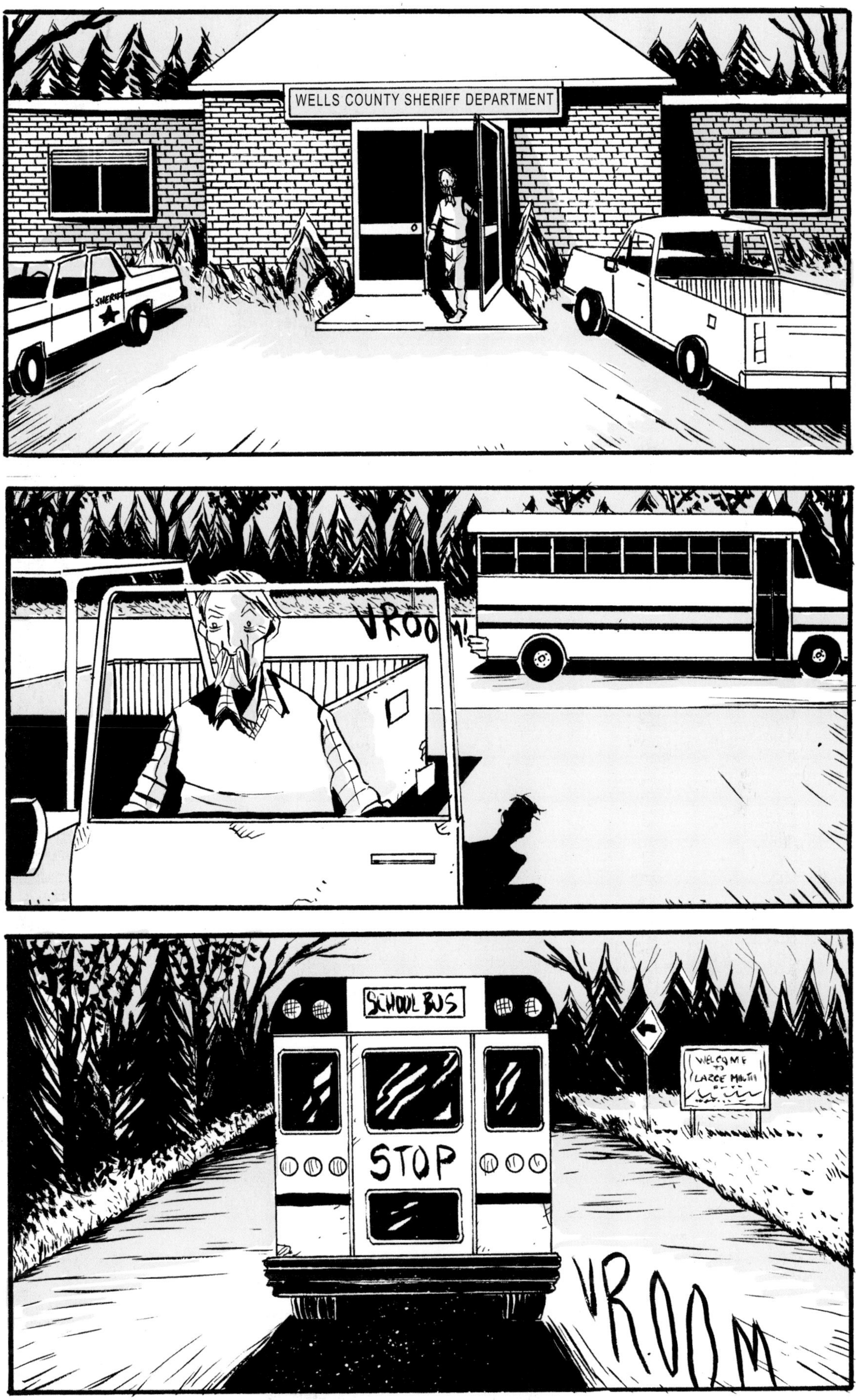
WELLS COUNTY SHERIFF DEPARTMENT
SHERIFF
VROOM!
SCHOOL BUS
STOP
WELCOME TO LARGE MOUTH
VROOM

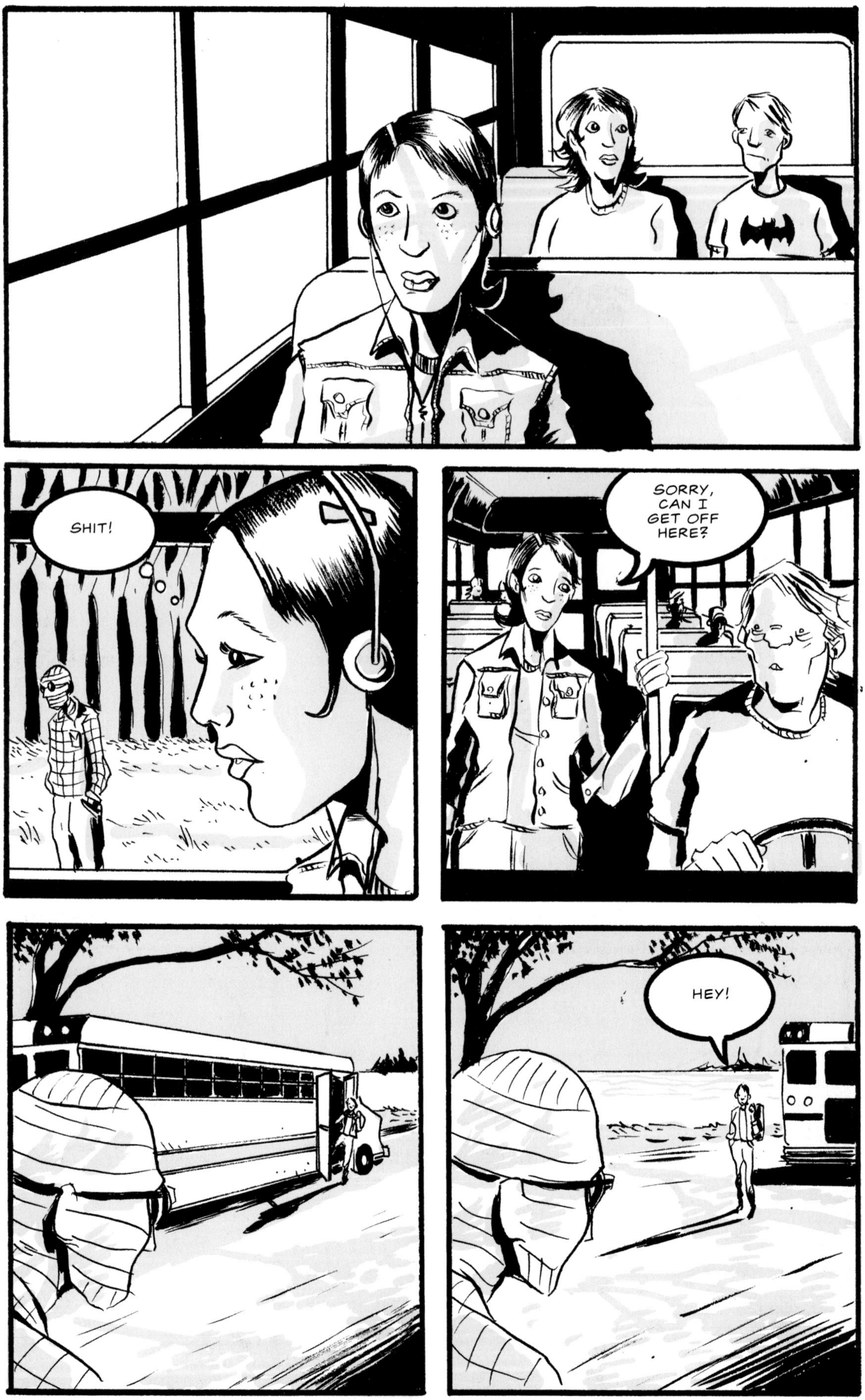
SHIT!
SORRY, CAN I GET OFF HERE?
HEY!

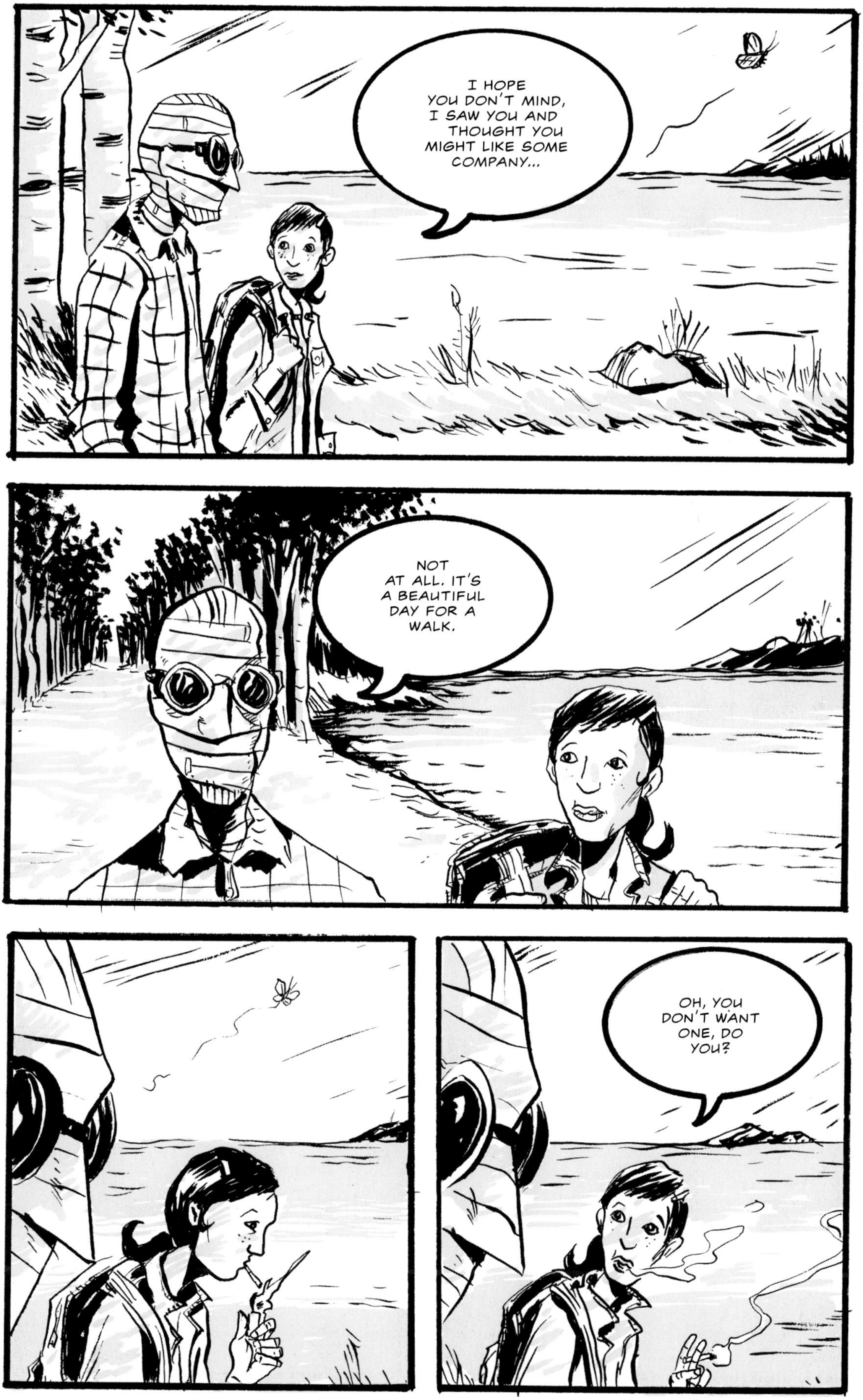
I HOPE YOU DON'T MIND, I SAW YOU AND THOUGHT YOU MIGHT LIKE SOME COMPANY...
NOT AT ALL. IT'S A BEAUTIFUL DAY FOR A WALK.
OH, YOU DON'T WANT ONE, DO YOU?

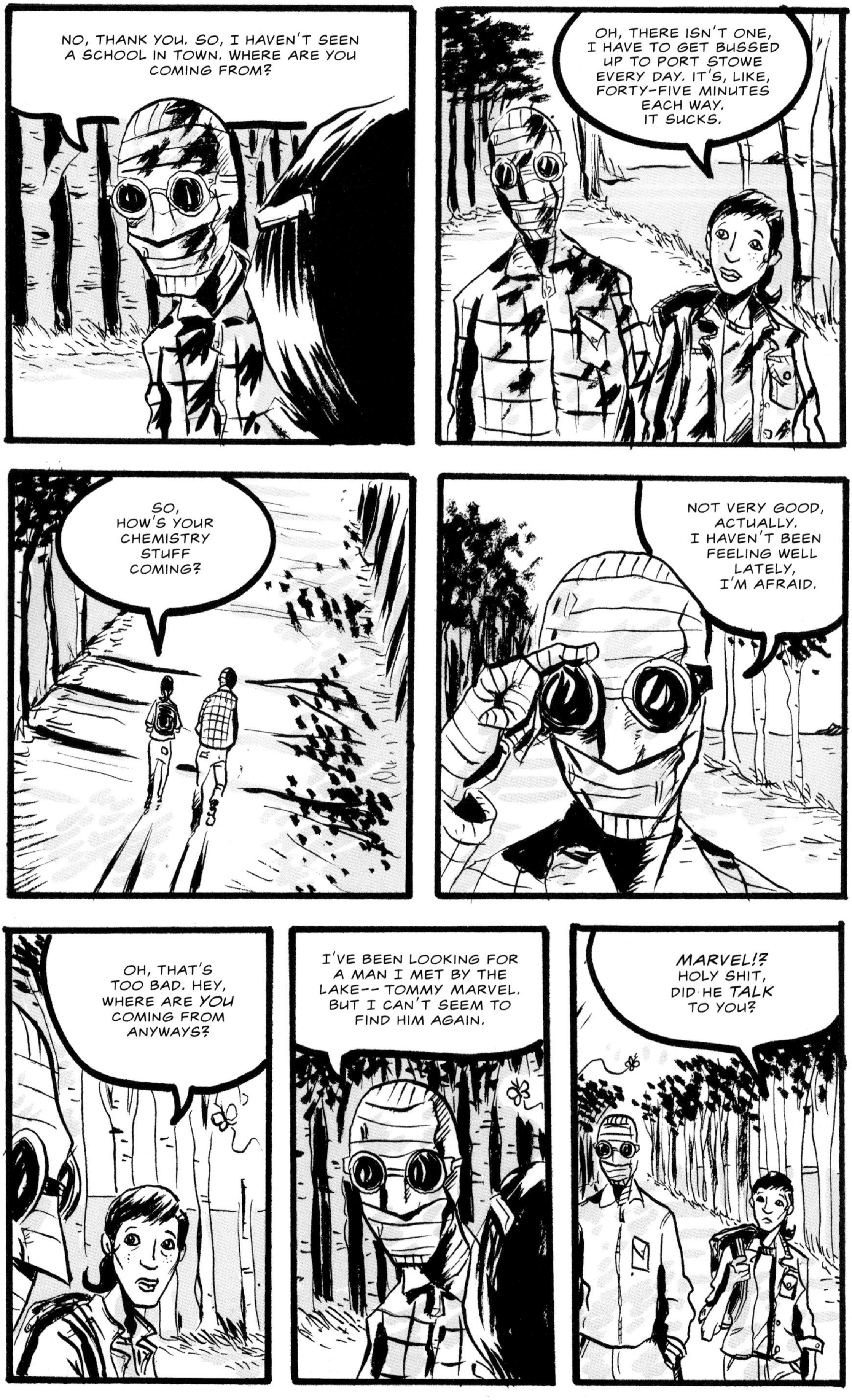
NO, THANK YOU. SO, I HAVEN'T SEEN A SCHOOL IN TOWN. WHERE ARE YOU COMING FROM?
OH, THERE ISN'T ONE, I HAVE TO GET BUSSED UP TO PORT STOWE EVERY DAY. IT'S, LIKE, FORTY-FIVE MINUTES EACH WAY. IT SUCKS.
SO, HOW'S YOUR CHEMISTRY STUFF COMING?
NOT VERY GOOD, ACTUALLY. I HAVEN'T BEEN FEELING WELL LATELY, I'M AFRAID.
OH, THAT'S TOO BAD. HEY, WHERE ARE *YOU* COMING FROM ANYWAYS?
I'VE BEEN LOOKING FOR A MAN I MET BY THE LAKE-- TOMMY MARVEL. BUT I CAN'T SEEM TO FIND HIM AGAIN.
MARVEL!? HOLY SHIT, DID HE *TALK* TO YOU?

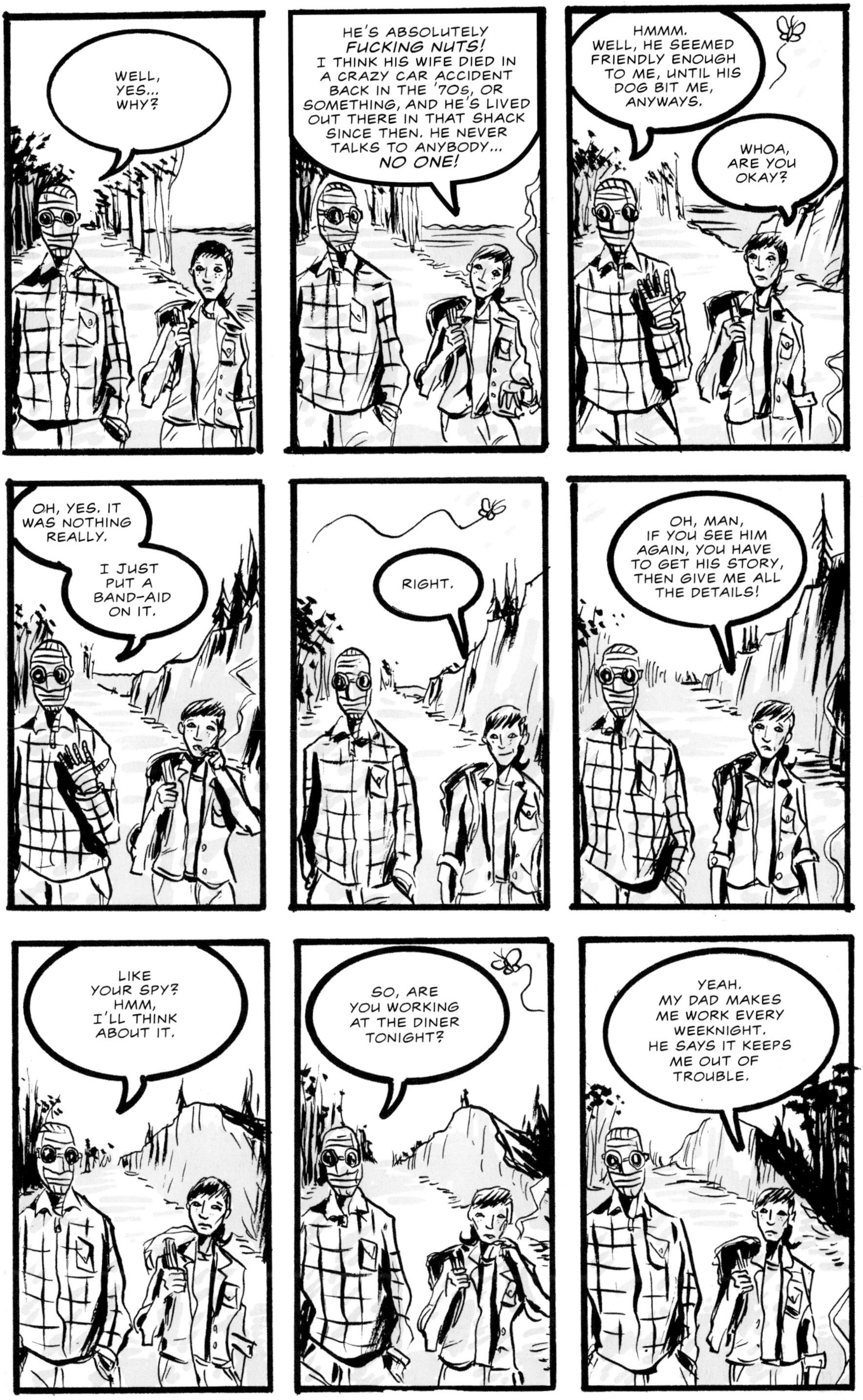
WELL, YES... WHY?
HE'S ABSOLUTELY FUCKING NUTS! I THINK HIS WIFE DIED IN A CRAZY CAR ACCIDENT BACK IN THE '70s, OR SOMETHING, AND HE'S LIVED OUT THERE IN THAT SHACK SINCE THEN. HE NEVER TALKS TO ANYBODY... NO ONE!
HMMM. WELL, HE SEEMED FRIENDLY ENOUGH TO ME, UNTIL HIS DOG BIT ME, ANYWAYS.
WHOA, ARE YOU OKAY?
OH, YES. IT WAS NOTHING REALLY.
I JUST PUT A BAND-AID ON IT.
RIGHT.
OH, MAN, IF YOU SEE HIM AGAIN, YOU HAVE TO GET HIS STORY, THEN GIVE ME ALL THE DETAILS!
LIKE YOUR SPY? HMM, I'LL THINK ABOUT IT.
SO, ARE YOU WORKING AT THE DINER TONIGHT?
YEAH. MY DAD MAKES ME WORK EVERY WEEKNIGHT. HE SAYS IT KEEPS ME OUT OF TROUBLE.

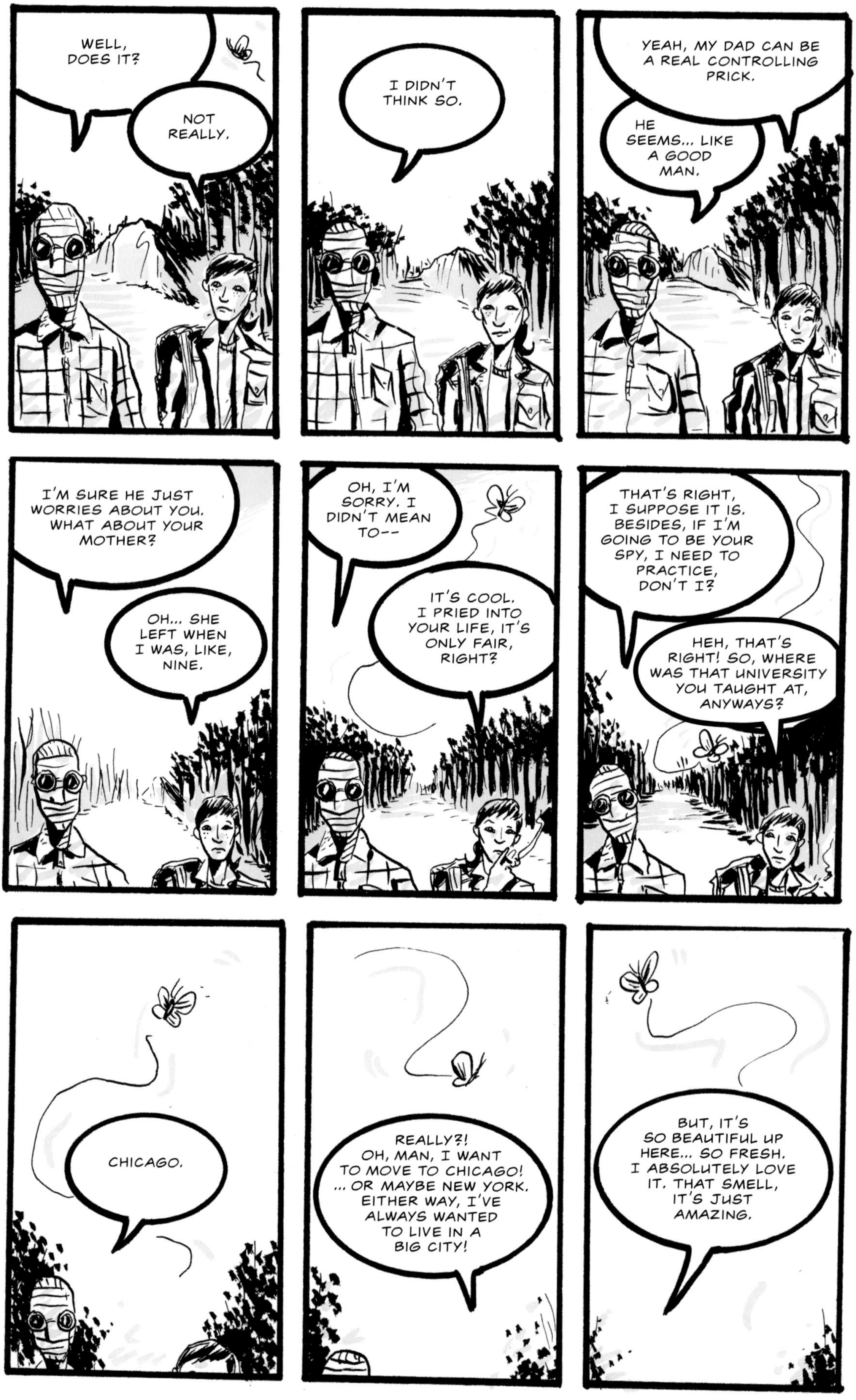
WELL, DOES IT?
NOT REALLY.
I DIDN'T THINK SO.
YEAH, MY DAD CAN BE A REAL CONTROLLING PRICK.
HE SEEMS... LIKE A GOOD MAN.
I'M SURE HE JUST WORRIES ABOUT YOU. WHAT ABOUT YOUR MOTHER?
OH... SHE LEFT WHEN I WAS, LIKE, NINE.
OH, I'M SORRY. I DIDN'T MEAN TO--
IT'S COOL. I PRIED INTO YOUR LIFE, IT'S ONLY FAIR, RIGHT?
THAT'S RIGHT, I SUPPOSE IT IS. BESIDES, IF I'M GOING TO BE YOUR SPY, I NEED TO PRACTICE, DON'T I?
HEH, THAT'S RIGHT! SO, WHERE WAS THAT UNIVERSITY YOU TAUGHT AT, ANYWAYS?
CHICAGO.
REALLY?! OH, MAN, I WANT TO MOVE TO CHICAGO! ...OR MAYBE NEW YORK. EITHER WAY, I'VE ALWAYS WANTED TO LIVE IN A BIG CITY!
BUT, IT'S SO BEAUTIFUL UP HERE... SO FRESH. I ABSOLUTELY LOVE IT. THAT SMELL, IT'S JUST AMAZING.

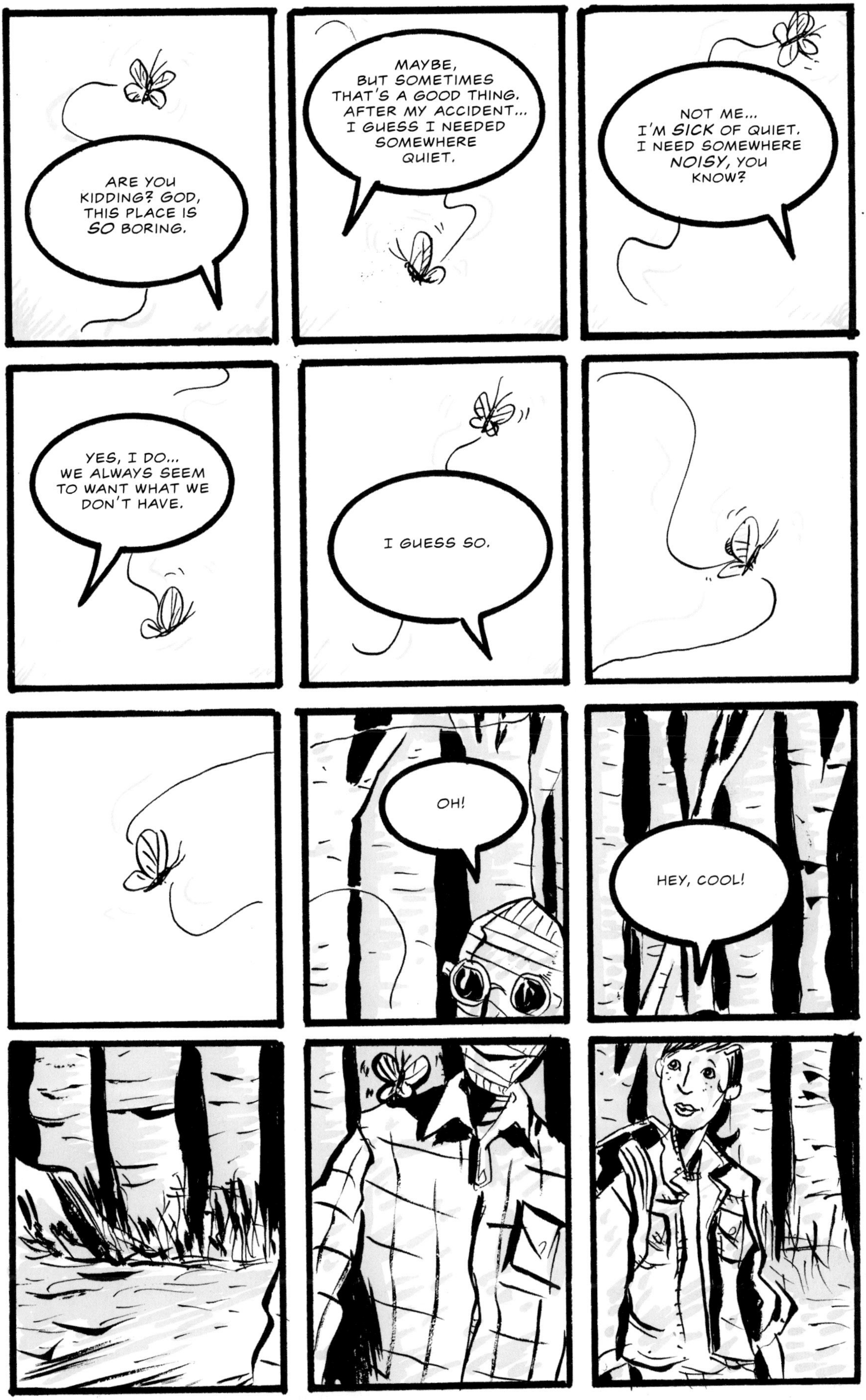
ARE YOU KIDDING? GOD, THIS PLACE IS SO BORING.
MAYBE, BUT SOMETIMES THAT'S A GOOD THING. AFTER MY ACCIDENT... I GUESS I NEEDED SOMEWHERE QUIET.
NOT ME... I'M SICK OF QUIET. I NEED SOMEWHERE NOISY, YOU KNOW?
YES, I DO... WE ALWAYS SEEM TO WANT WHAT WE DON'T HAVE.
I GUESS SO.
OH!
HEY, COOL!

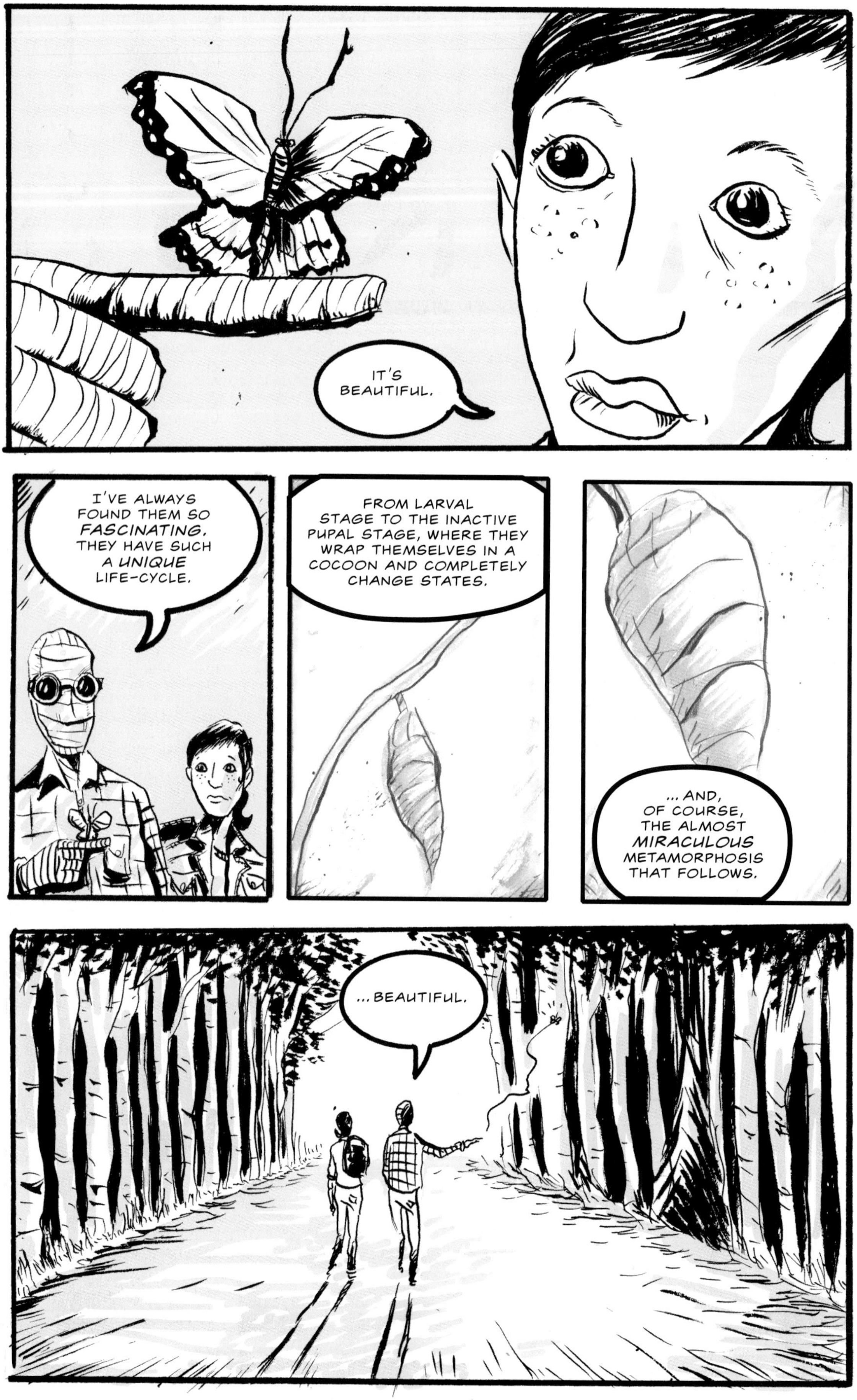
IT'S BEAUTIFUL.
I'VE ALWAYS FOUND THEM SO FASCINATING. THEY HAVE SUCH A UNIQUE LIFE-CYCLE.
FROM LARVAL STAGE TO THE INACTIVE PUPAL STAGE, WHERE THEY WRAP THEMSELVES IN A COCOON AND COMPLETELY CHANGE STATES.
...AND, OF COURSE, THE ALMOST MIRACULOUS METAMORPHOSIS THAT FOLLOWS.
...BEAUTIFUL.

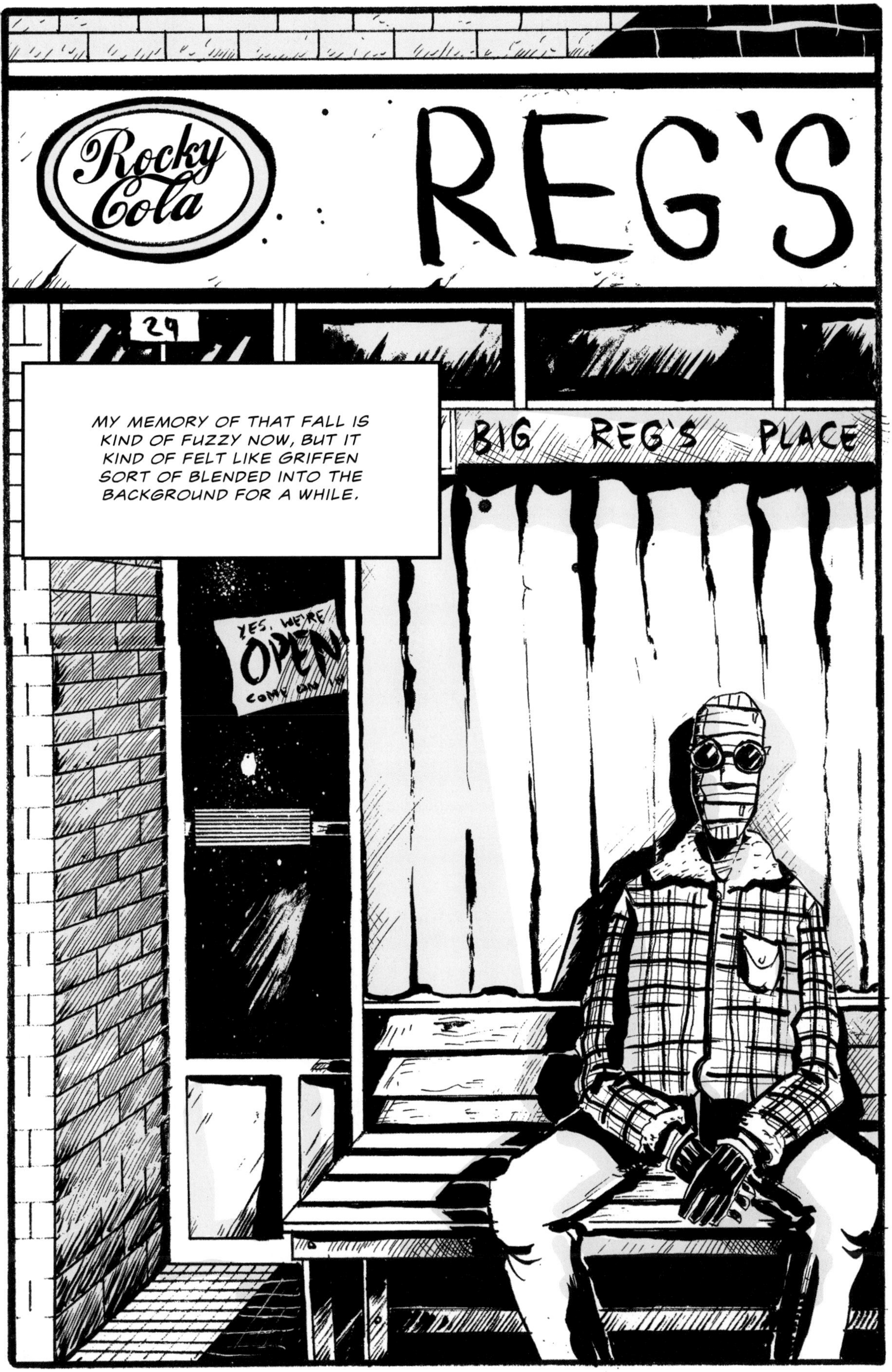
Rocky Cola
REG'S
29
MY MEMORY OF THAT FALL IS KIND OF FUZZY NOW, BUT IT KIND OF FELT LIKE GRIFFEN SORT OF BLENDED INTO THE BACKGROUND FOR A WHILE.
BIG REG'S PLACE
YES, WE'RE
OPEN

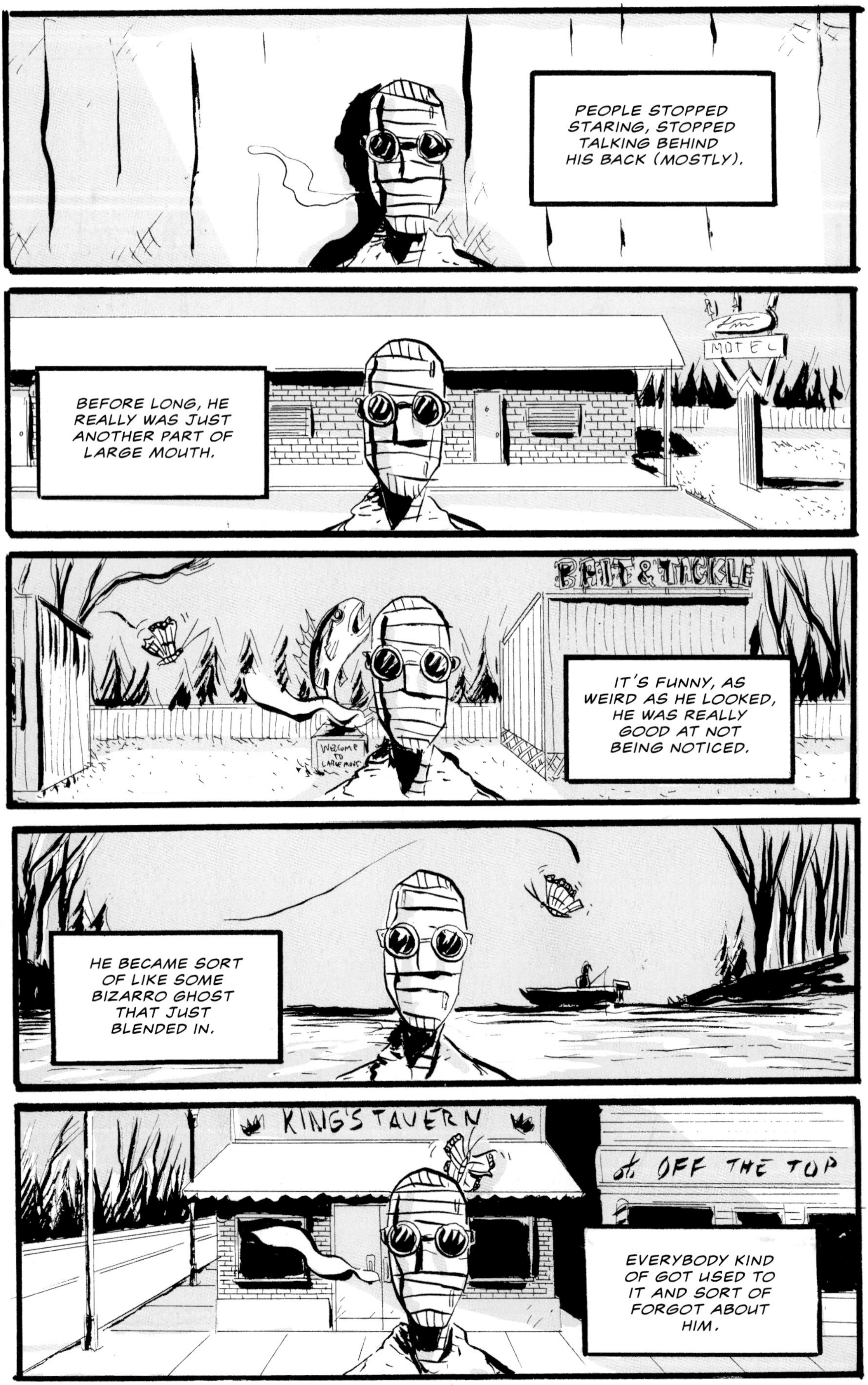
PEOPLE STOPPED STARING, STOPPED TALKING BEHIND HIS BACK (MOSTLY).
MOTEL
BEFORE LONG, HE REALLY WAS JUST ANOTHER PART OF LARGE MOUTH.
BAIT & TACKLE
IT'S FUNNY, AS WEIRD AS HE LOOKED, HE WAS REALLY GOOD AT NOT BEING NOTICED.
HE BECAME SORT OF LIKE SOME BIZARRO GHOST THAT JUST BLENDED IN.
KING'S TAVERN
OFF THE TOP
EVERYBODY KIND OF GOT USED TO IT AND SORT OF FORGOT ABOUT HIM.

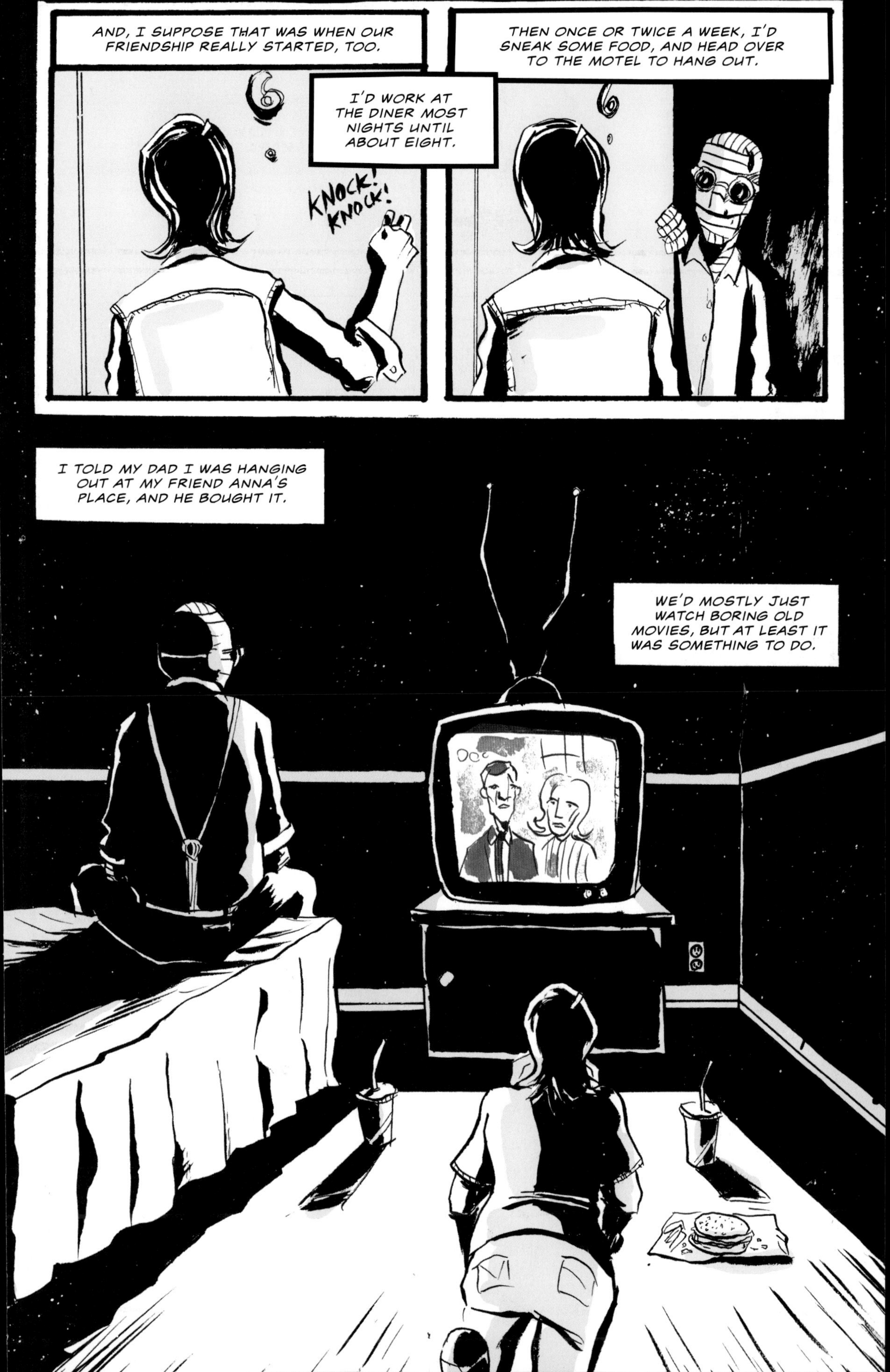
AND, I SUPPOSE THAT WAS WHEN OUR FRIENDSHIP REALLY STARTED, TOO.
I'D WORK AT THE DINER MOST NIGHTS UNTIL ABOUT EIGHT.
KNOCK! KNOCK!
THEN ONCE OR TWICE A WEEK, I'D SNEAK SOME FOOD, AND HEAD OVER TO THE MOTEL TO HANG OUT.
I TOLD MY DAD I WAS HANGING OUT AT MY FRIEND ANNA'S PLACE, AND HE BOUGHT IT.
WE'D MOSTLY JUST WATCH BORING OLD MOVIES, BUT AT LEAST IT WAS SOMETHING TO DO.

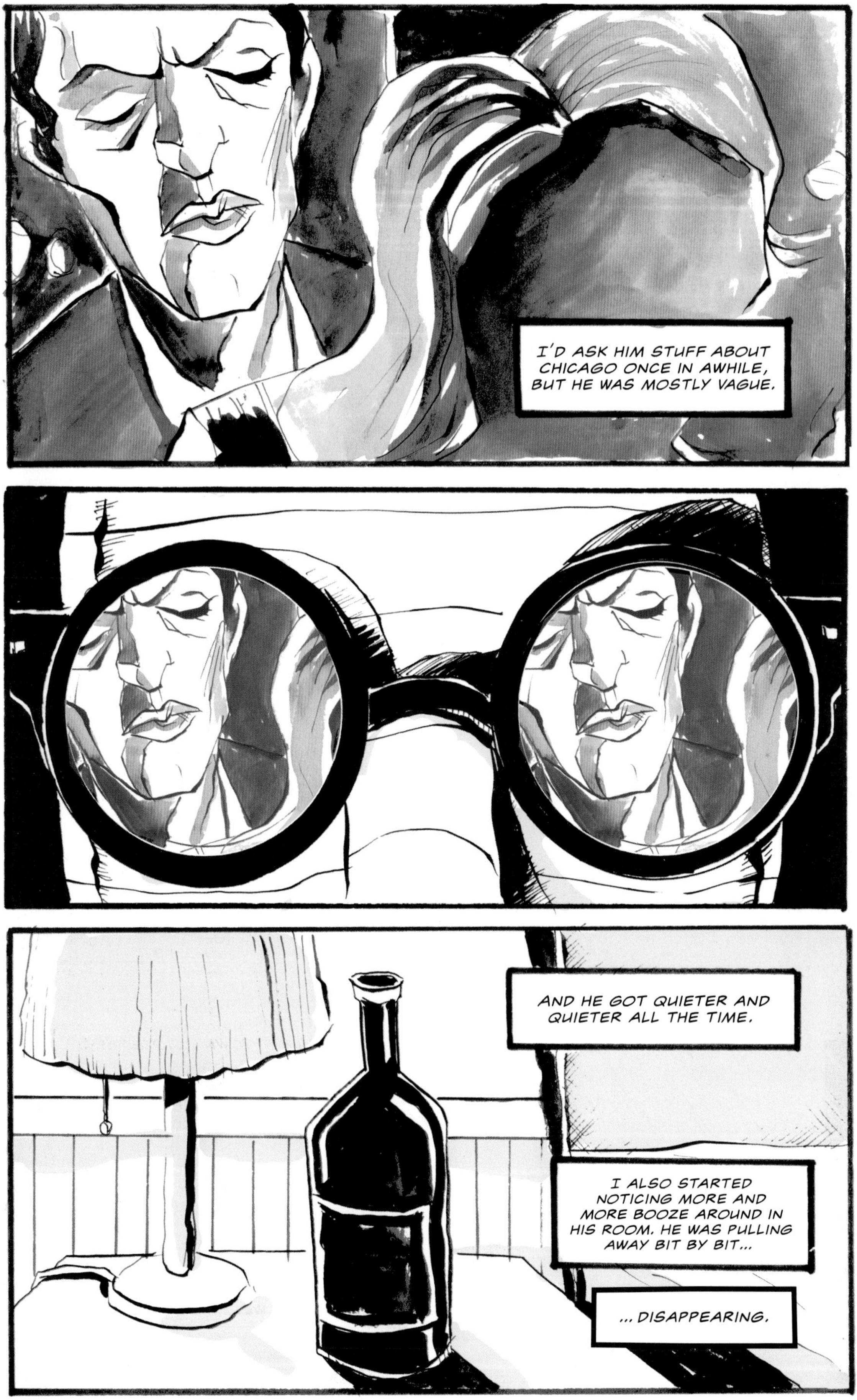
I'D ASK HIM STUFF ABOUT CHICAGO ONCE IN AWHILE, BUT HE WAS MOSTLY VAGUE.
AND HE GOT QUIETER AND QUIETER ALL THE TIME.
I ALSO STARTED NOTICING MORE AND MORE BOOZE AROUND IN HIS ROOM. HE WAS PULLING AWAY BIT BY BIT...
...DISAPPEARING.

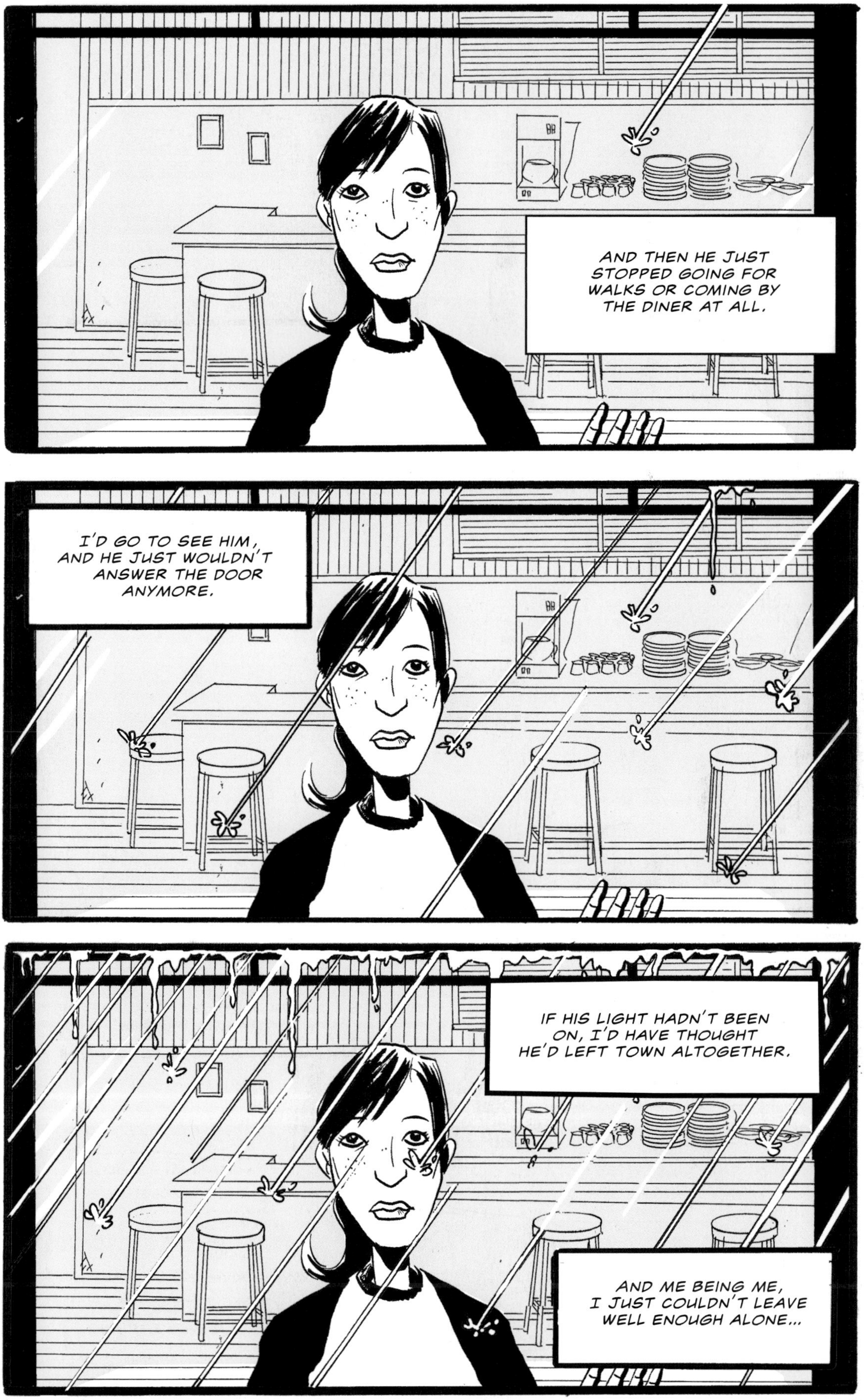
AND THEN HE JUST STOPPED GOING FOR WALKS OR COMING BY THE DINER AT ALL.
I'D GO TO SEE HIM, AND HE JUST WOULDN'T ANSWER THE DOOR ANYMORE.
IF HIS LIGHT HADN'T BEEN ON, I'D HAVE THOUGHT HE'D LEFT TOWN ALTOGETHER.
AND ME BEING ME, I JUST COULDN'T LEAVE WELL ENOUGH ALONE...

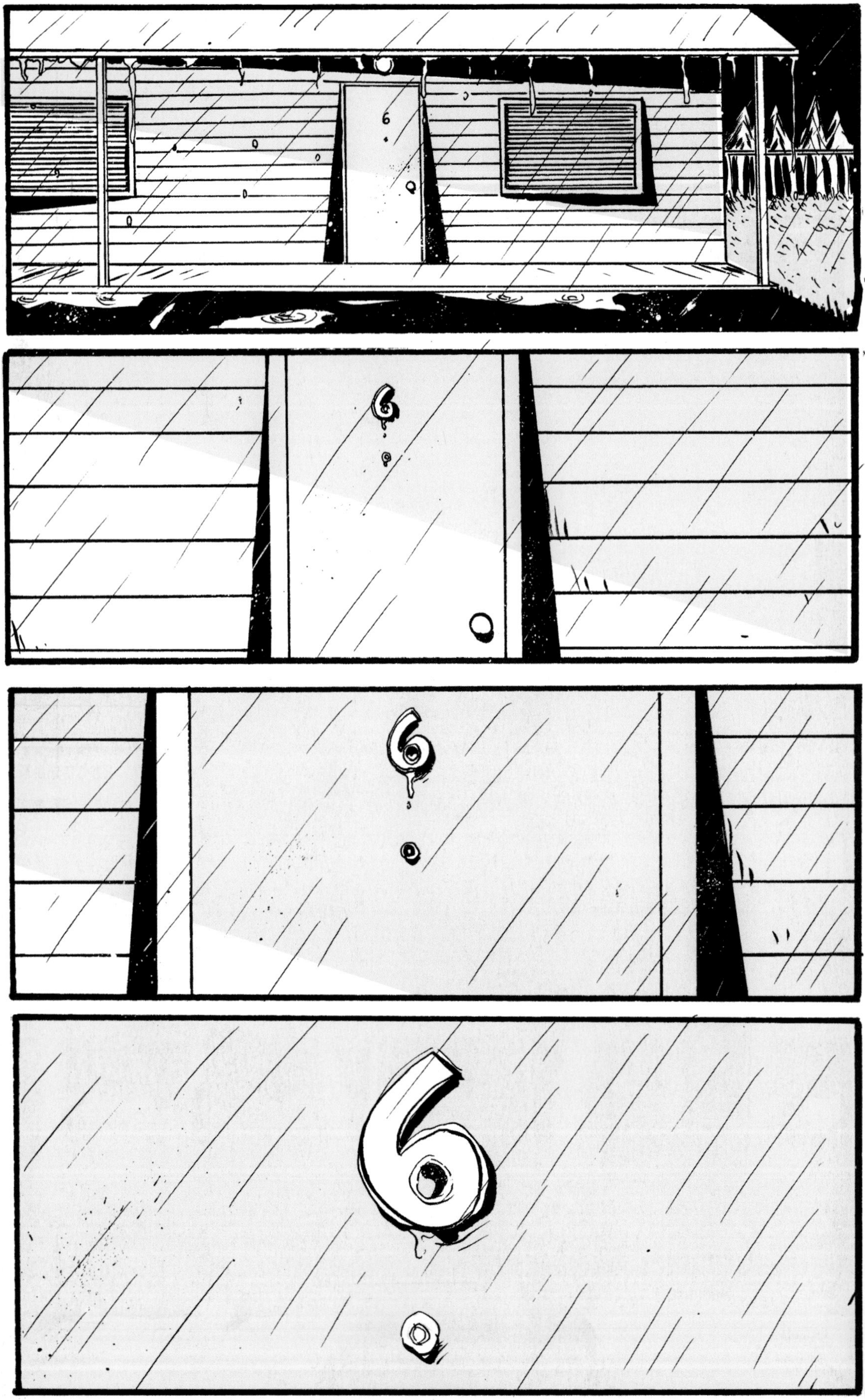
6

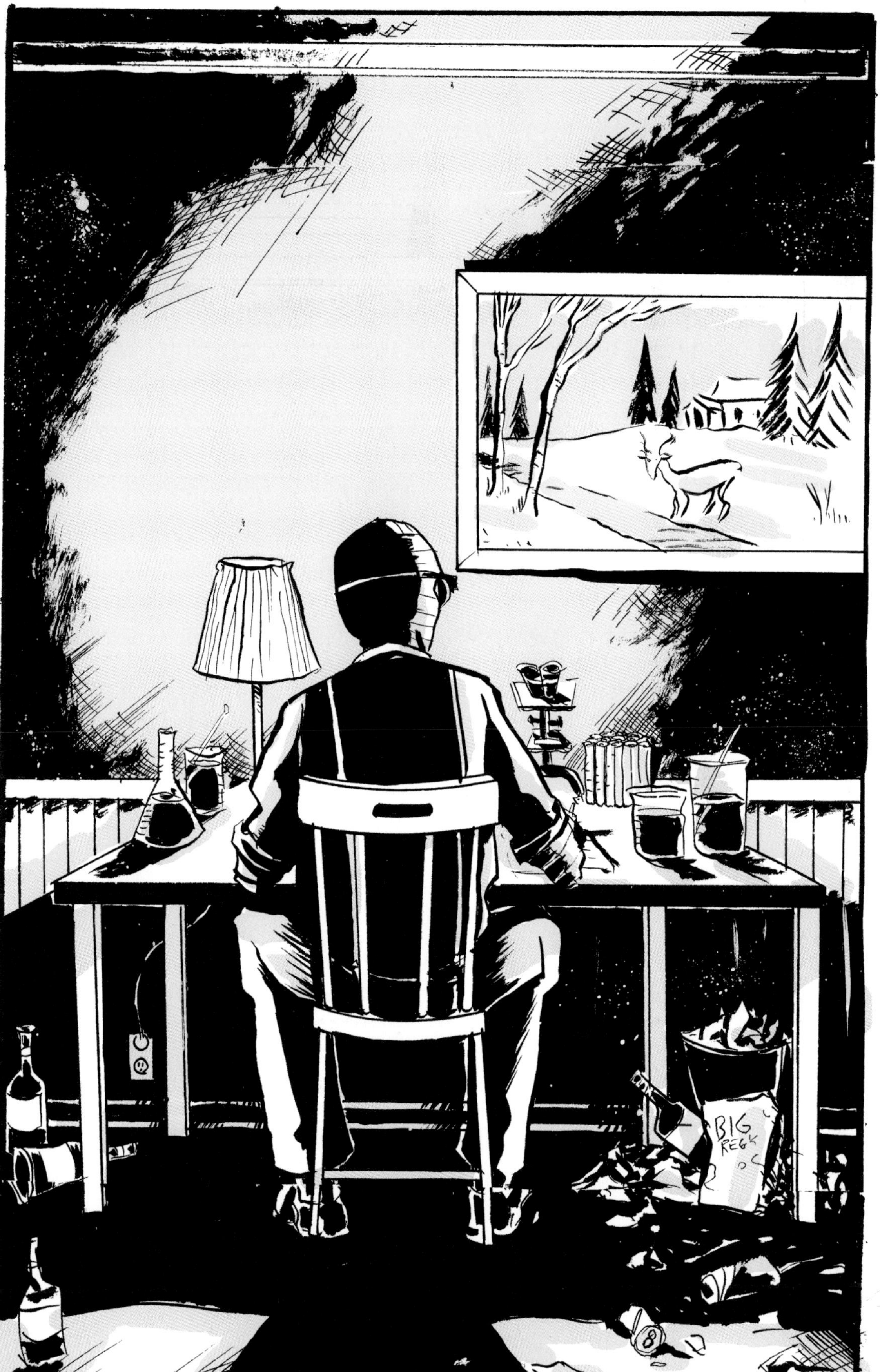
BIG
REGK

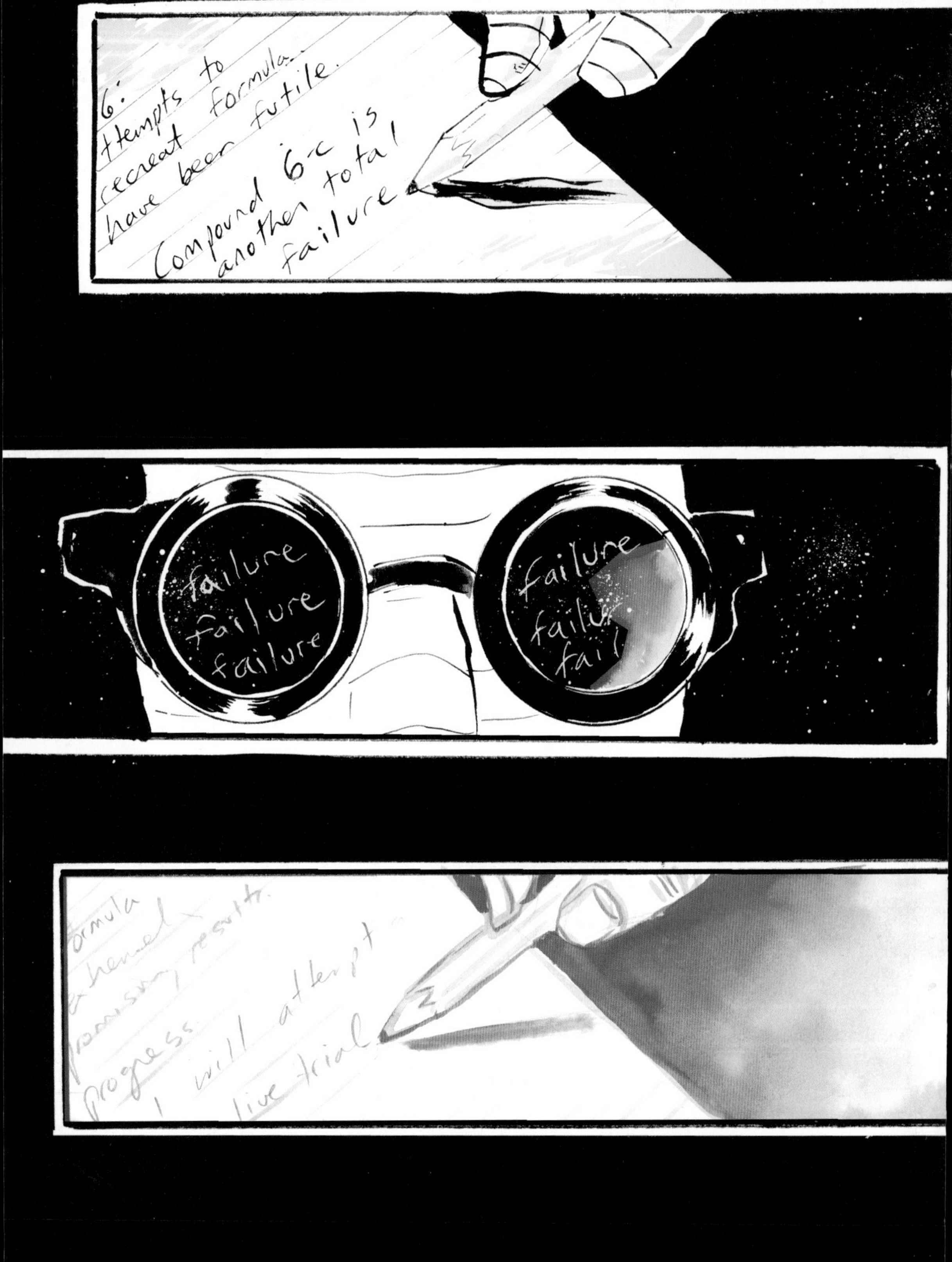
6:
ttempts to recreat formula have been futile.
Compound 6-c is another total failure
failure
failure
failure
failure
failu
fail
ormula
progress.
I will attempt a
live trial.

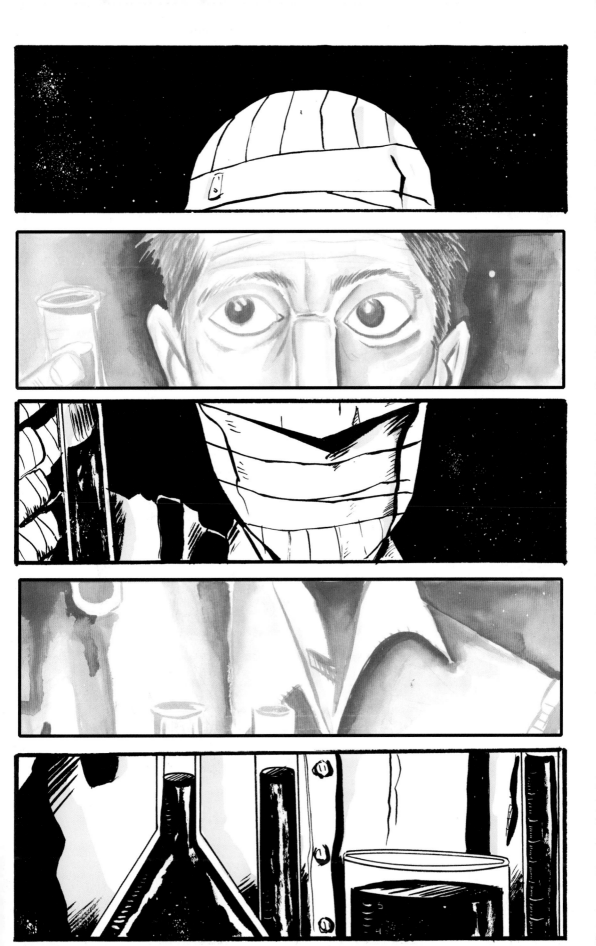

will
attempt
live

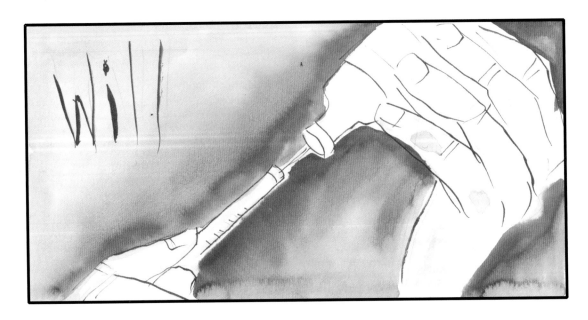

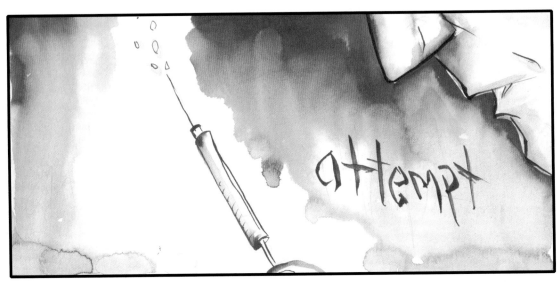

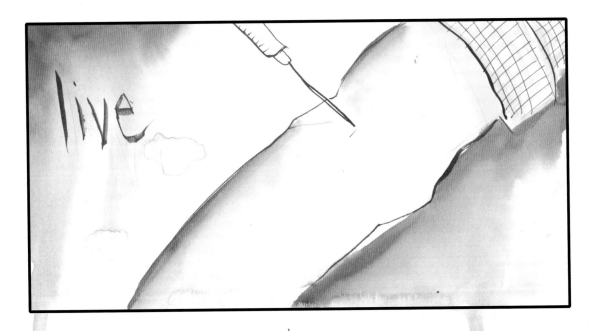

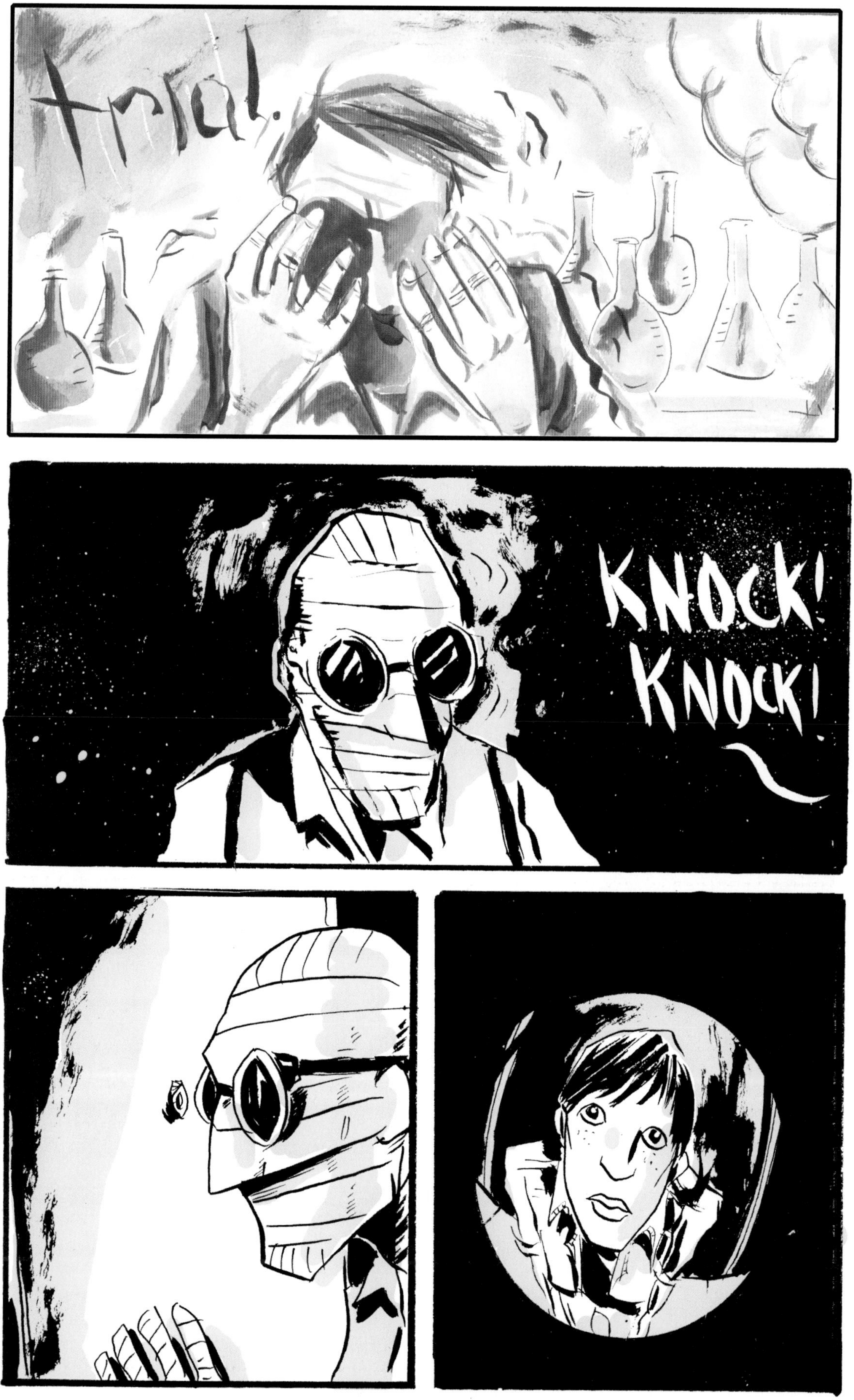
thud.
KNOCK! KNOCK!

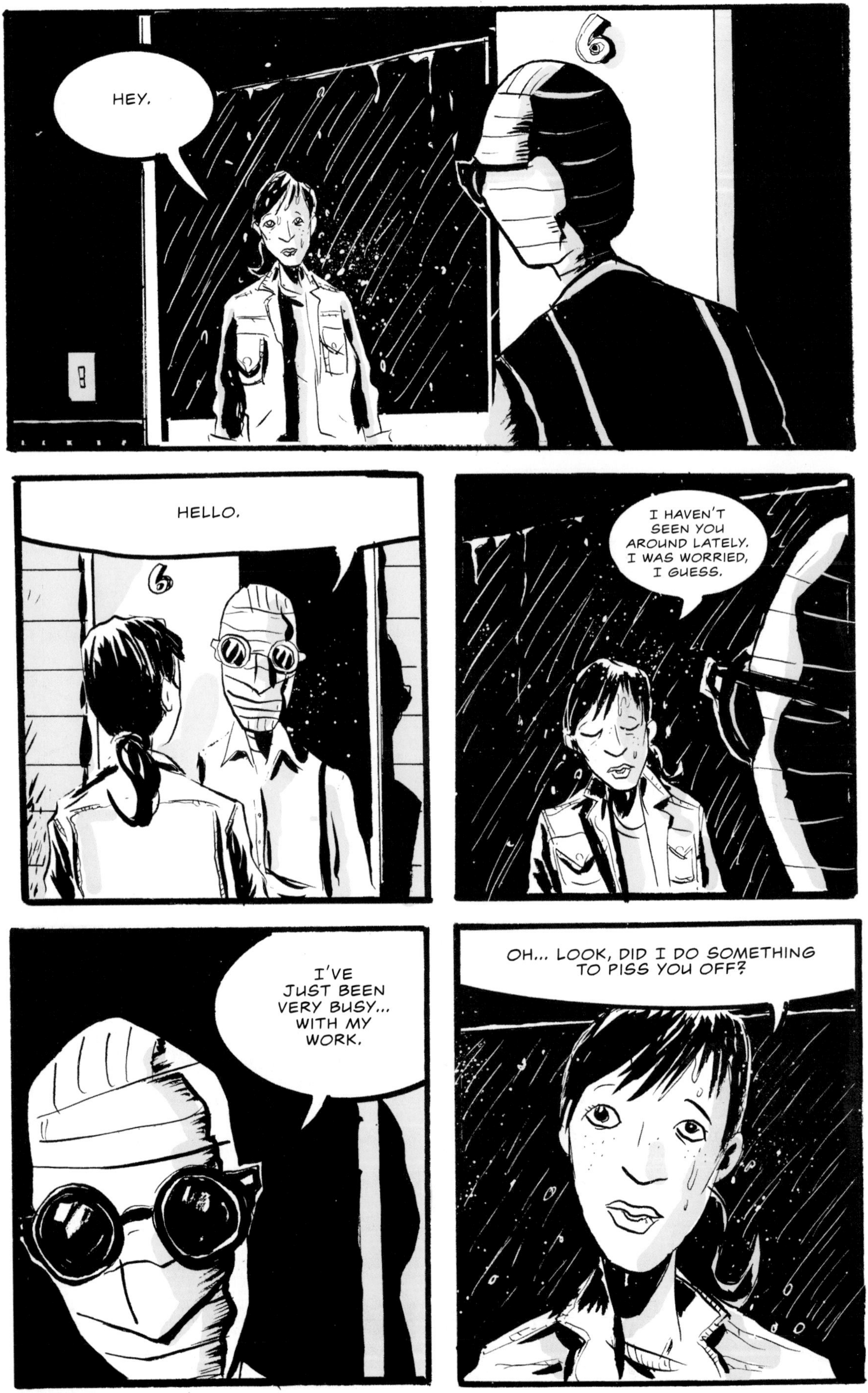
HEY.
HELLO.
I HAVEN'T SEEN YOU AROUND LATELY. I WAS WORRIED, I GUESS.
I'VE JUST BEEN VERY BUSY... WITH MY WORK.
OH... LOOK, DID I DO SOMETHING TO PISS YOU OFF?

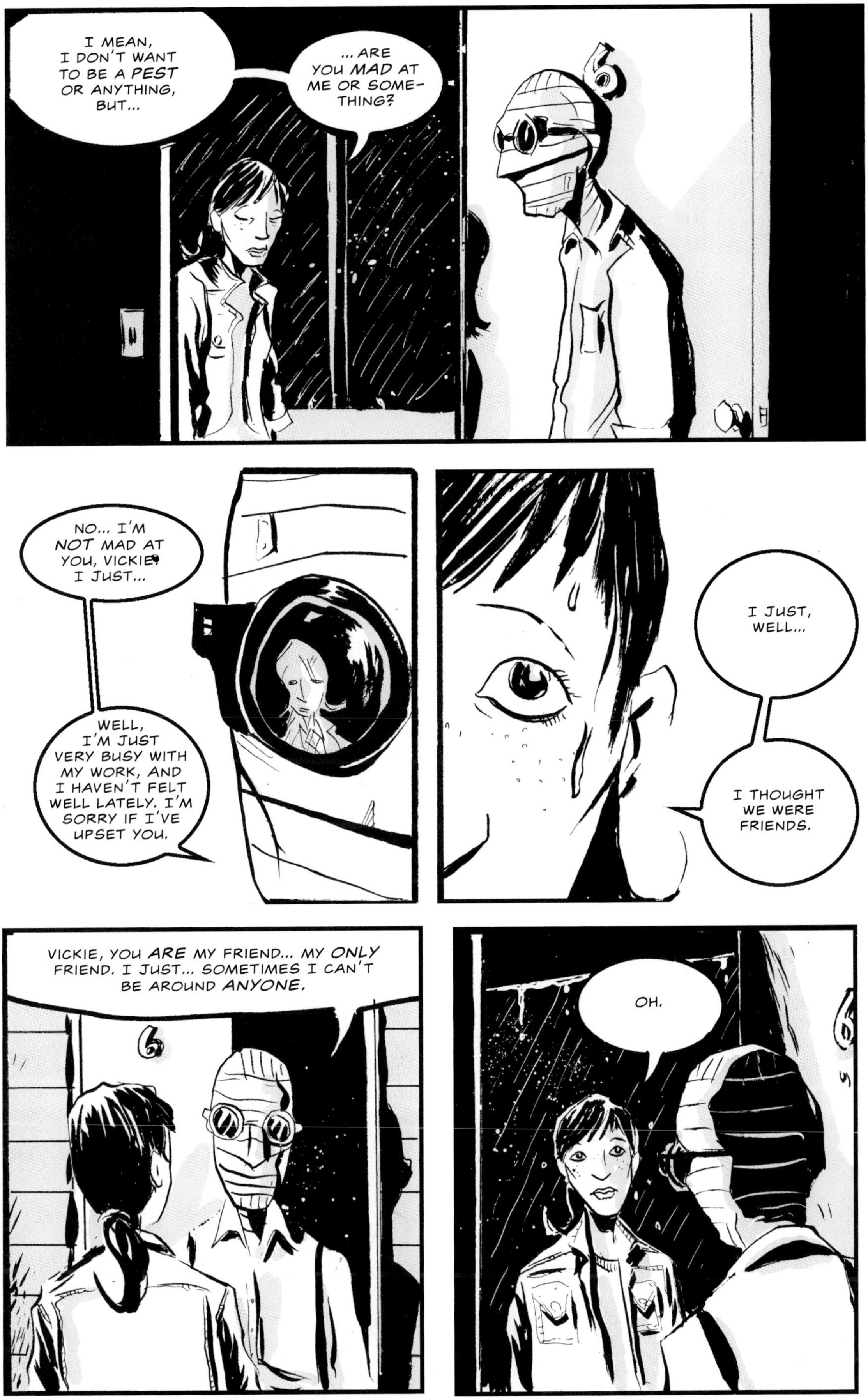
I MEAN, I DON'T WANT TO BE A PEST OR ANYTHING, BUT...
...ARE YOU MAD AT ME OR SOME-THING?
NO... I'M NOT MAD AT YOU, VICKIE. I JUST...
WELL, I'M JUST VERY BUSY WITH MY WORK, AND I HAVEN'T FELT WELL LATELY. I'M SORRY IF I'VE UPSET YOU.
I JUST, WELL...
I THOUGHT WE WERE FRIENDS.
VICKIE, YOU ARE MY FRIEND... MY ONLY FRIEND. I JUST... SOMETIMES I CAN'T BE AROUND ANYONE.
OH.

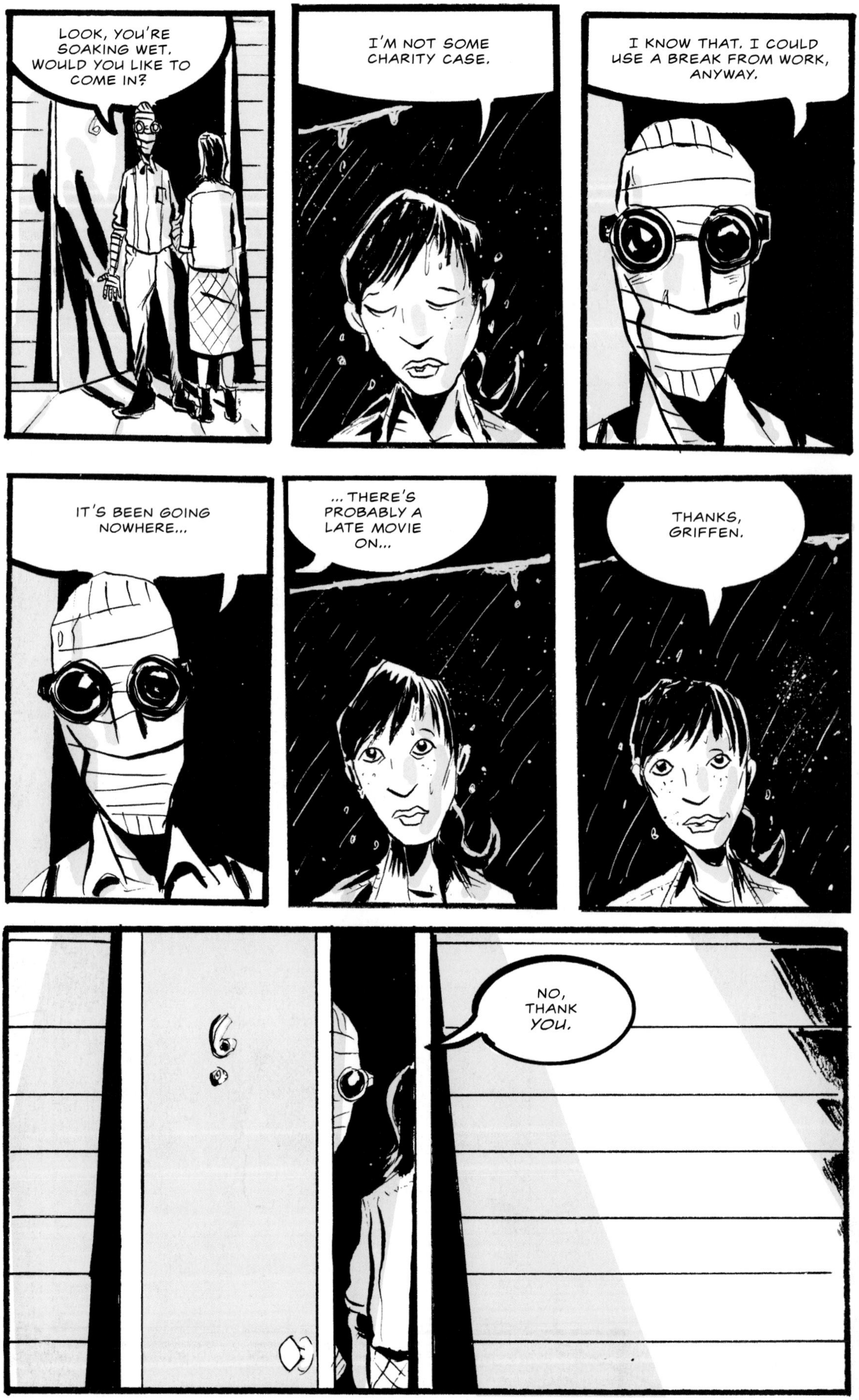
LOOK, YOU'RE SOAKING WET. WOULD YOU LIKE TO COME IN?
I'M NOT SOME CHARITY CASE.
I KNOW THAT. I COULD USE A BREAK FROM WORK, ANYWAY.
IT'S BEEN GOING NOWHERE...
...THERE'S PROBABLY A LATE MOVIE ON...
THANKS, GRIFFEN.
NO, THANK YOU.

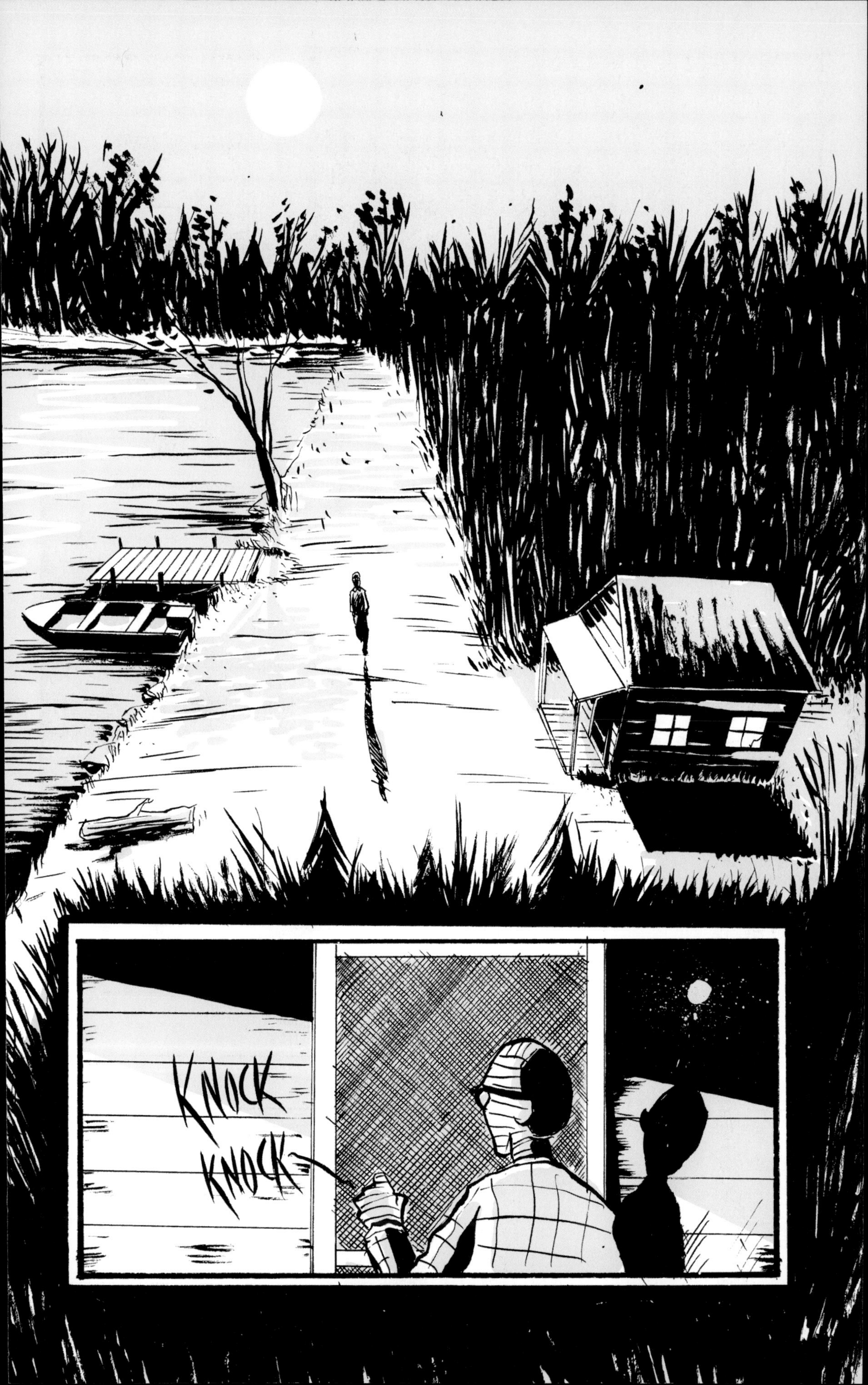
KNOCK
KNOCK

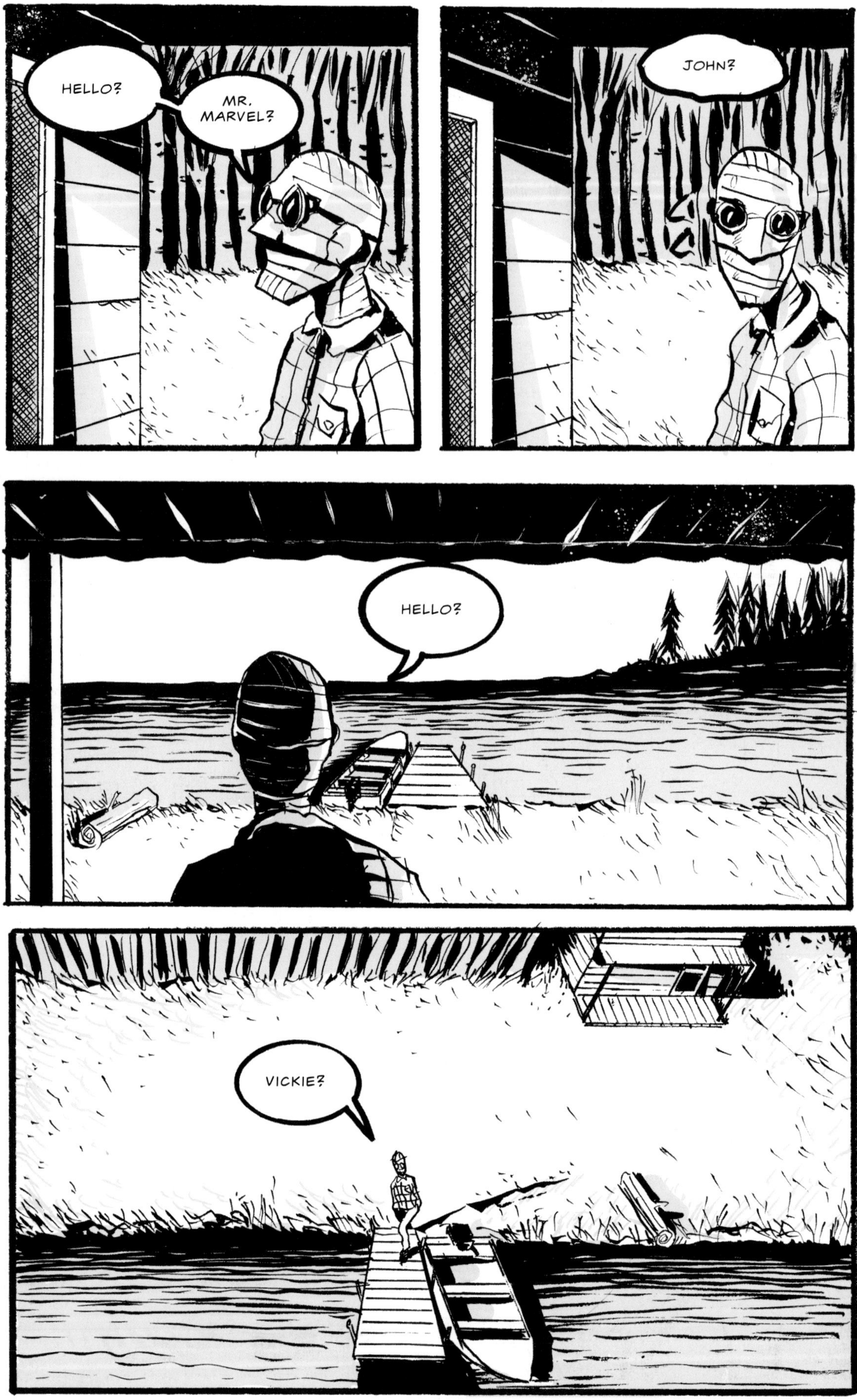
HELLO?
MR. MARVEL?
JOHN?
HELLO?
VICKIE?

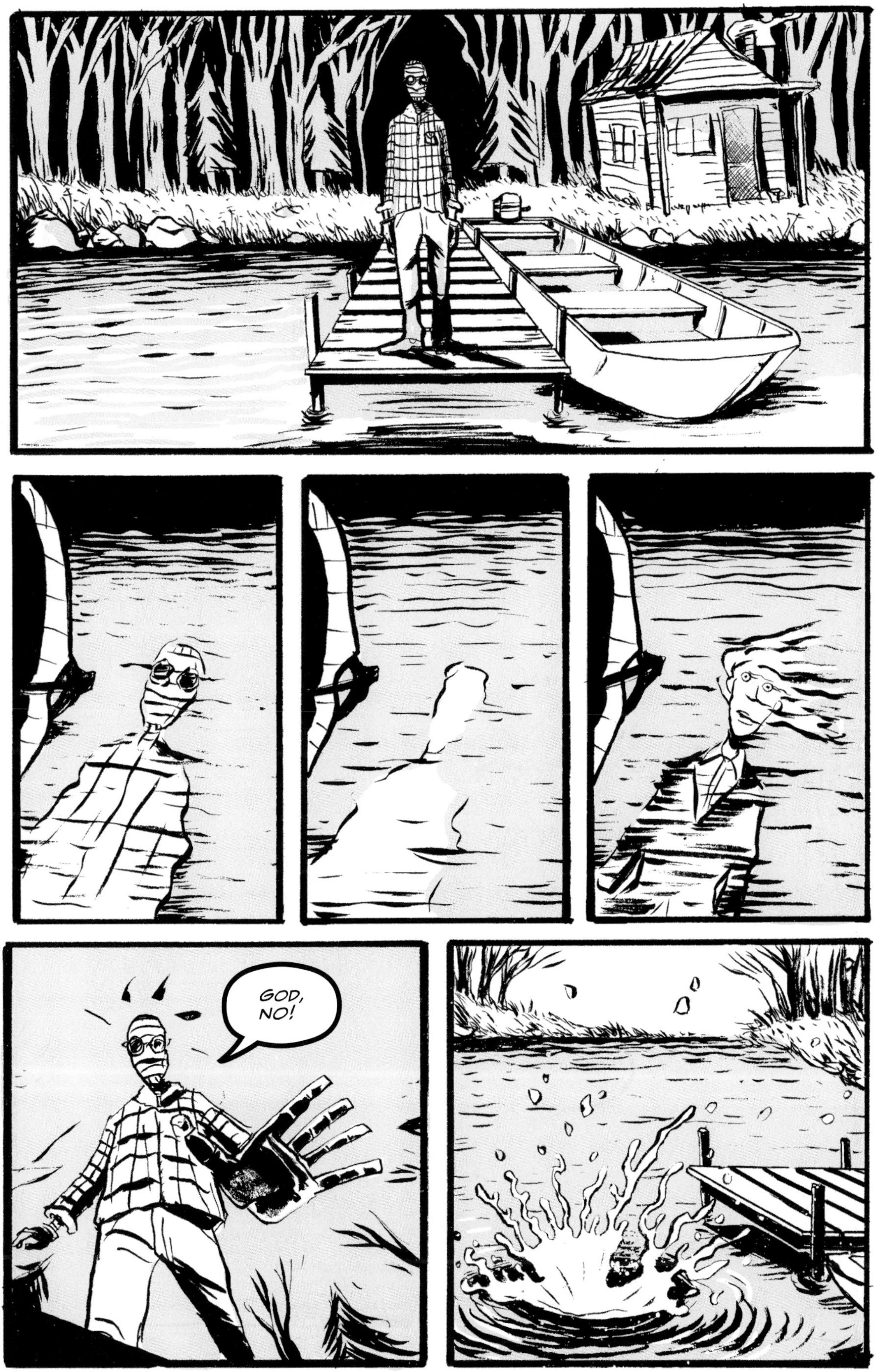
GOD, NO!

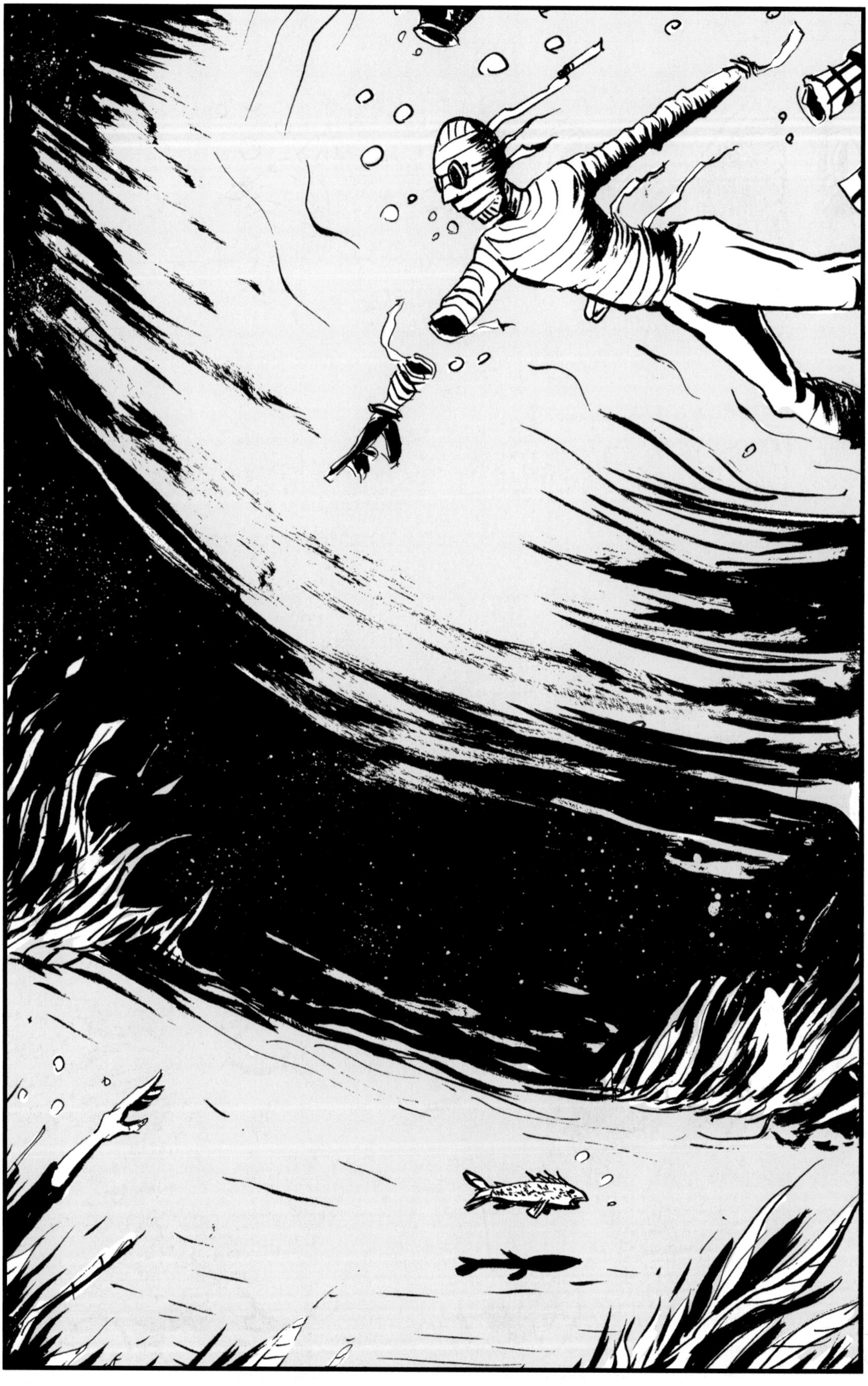

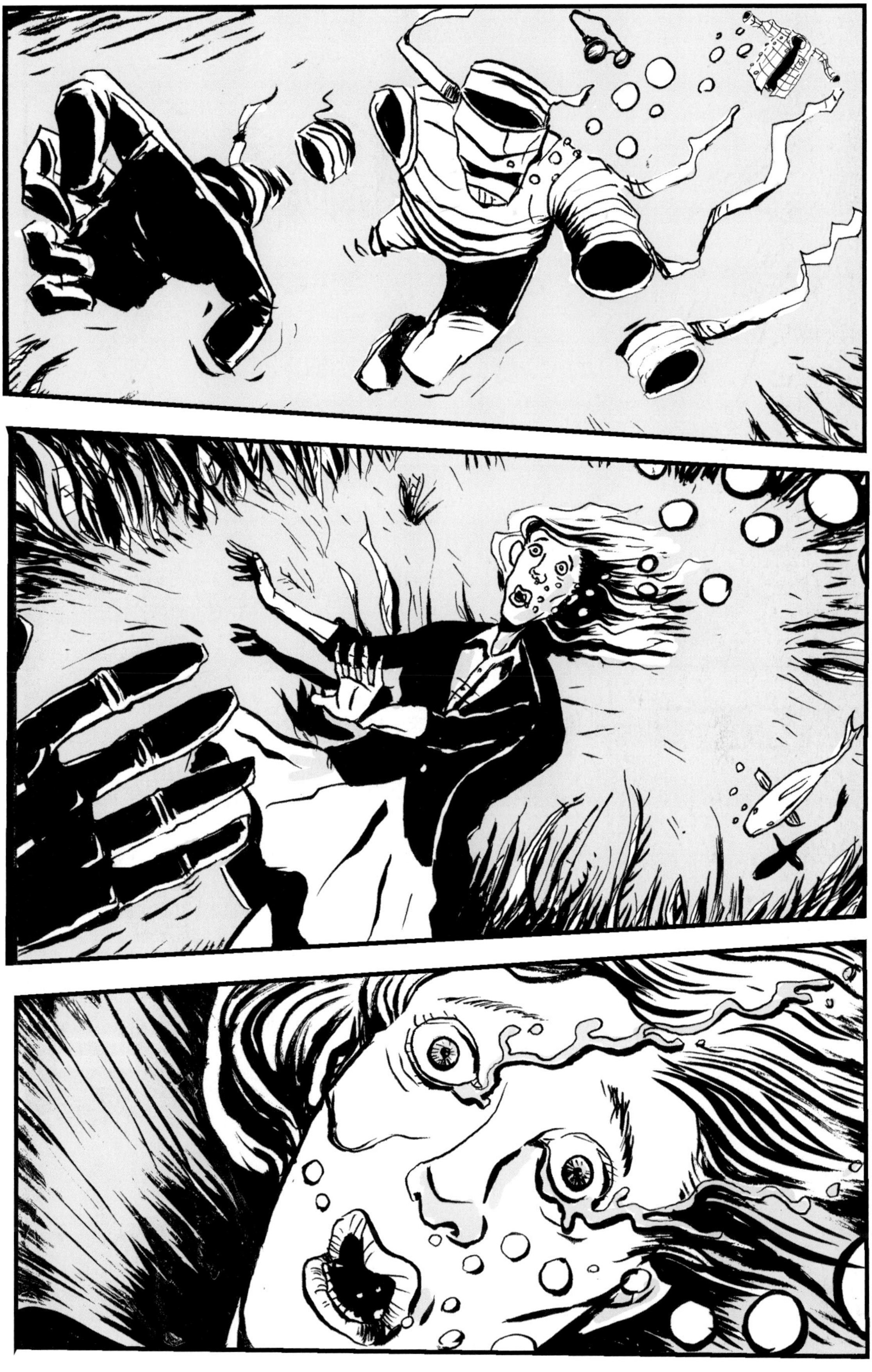

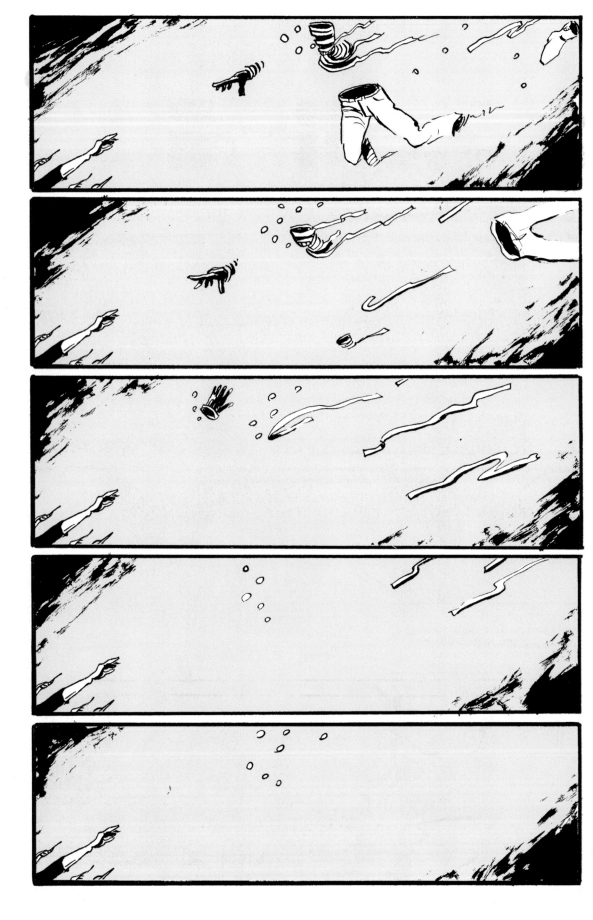

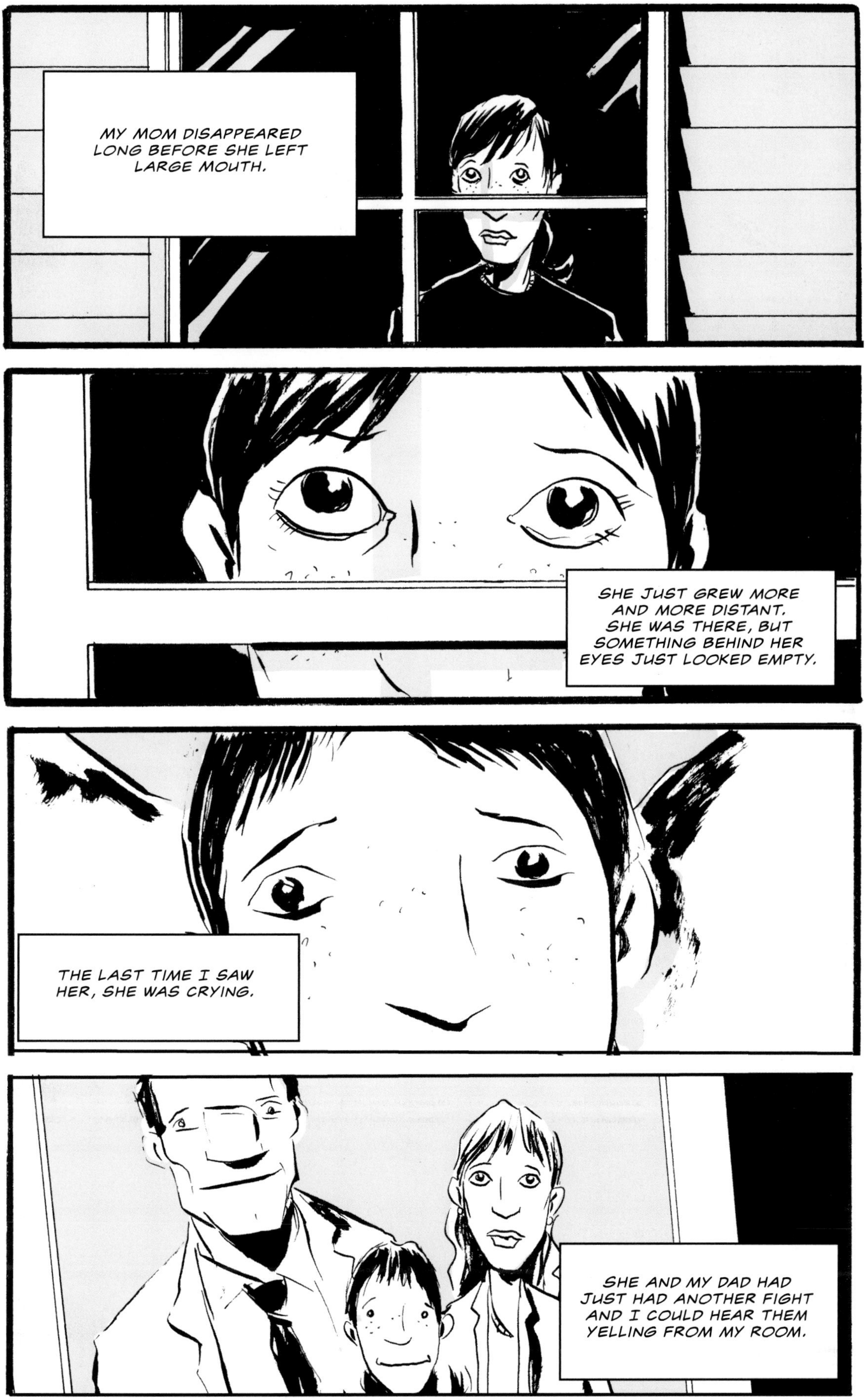
MY MOM DISAPPEARED LONG BEFORE SHE LEFT LARGE MOUTH.
SHE JUST GREW MORE AND MORE DISTANT. SHE WAS THERE, BUT SOMETHING BEHIND HER EYES JUST LOOKED EMPTY.
THE LAST TIME I SAW HER, SHE WAS CRYING.
SHE AND MY DAD HAD JUST HAD ANOTHER FIGHT AND I COULD HEAR THEM YELLING FROM MY ROOM.

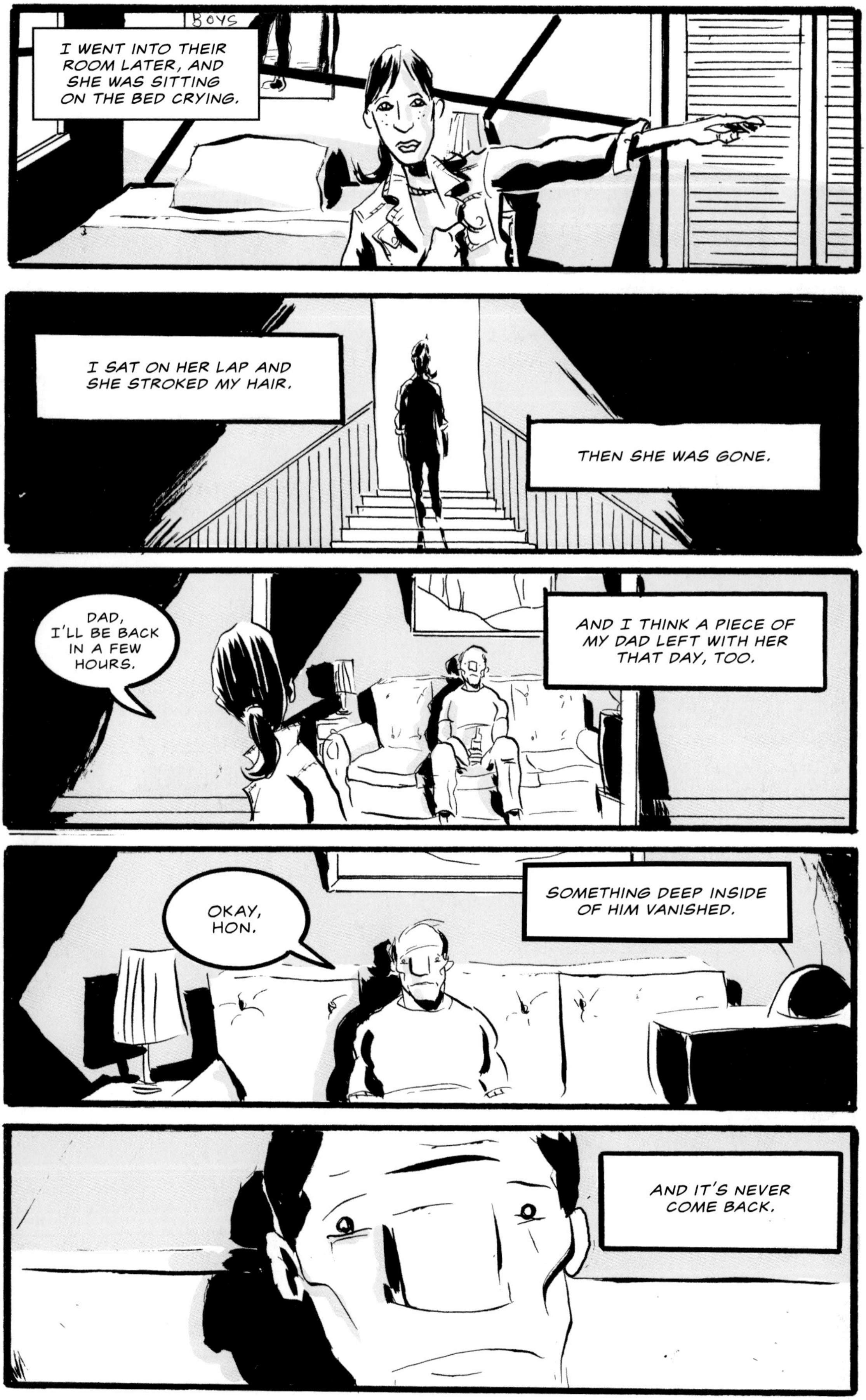
BOYS
I WENT INTO THEIR ROOM LATER, AND SHE WAS SITTING ON THE BED CRYING.
I SAT ON HER LAP AND SHE STROKED MY HAIR.
THEN SHE WAS GONE.
DAD, I'LL BE BACK IN A FEW HOURS.
AND I THINK A PIECE OF MY DAD LEFT WITH HER THAT DAY, TOO.
OKAY, HON.
SOMETHING DEEP INSIDE OF HIM VANISHED.
AND IT'S NEVER COME BACK.

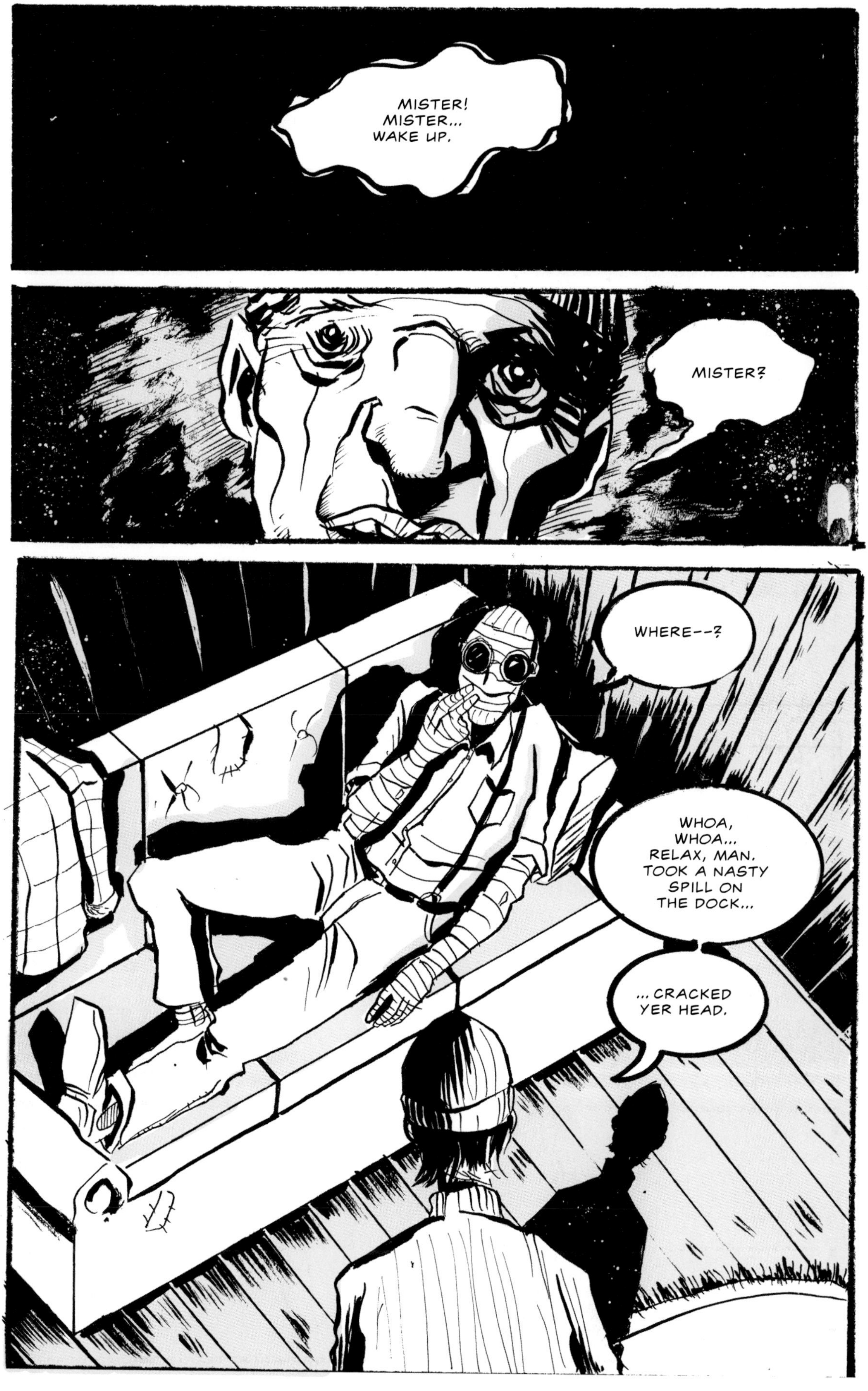
MISTER! MISTER... WAKE UP.
MISTER?
WHERE--?
WHOA, WHOA... RELAX, MAN. TOOK A NASTY SPILL ON THE DOCK...
...CRACKED YER HEAD.

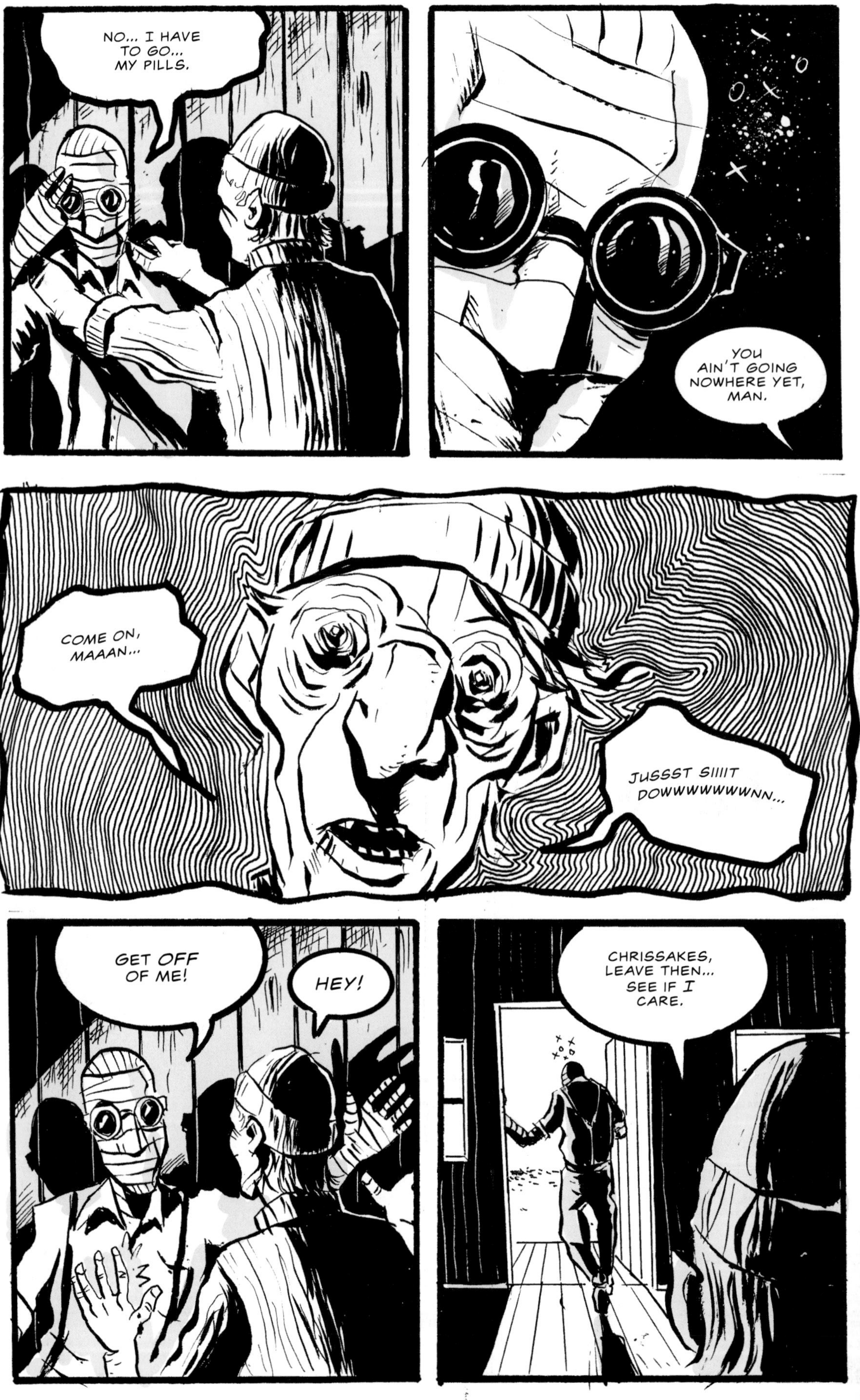
NO... I HAVE TO GO... MY PILLS.
YOU AIN'T GOING NOWHERE YET, MAN.
COME ON, MAAAN...
JUSSST SIIIIT DOWWWWWWWNN...
GET OFF OF ME!
HEY!
CHRISSAKES, LEAVE THEN... SEE IF I CARE.

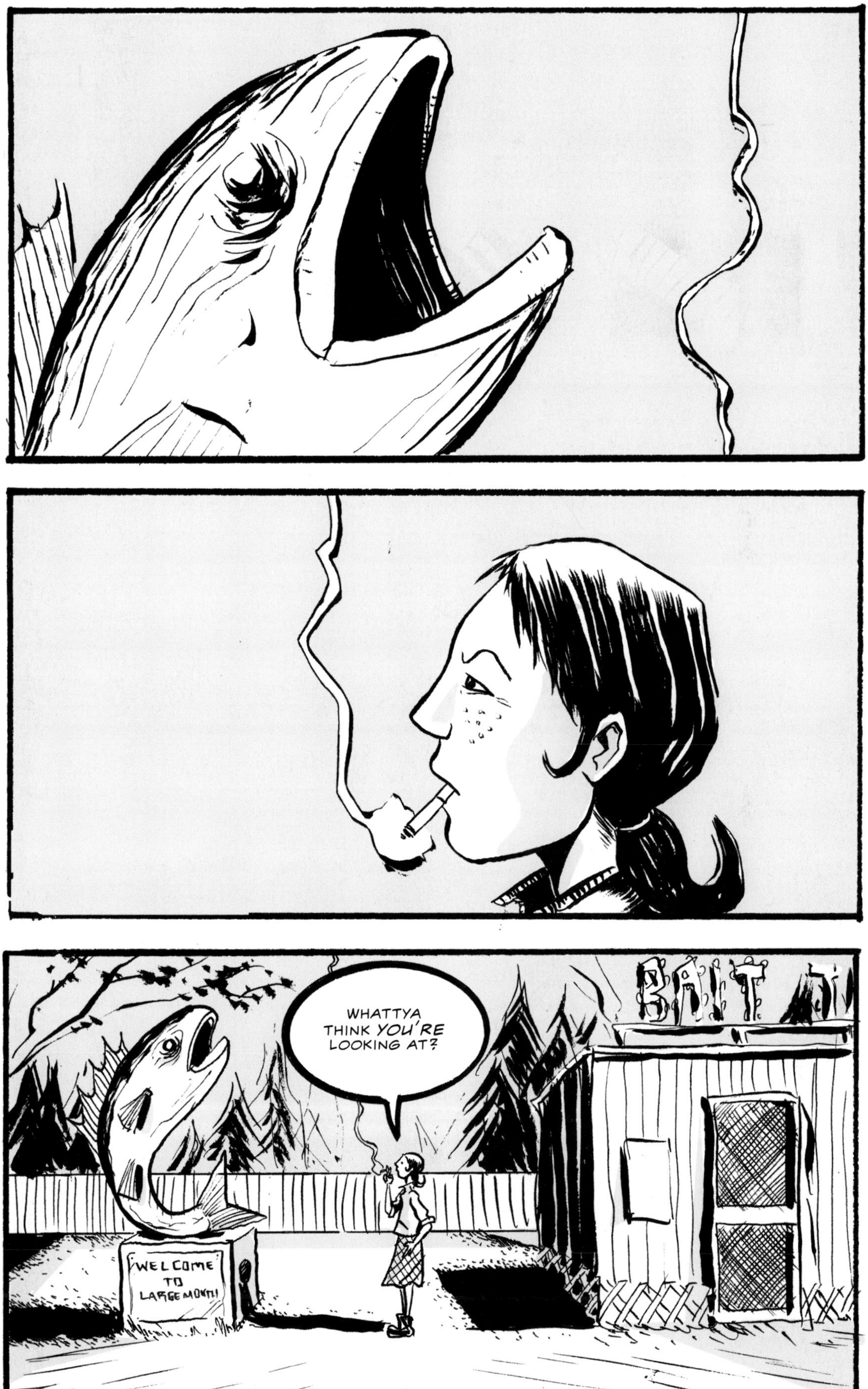
WHATTYA THINK *YOU'RE* LOOKING AT?
WELCOME TO LARGEMOUTH
BAIT

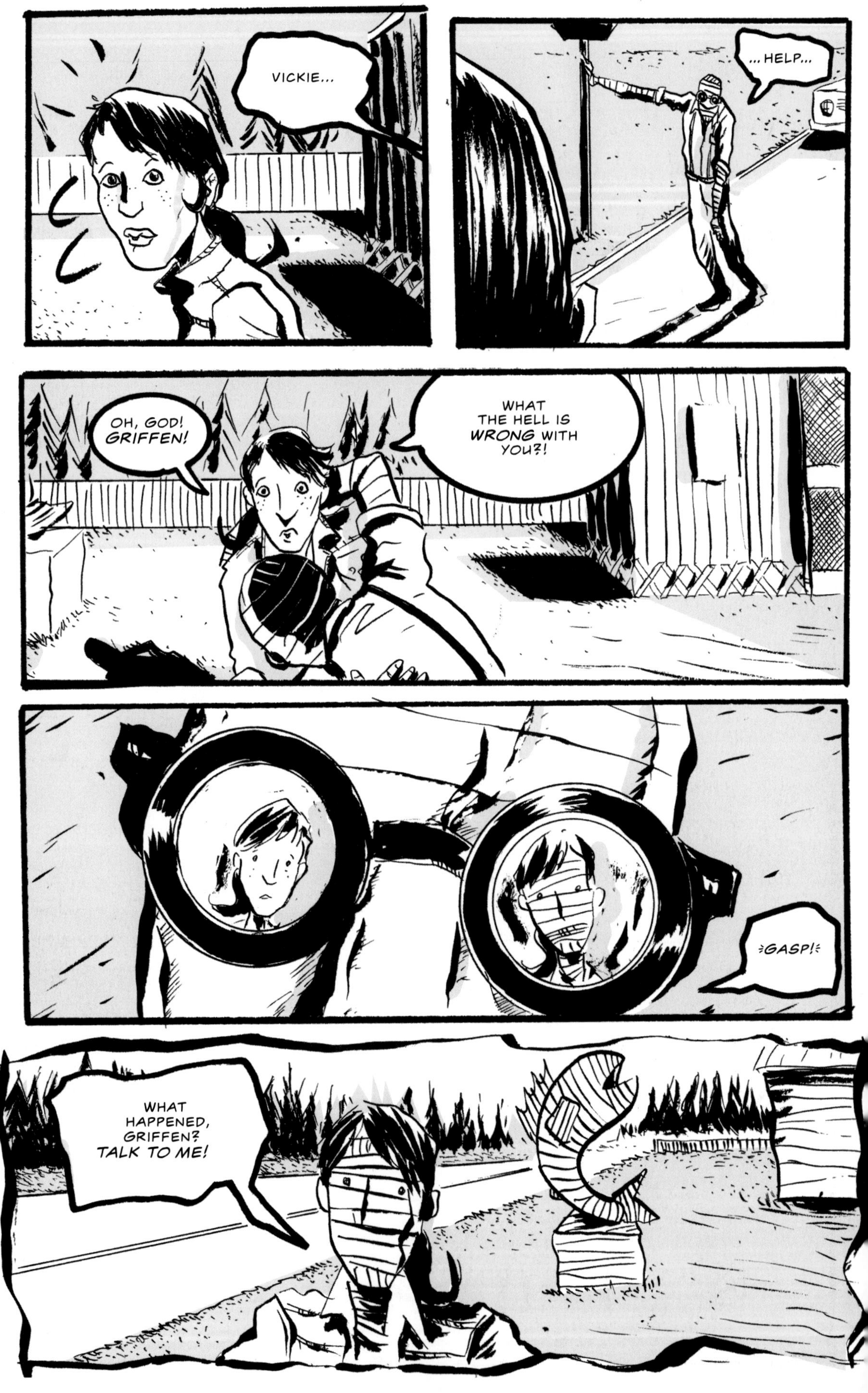
VICKIE...
...HELP...
OH, GOD! GRIFFEN!
WHAT THE HELL IS WRONG WITH YOU?!
GASP!
WHAT HAPPENED, GRIFFEN? TALK TO ME!

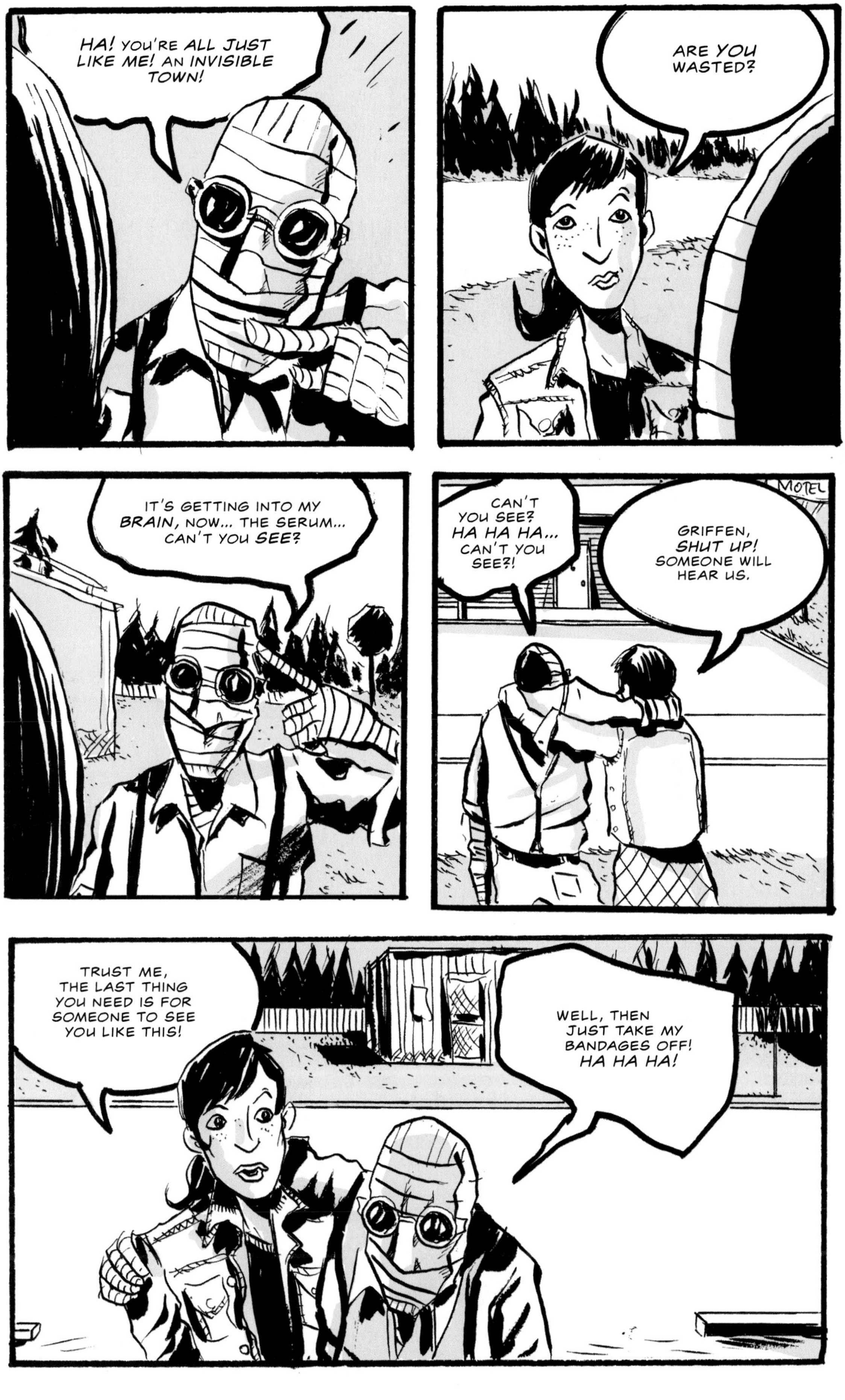
HA! YOU'RE ALL JUST LIKE ME! AN INVISIBLE TOWN!
ARE YOU WASTED?
IT'S GETTING INTO MY BRAIN, NOW... THE SERUM... CAN'T YOU SEE?
MOTEL
CAN'T YOU SEE? HA HA HA... CAN'T YOU SEE?!
GRIFFEN, SHUT UP! SOMEONE WILL HEAR US.
TRUST ME, THE LAST THING YOU NEED IS FOR SOMEONE TO SEE YOU LIKE THIS!
WELL, THEN JUST TAKE MY BANDAGES OFF! HA HA HA!

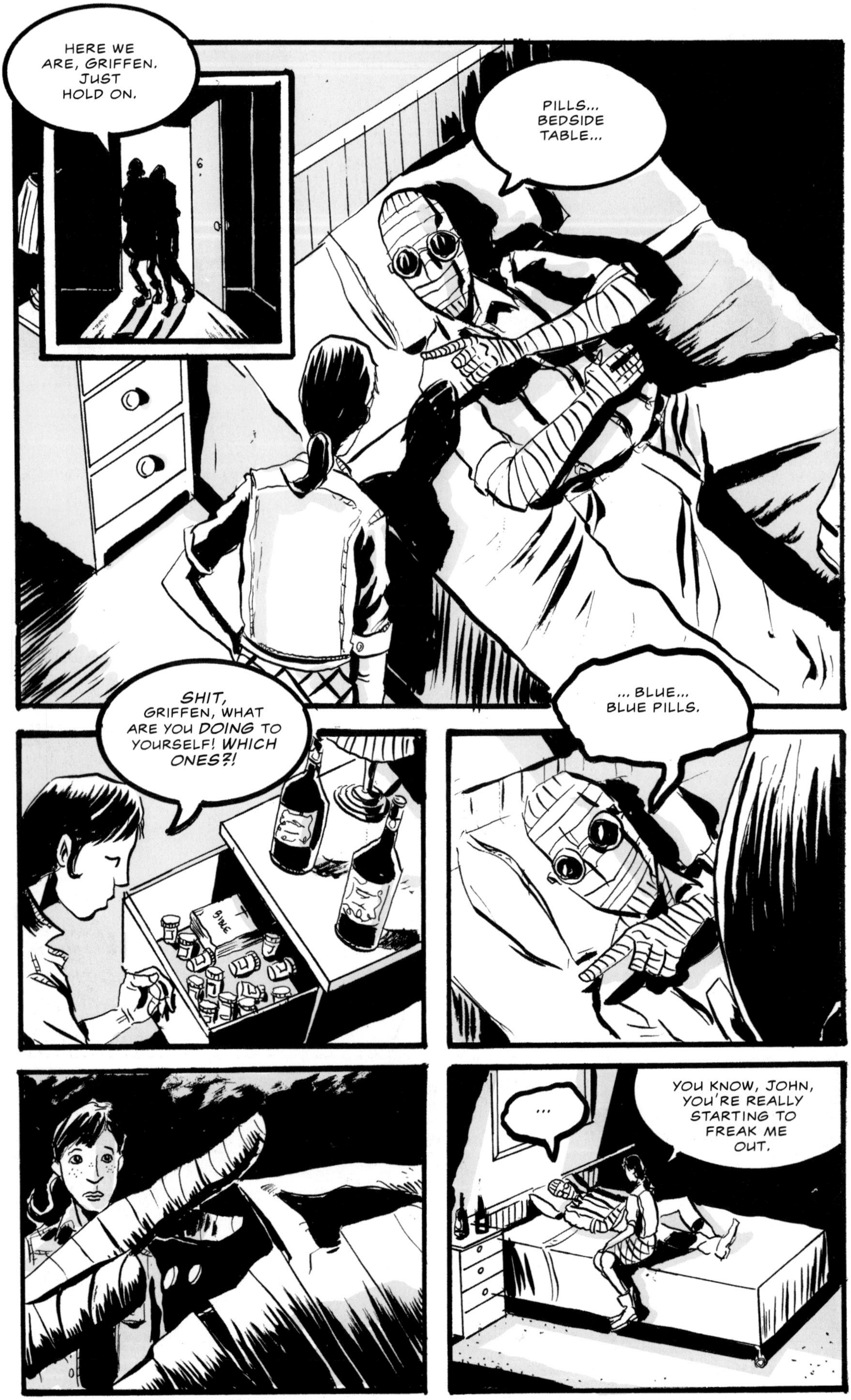
HERE WE ARE, GRIFFEN. JUST HOLD ON.
PILLS... BEDSIDE TABLE...
SHIT, GRIFFEN, WHAT ARE YOU DOING TO YOURSELF! WHICH ONES?!
... BLUE... BLUE PILLS.
BIBLE
...
YOU KNOW, JOHN, YOU'RE REALLY STARTING TO FREAK ME OUT.

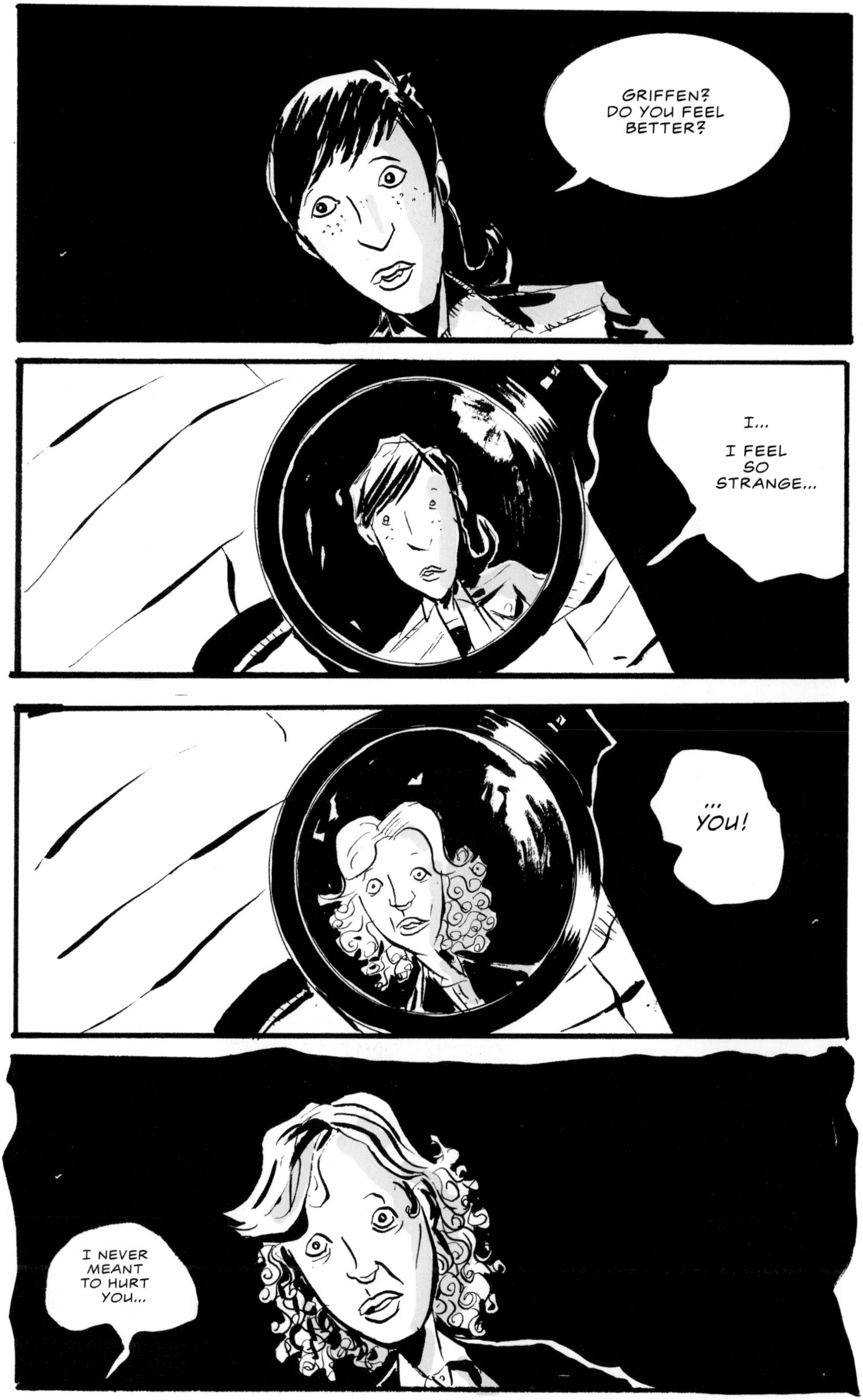
GRIFFEN? DO YOU FEEL BETTER?
I...
I FEEL SO STRANGE...
...YOU!
I NEVER MEANT TO HURT YOU...

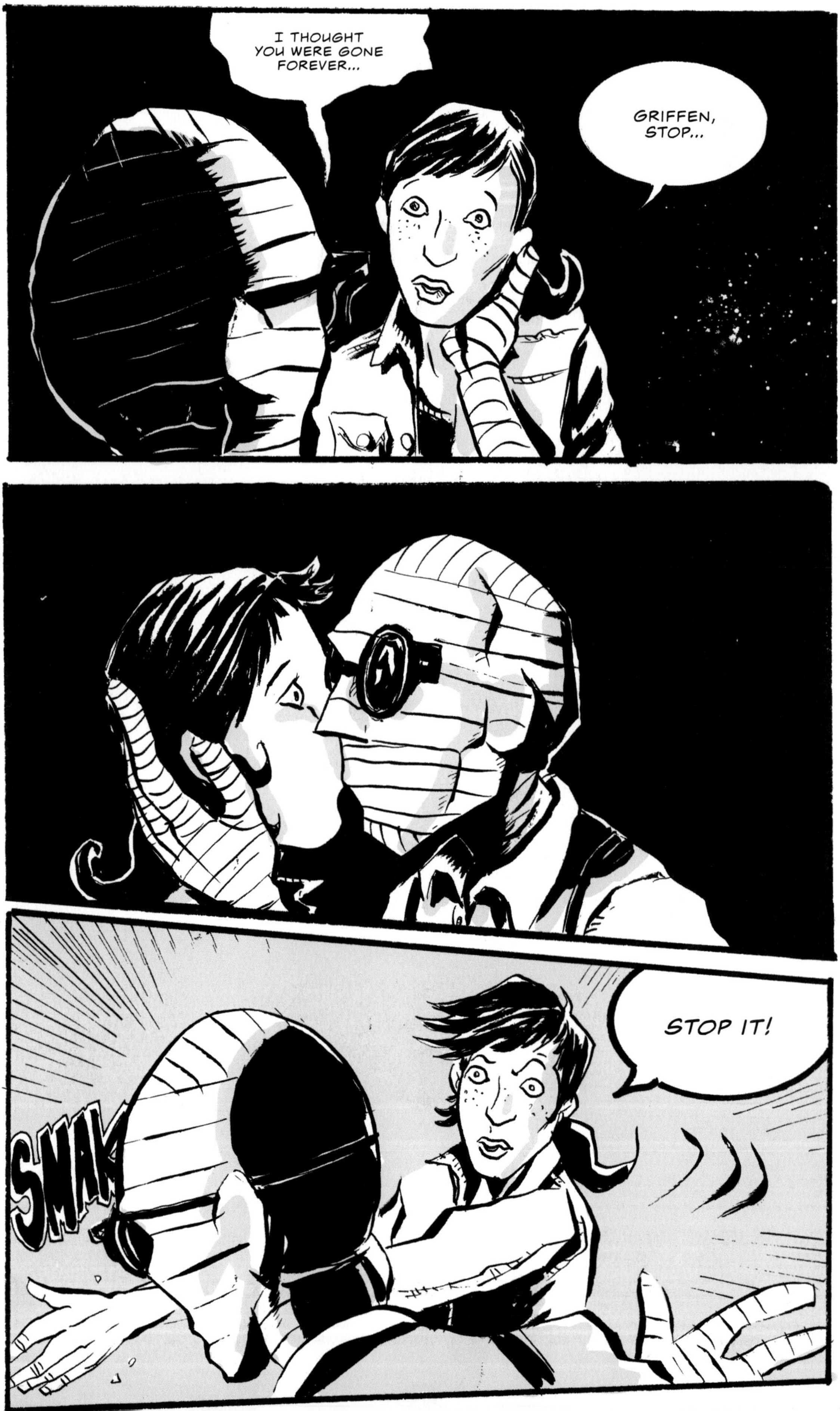
I THOUGHT YOU WERE GONE FOREVER...
GRIFFEN, STOP...
STOP IT!
SMAK

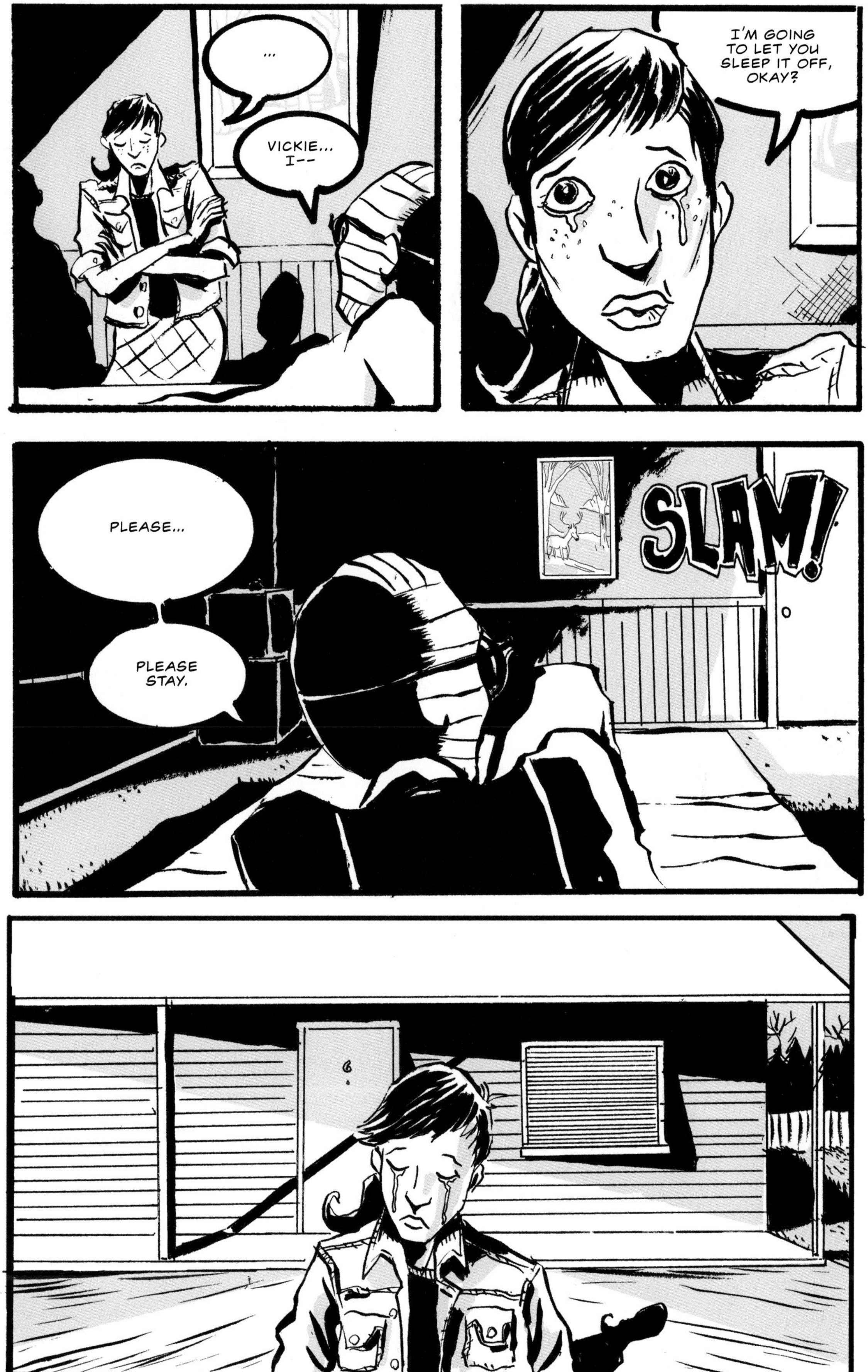
...
VICKIE... I--
I'M GOING TO LET YOU SLEEP IT OFF, OKAY?
PLEASE...
PLEASE STAY.
SLAM!

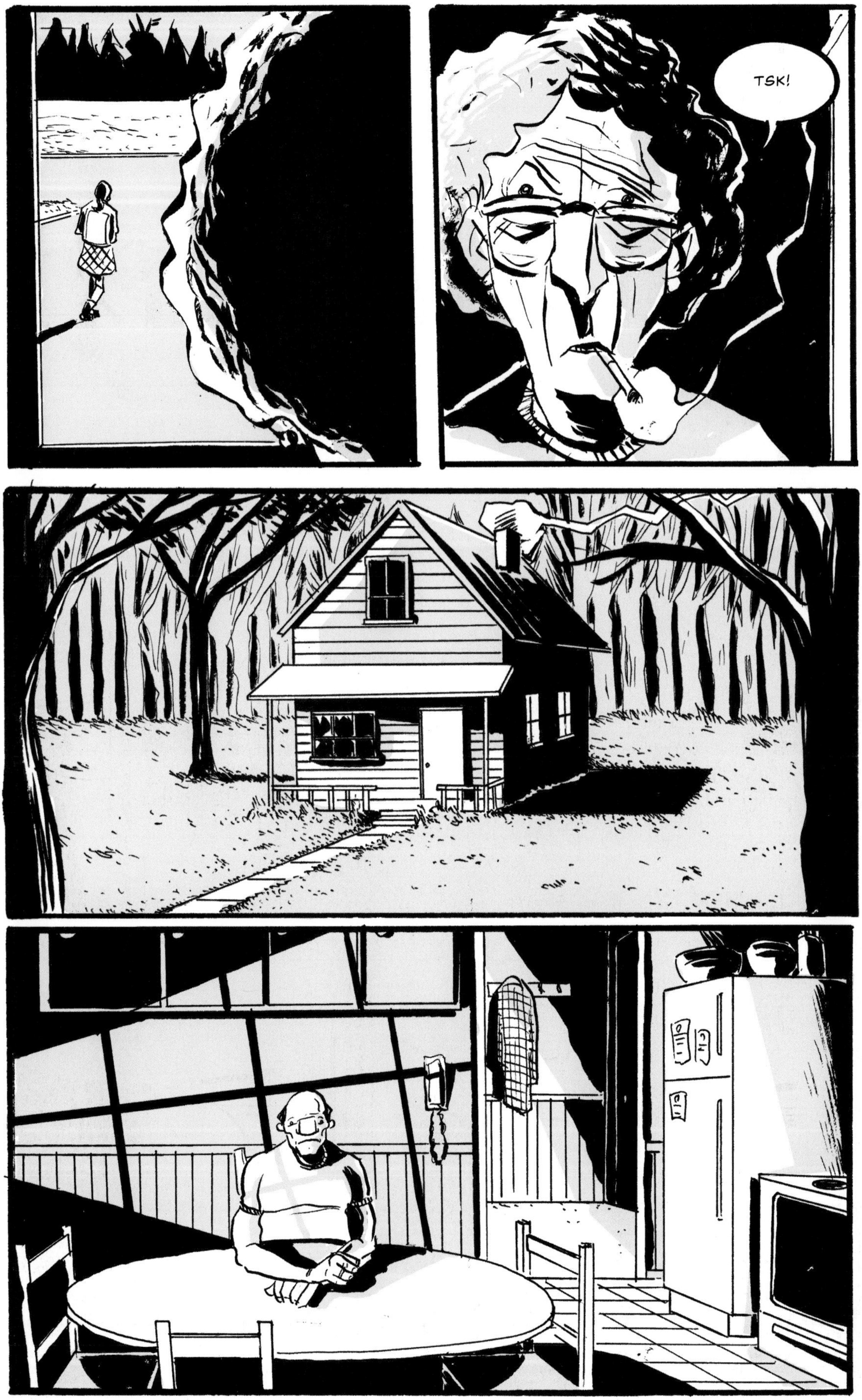
TSK!

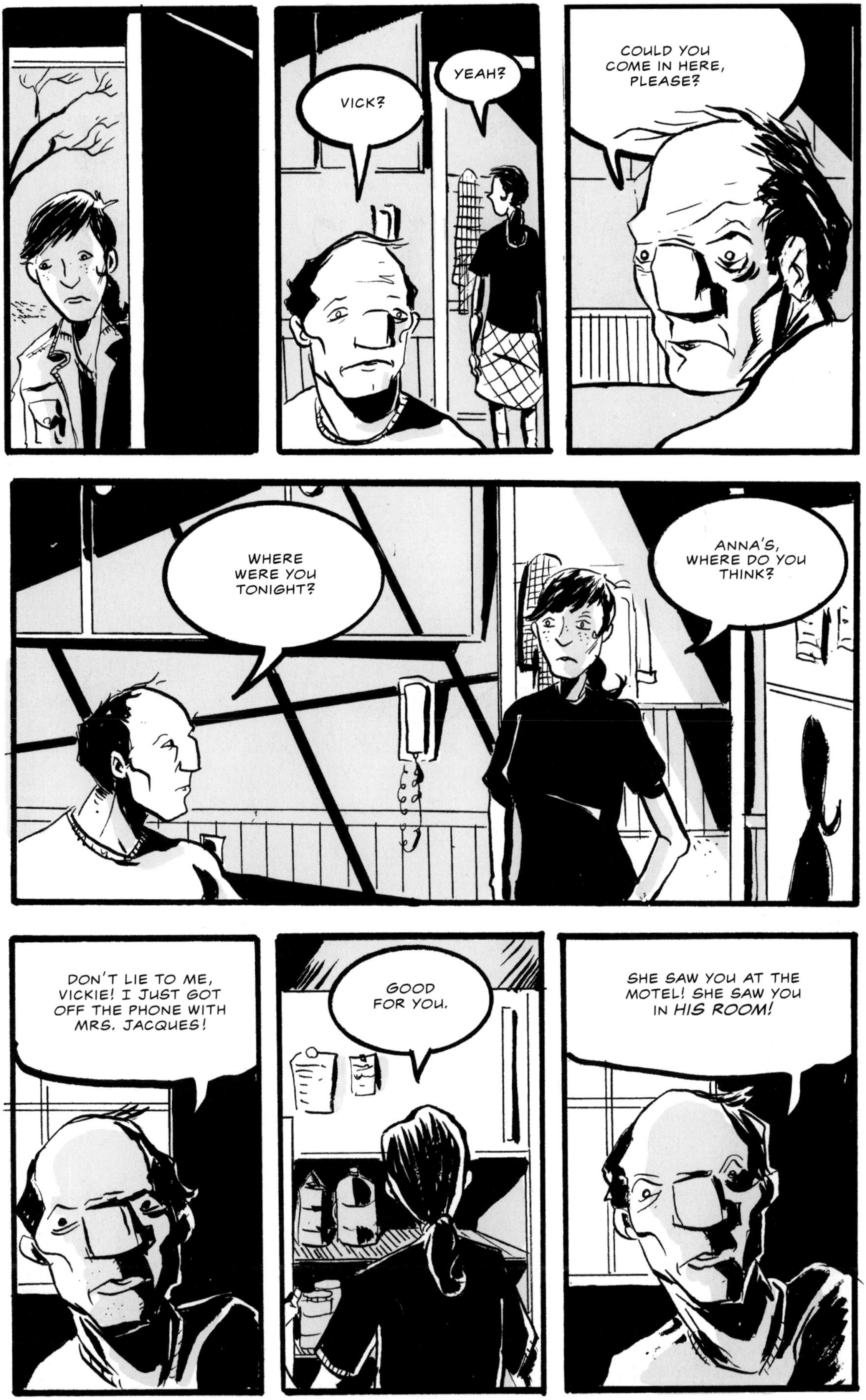
VICK?
YEAH?
COULD YOU COME IN HERE, PLEASE?
WHERE WERE YOU TONIGHT?
ANNA'S, WHERE DO YOU THINK?
DON'T LIE TO ME, VICKIE! I JUST GOT OFF THE PHONE WITH MRS. JACQUES!
GOOD FOR YOU.
SHE SAW YOU AT THE MOTEL! SHE SAW YOU IN HIS ROOM!

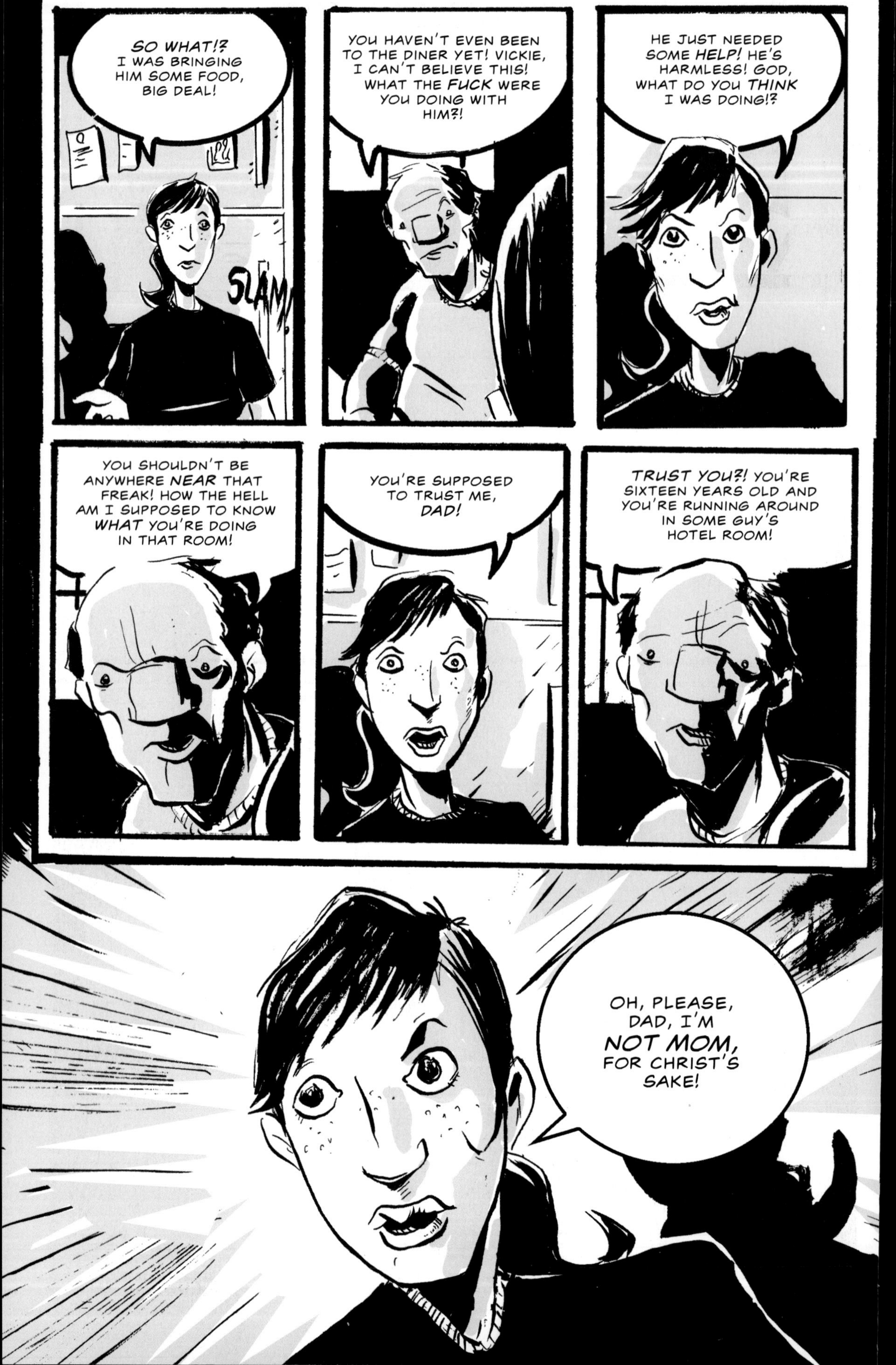
SO WHAT!? I WAS BRINGING HIM SOME FOOD, BIG DEAL!
SLAM
YOU HAVEN'T EVEN BEEN TO THE DINER YET! VICKIE, I CAN'T BELIEVE THIS! WHAT THE FUCK WERE YOU DOING WITH HIM?!
HE JUST NEEDED SOME HELP! HE'S HARMLESS! GOD, WHAT DO YOU THINK I WAS DOING!?
YOU SHOULDN'T BE ANYWHERE NEAR THAT FREAK! HOW THE HELL AM I SUPPOSED TO KNOW WHAT YOU'RE DOING IN THAT ROOM!
YOU'RE SUPPOSED TO TRUST ME, DAD!
TRUST YOU?! YOU'RE SIXTEEN YEARS OLD AND YOU'RE RUNNING AROUND IN SOME GUY'S HOTEL ROOM!
OH, PLEASE, DAD, I'M NOT MOM, FOR CHRIST'S SAKE!

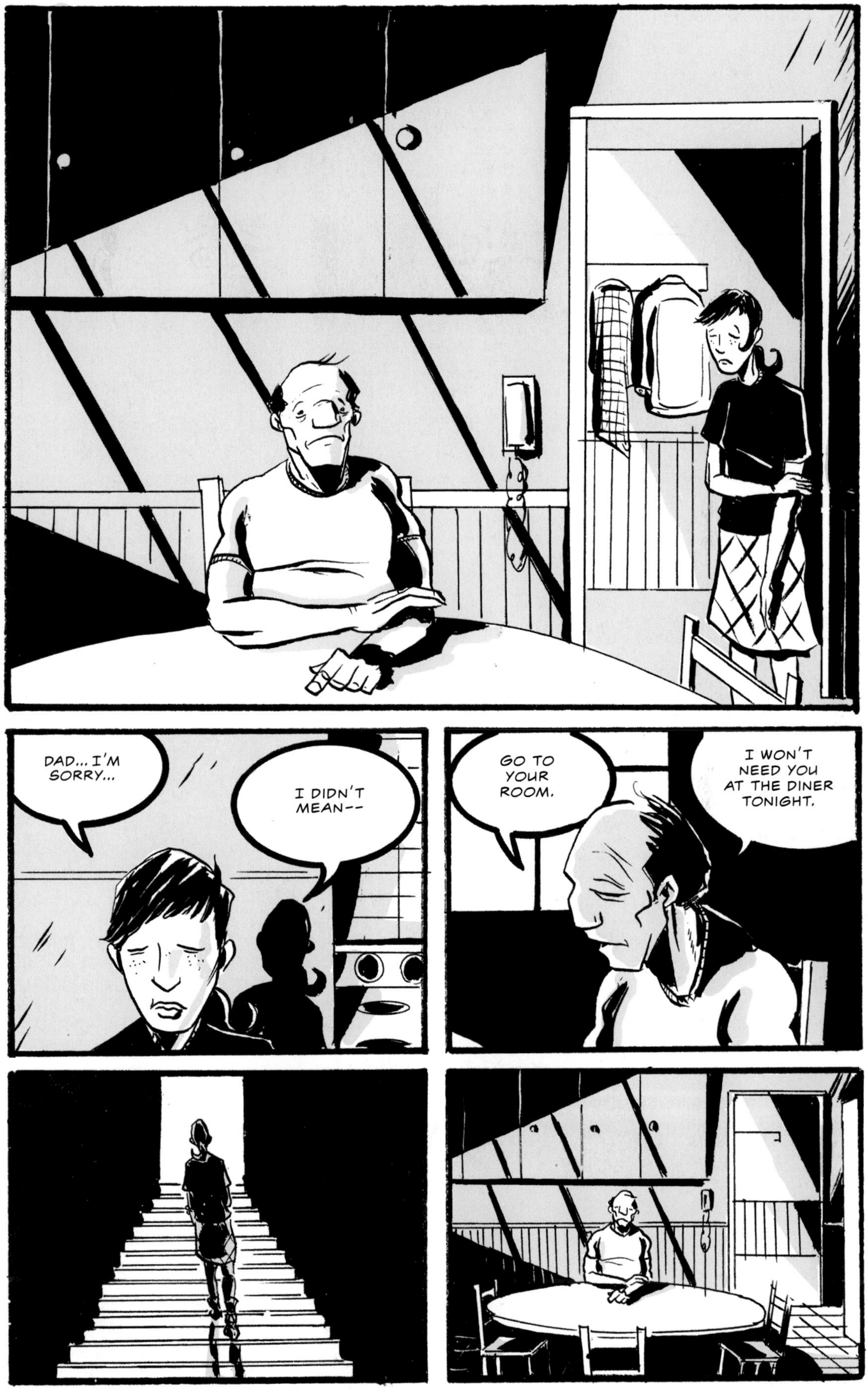
DAD... I'M SORRY...
I DIDN'T MEAN--
GO TO YOUR ROOM.
I WON'T NEED YOU AT THE DINER TONIGHT.

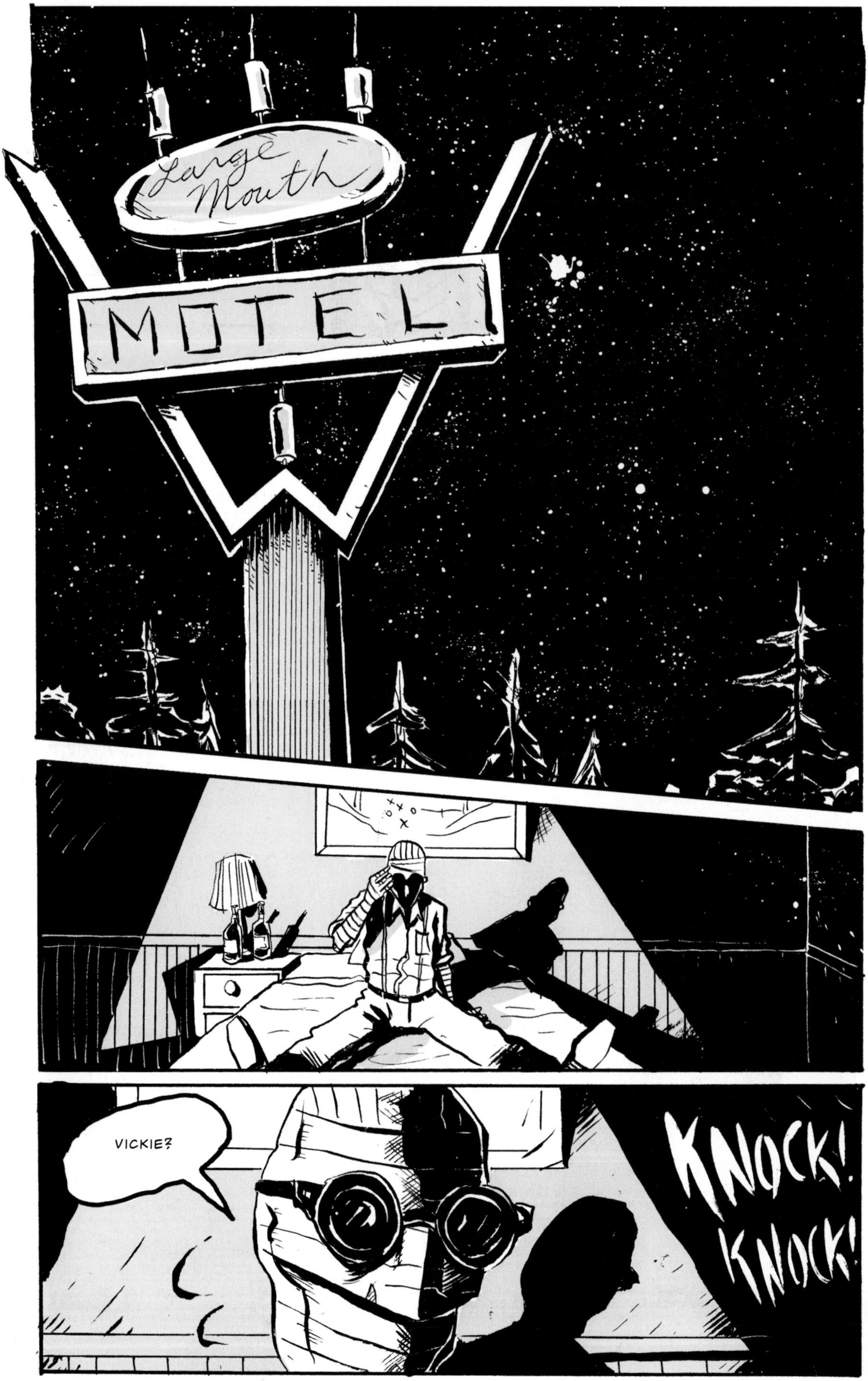

Large Mouth
MOTEL
VICKIE?
KNOCK!
KNOCK!

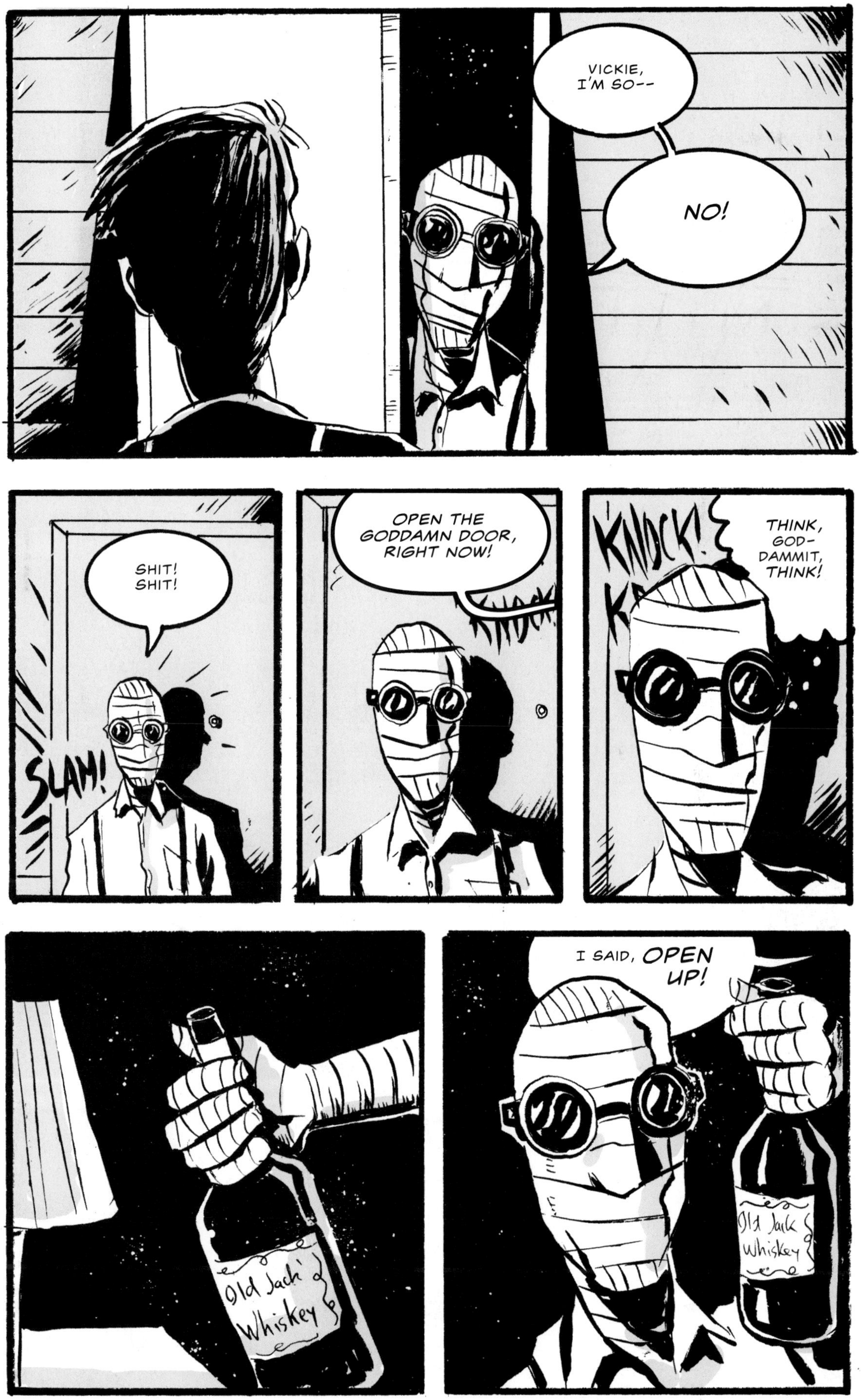
VICKIE, I'M SO--
NO!
SHIT! SHIT!
SLAM!
OPEN THE GODDAMN DOOR, RIGHT NOW!
KNOCK!
KNOCK!
THINK, GOD-DAMMIT, THINK!
Old Jack Whiskey
I SAID, OPEN UP!
Old Jack Whiskey

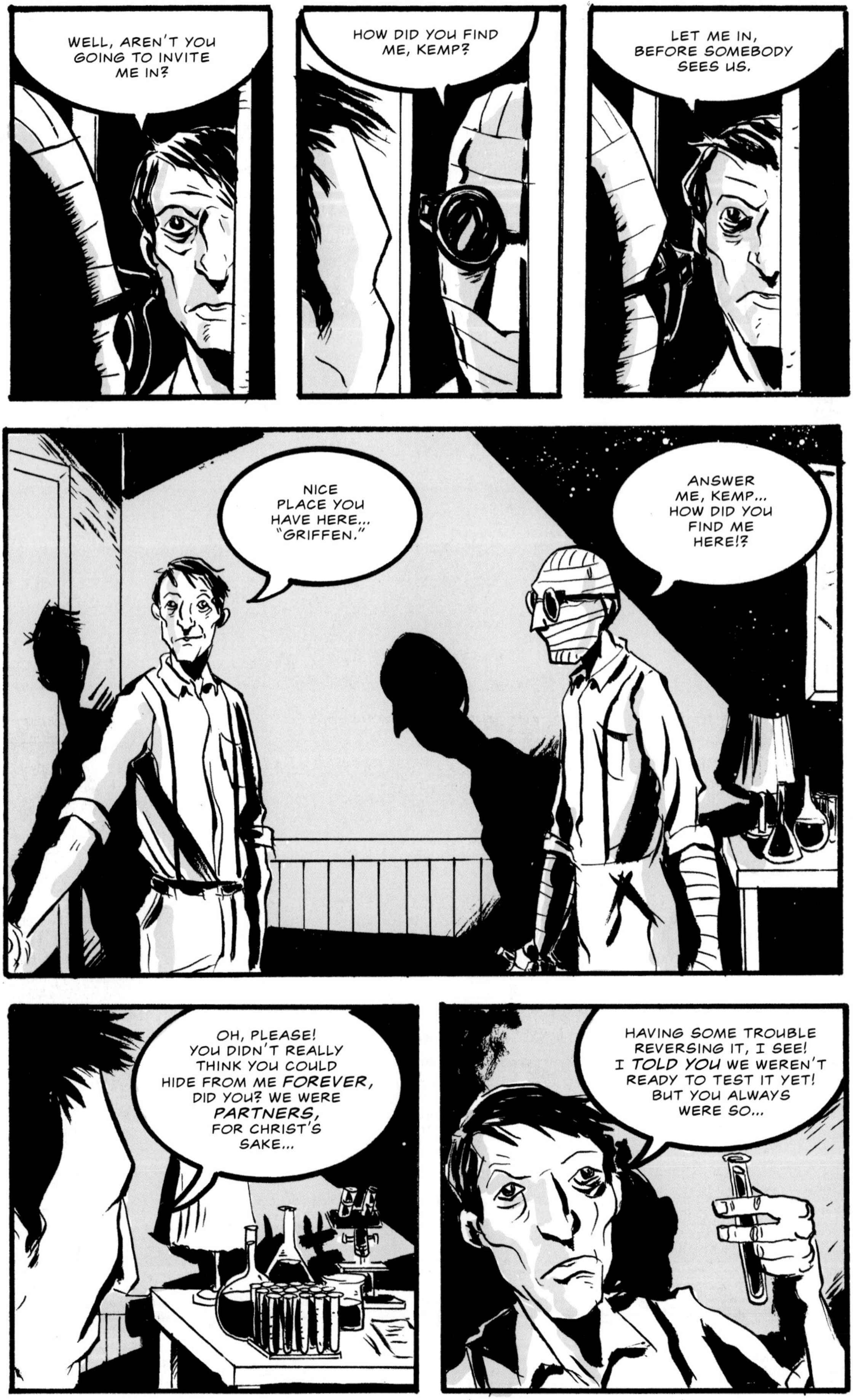

WELL, AREN'T YOU GOING TO INVITE ME IN?
HOW DID YOU FIND ME, KEMP?
LET ME IN, BEFORE SOMEBODY SEES US.
NICE PLACE YOU HAVE HERE... "GRIFFEN."
ANSWER ME, KEMP... HOW DID YOU FIND ME HERE!?
OH, PLEASE! YOU DIDN'T REALLY THINK YOU COULD HIDE FROM ME FOREVER, DID YOU? WE WERE PARTNERS, FOR CHRIST'S SAKE...
HAVING SOME TROUBLE REVERSING IT, I SEE! I TOLD YOU WE WEREN'T READY TO TEST IT YET! BUT YOU ALWAYS WERE SO...

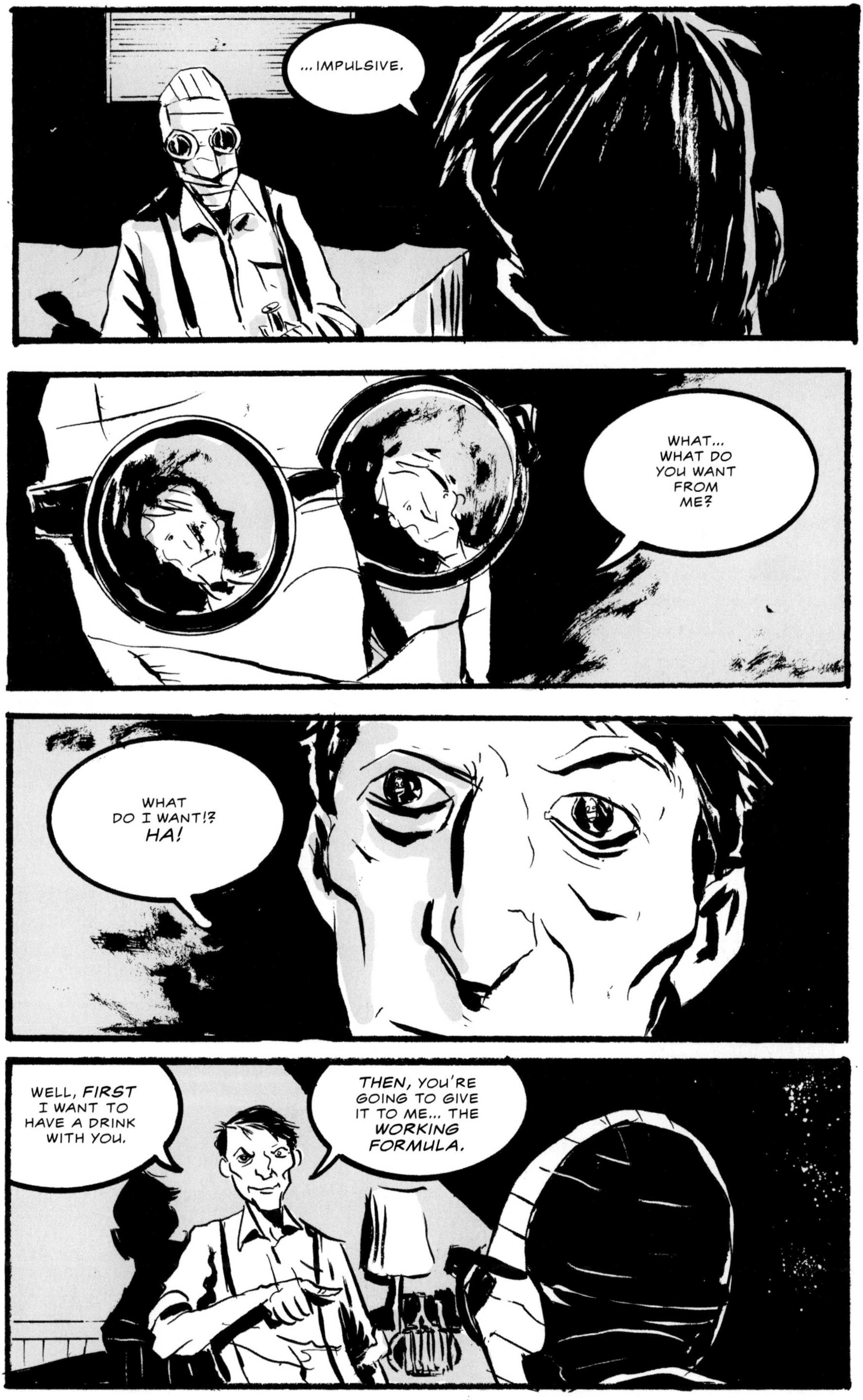
...IMPULSIVE.
WHAT... WHAT DO YOU WANT FROM ME?
WHAT DO I WANT!? HA!
WELL, FIRST I WANT TO HAVE A DRINK WITH YOU.
THEN, YOU'RE GOING TO GIVE IT TO ME... THE WORKING FORMULA.

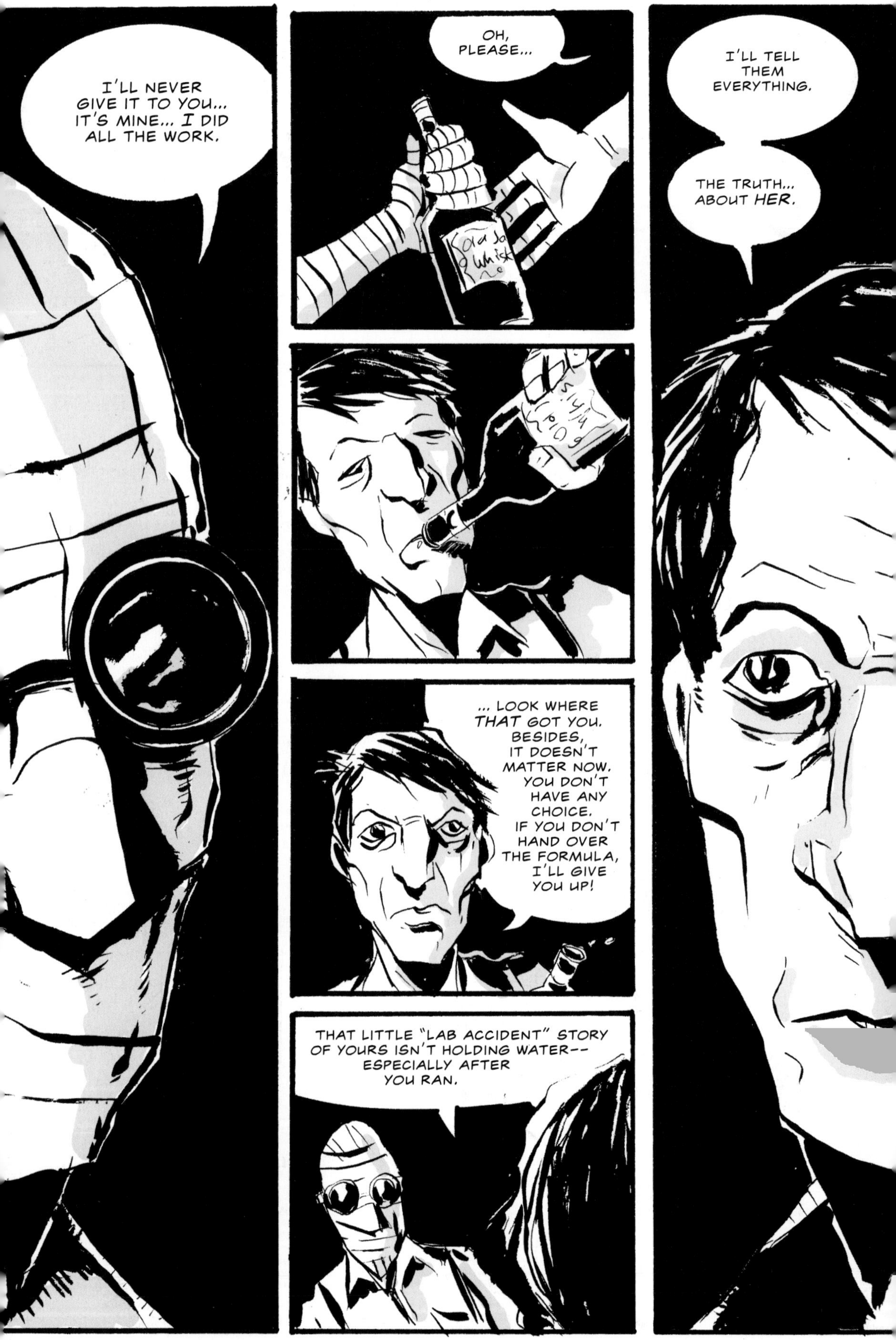

I'LL NEVER GIVE IT TO YOU... IT'S MINE... I DID ALL THE WORK.
OH, PLEASE...
... LOOK WHERE THAT GOT YOU. BESIDES, IT DOESN'T MATTER NOW. YOU DON'T HAVE ANY CHOICE. IF YOU DON'T HAND OVER THE FORMULA, I'LL GIVE YOU UP!
THAT LITTLE "LAB ACCIDENT" STORY OF YOURS ISN'T HOLDING WATER-- ESPECIALLY AFTER YOU RAN.
I'LL TELL THEM EVERYTHING.
THE TRUTH... ABOUT HER.

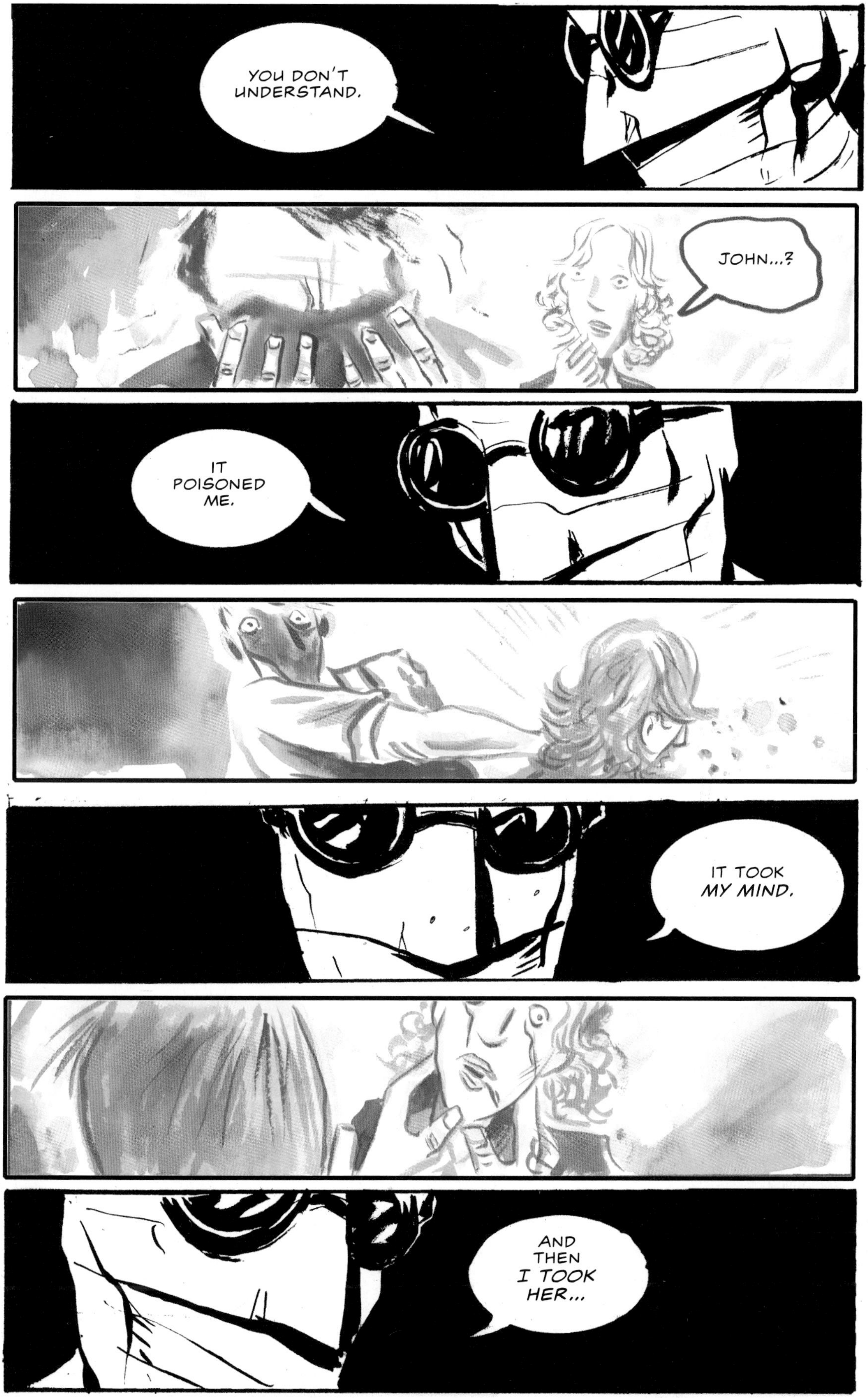
YOU DON'T UNDERSTAND.
JOHN...?
IT POISONED ME.
IT TOOK MY MIND.
AND THEN I TOOK HER...

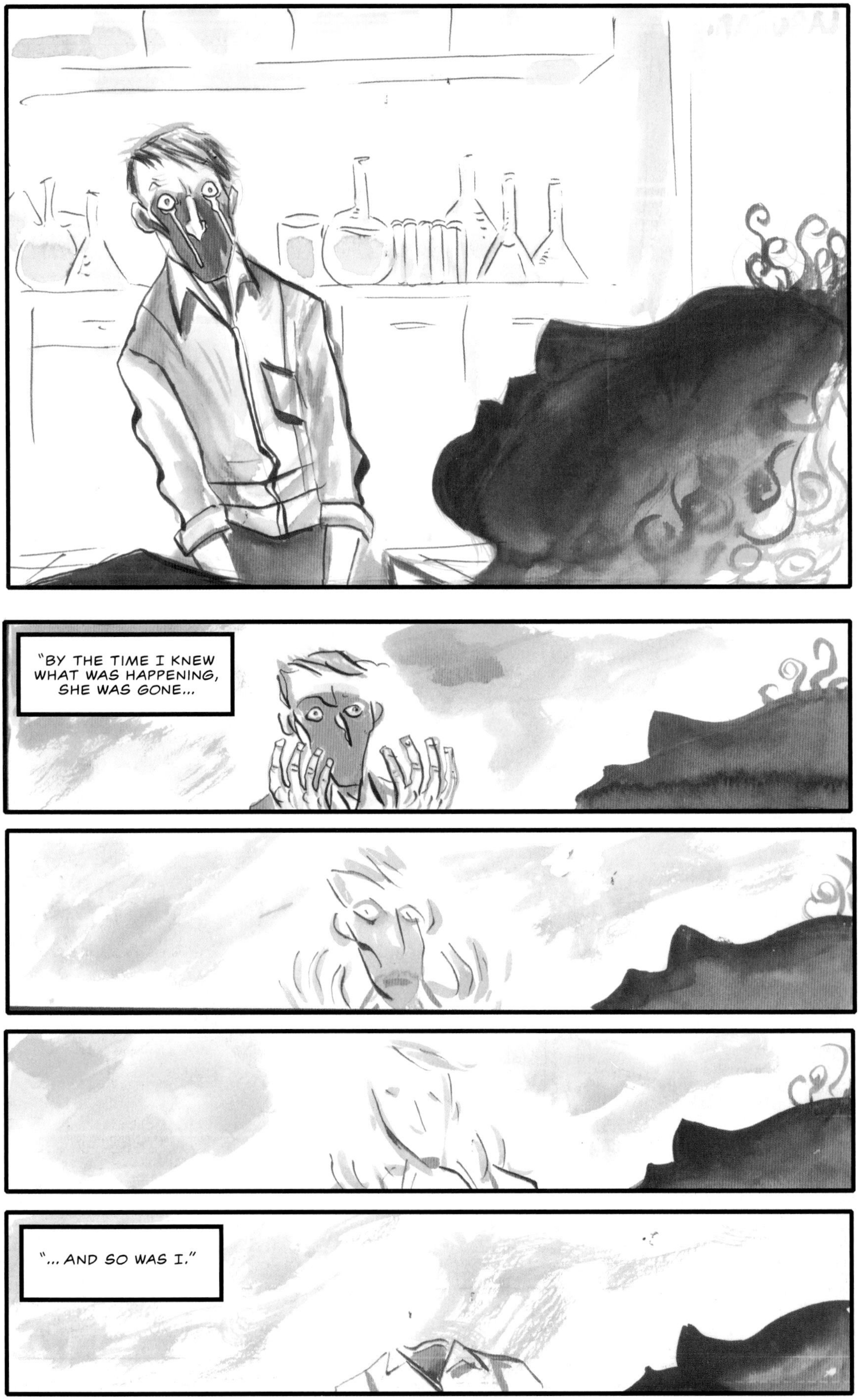
"BY THE TIME I KNEW WHAT WAS HAPPENING, SHE WAS GONE...
"... AND SO WAS I."

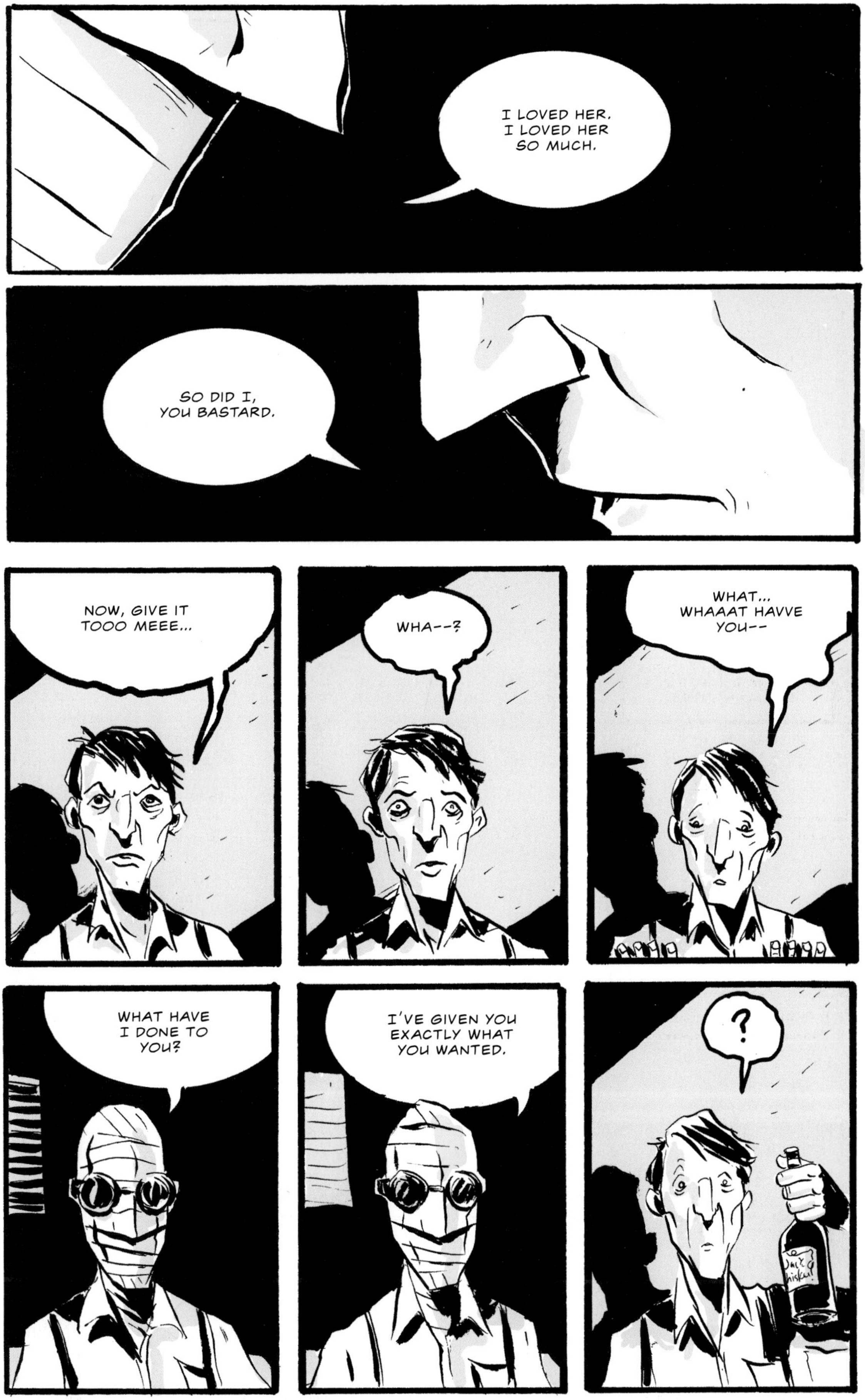
I LOVED HER. I LOVED HER SO MUCH.
SO DID I, YOU BASTARD.
NOW, GIVE IT TOOO MEEE...
WHA--?
WHAT... WHAAAT HAVVE YOU--
WHAT HAVE I DONE TO YOU?
I'VE GIVEN YOU EXACTLY WHAT YOU WANTED.
?

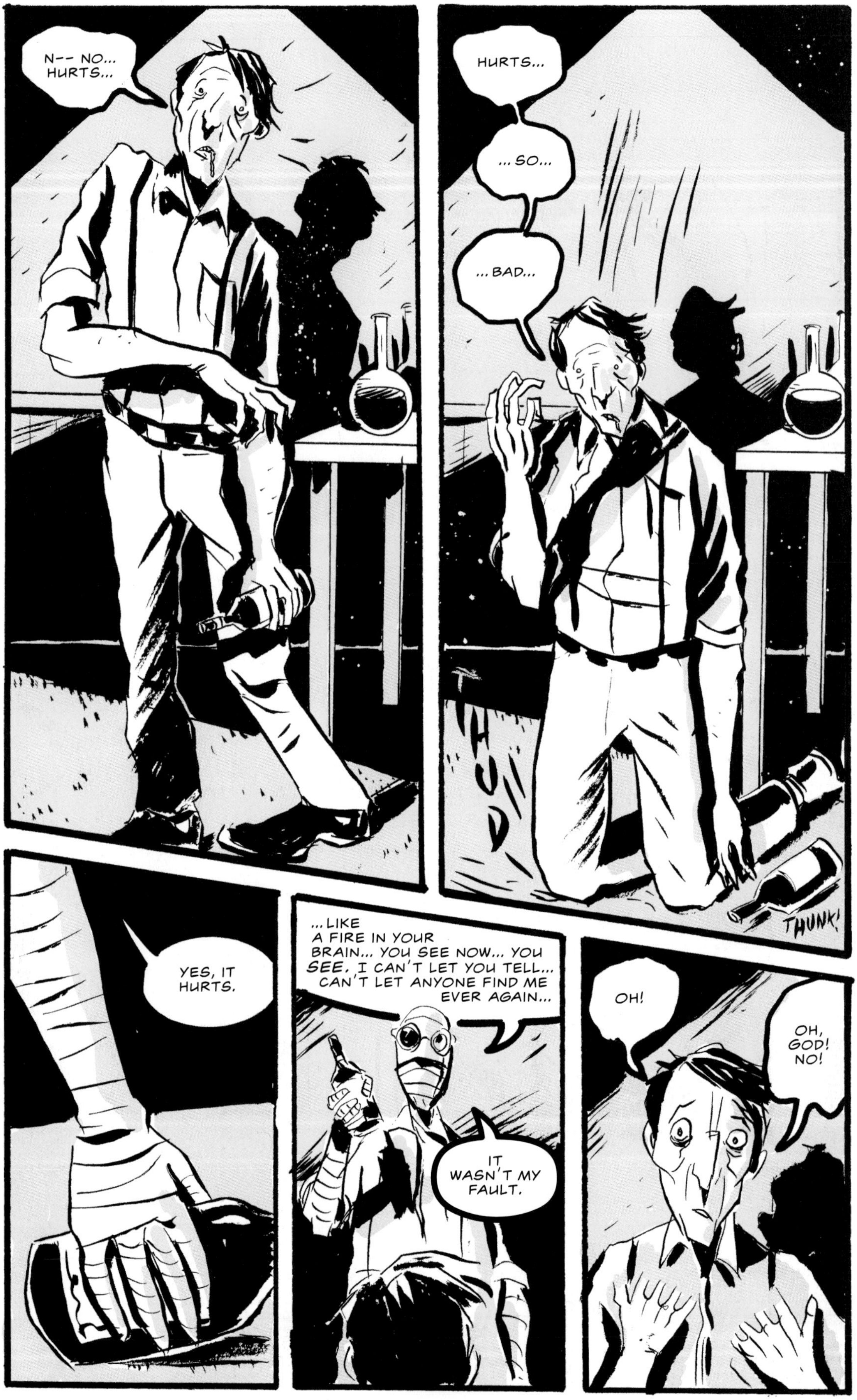
N-- NO...
HURTS...
HURTS...
...SO...
...BAD...
THUD
THUNK!
YES, IT HURTS.
...LIKE A FIRE IN YOUR BRAIN... YOU SEE NOW... YOU SEE. I CAN'T LET YOU TELL... CAN'T LET ANYONE FIND ME EVER AGAIN...
IT WASN'T MY FAULT.
OH!
OH, GOD! NO!

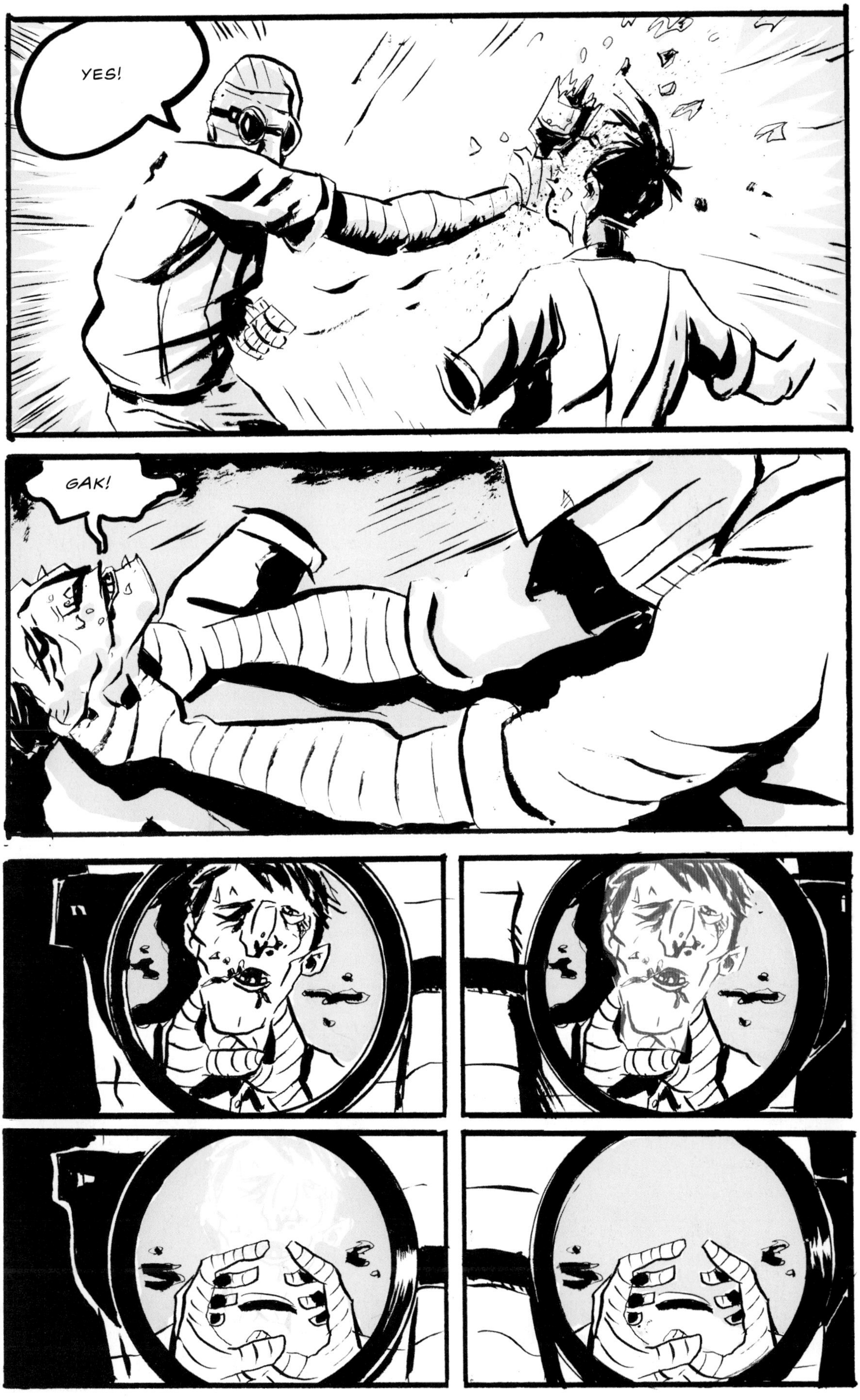
YES!
GAK!

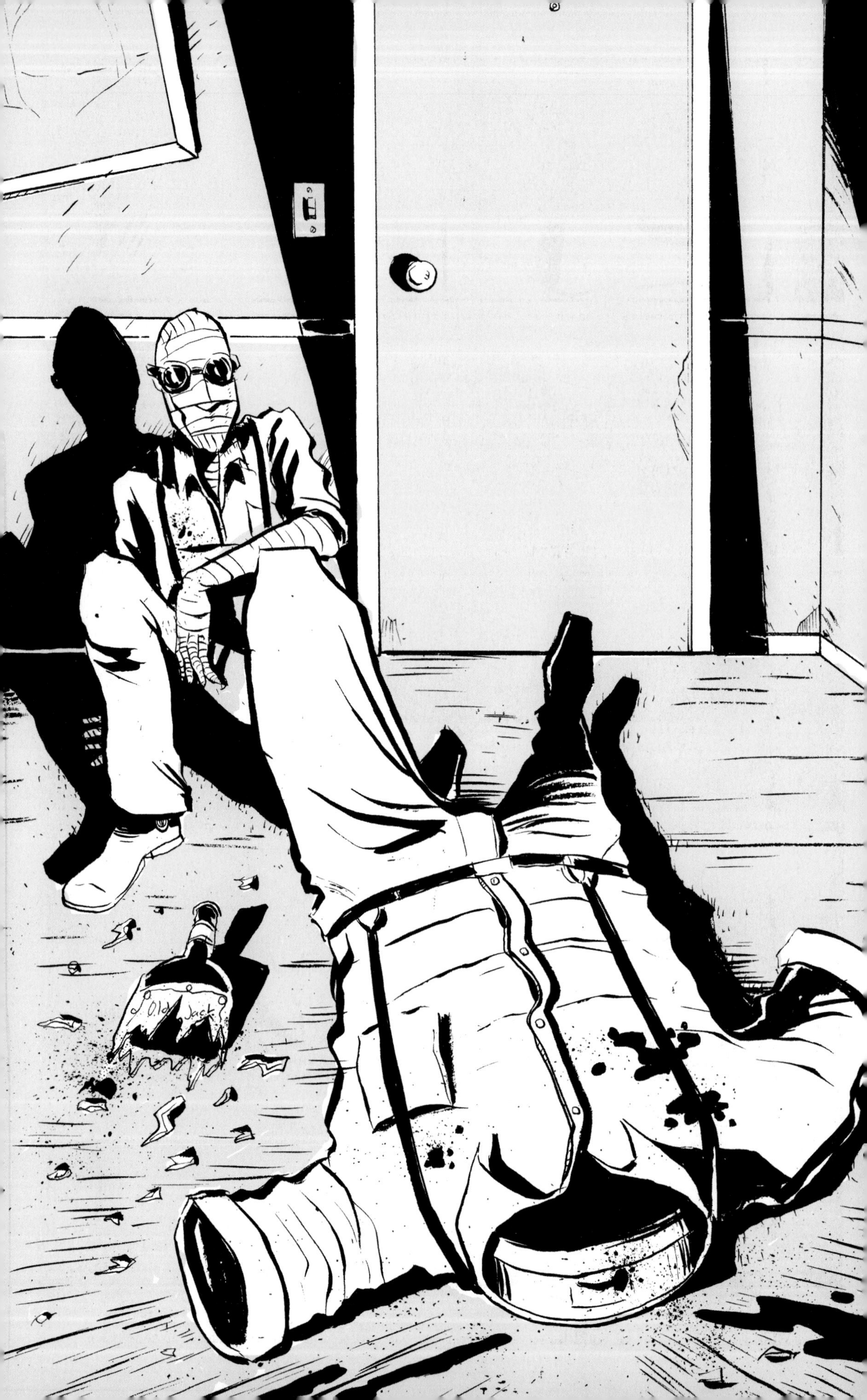
Old Jack

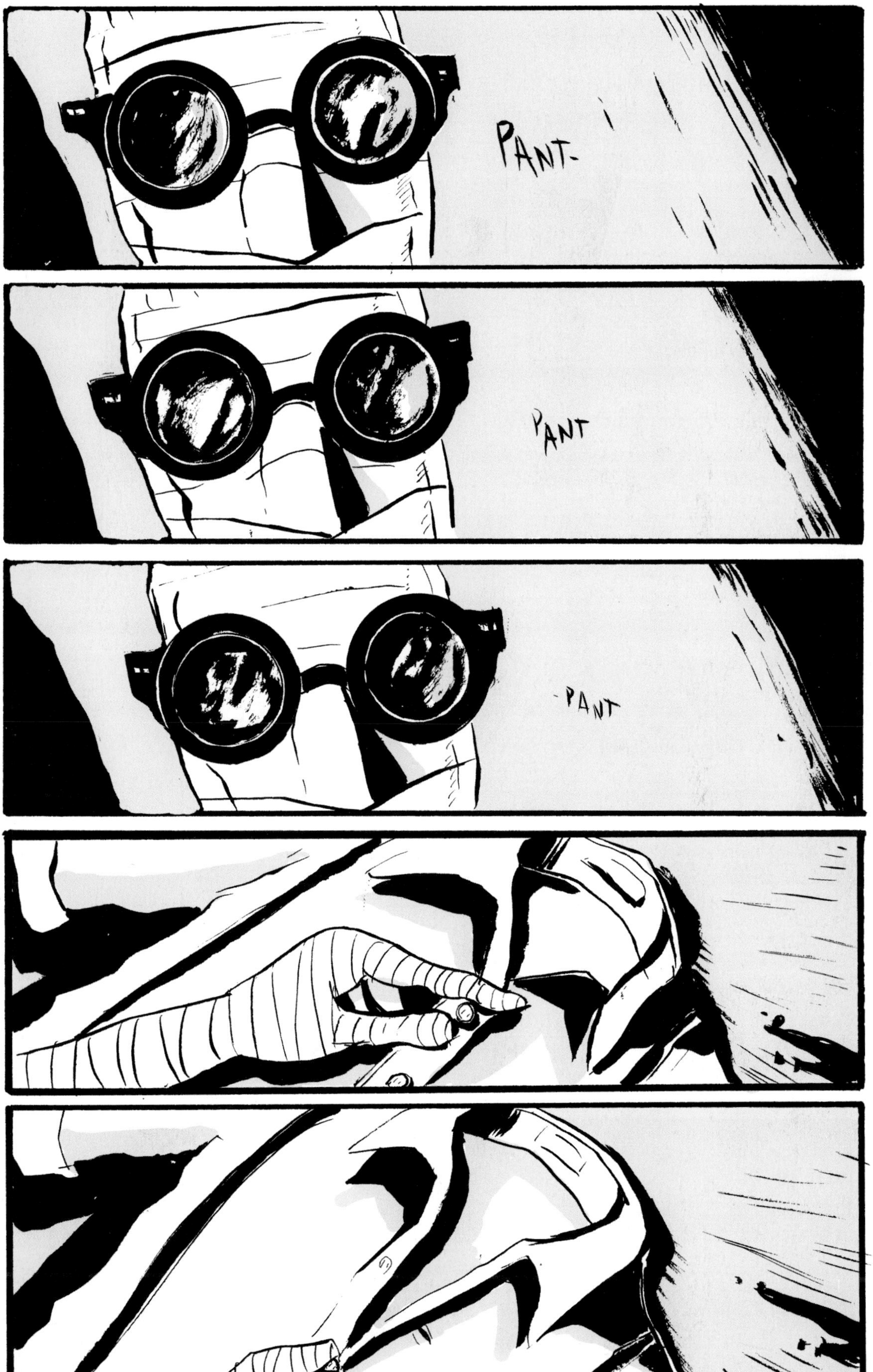
PANT-
PANT
-PANT

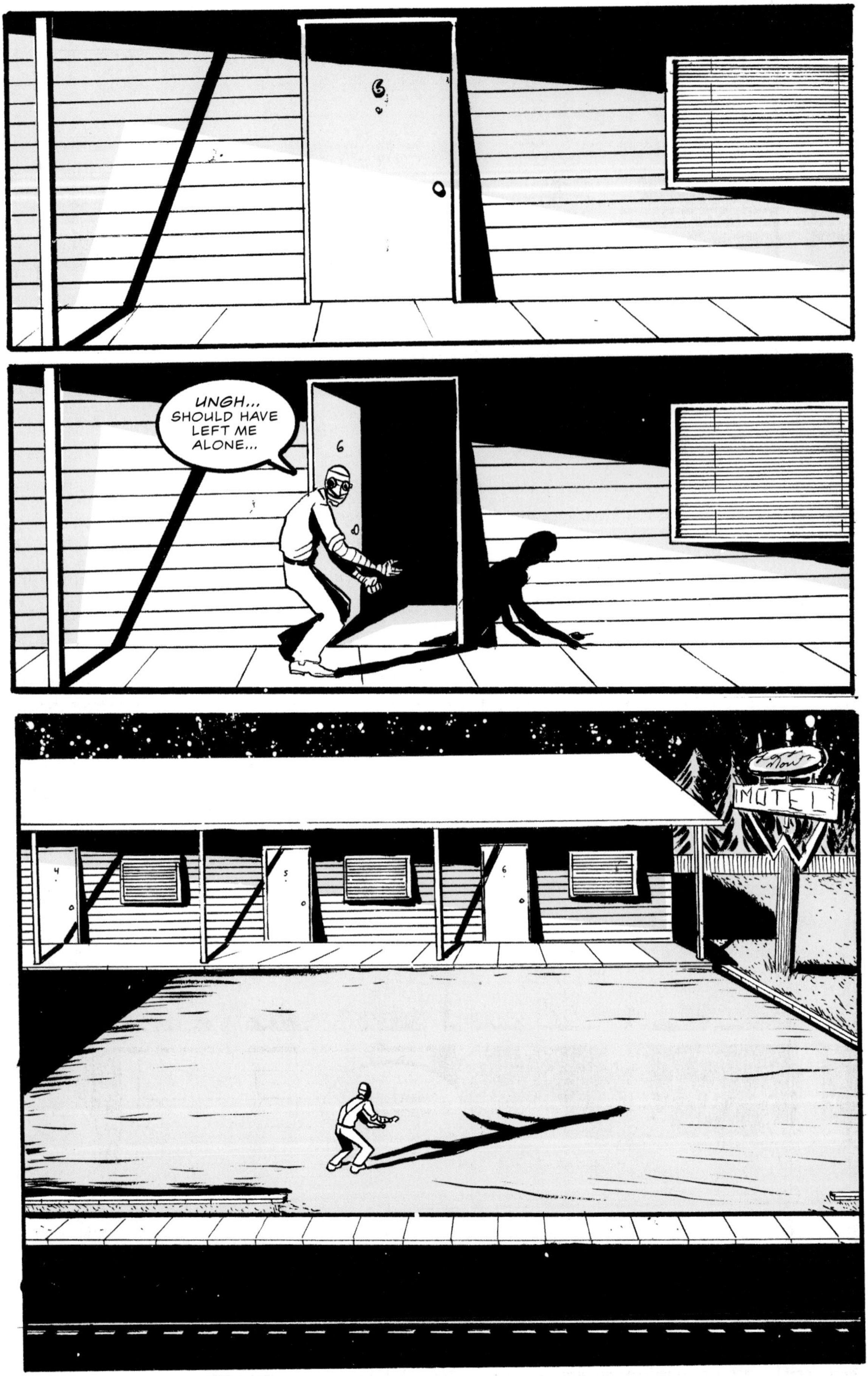
UNGH... SHOULD HAVE LEFT ME ALONE...
MOTEL

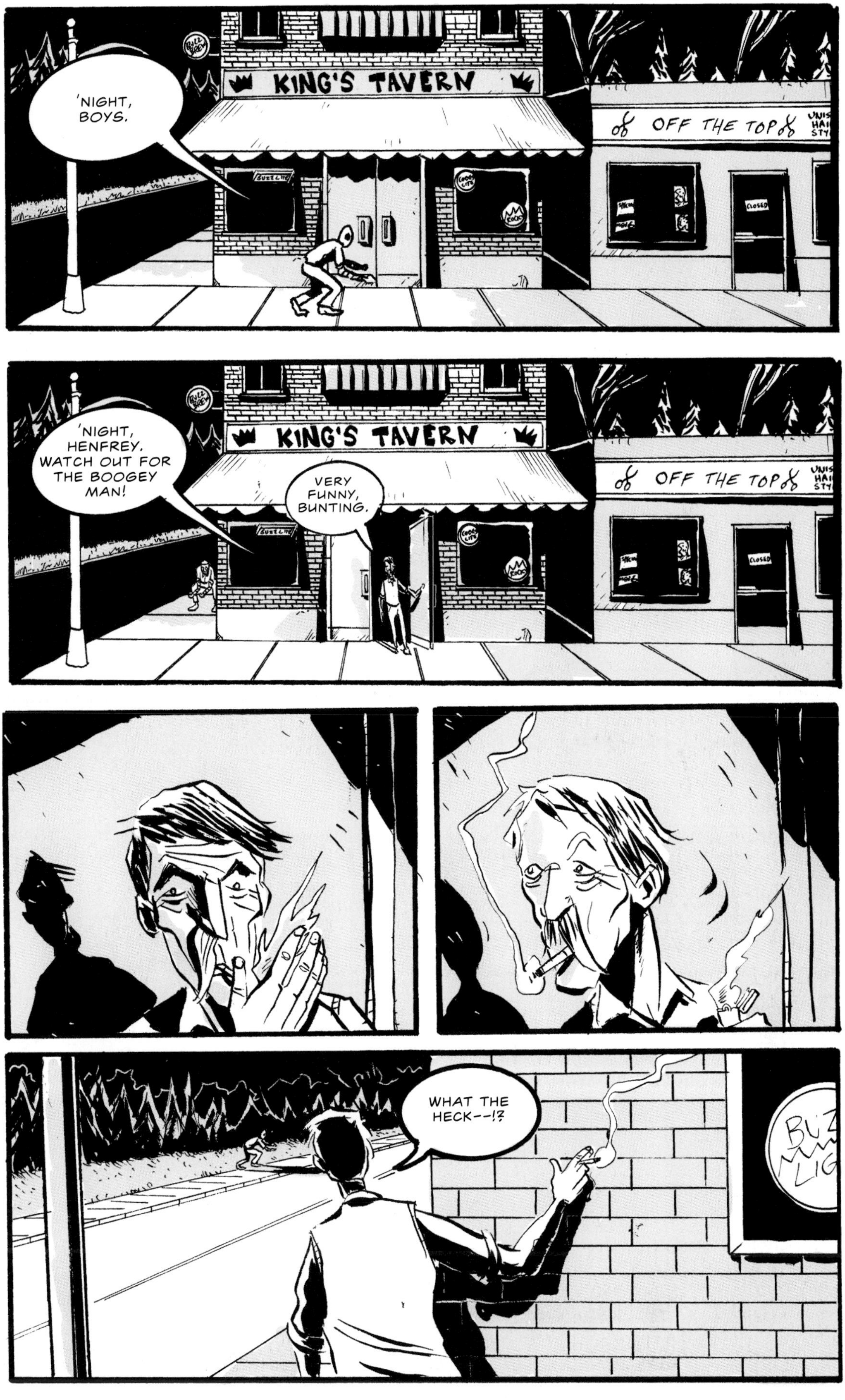
KING'S TAVERN
OFF THE TOP
'NIGHT, BOYS.
'NIGHT, HENFREY. WATCH OUT FOR THE BOOGEY MAN!
VERY FUNNY, BUNTING.
WHAT THE HECK--!?

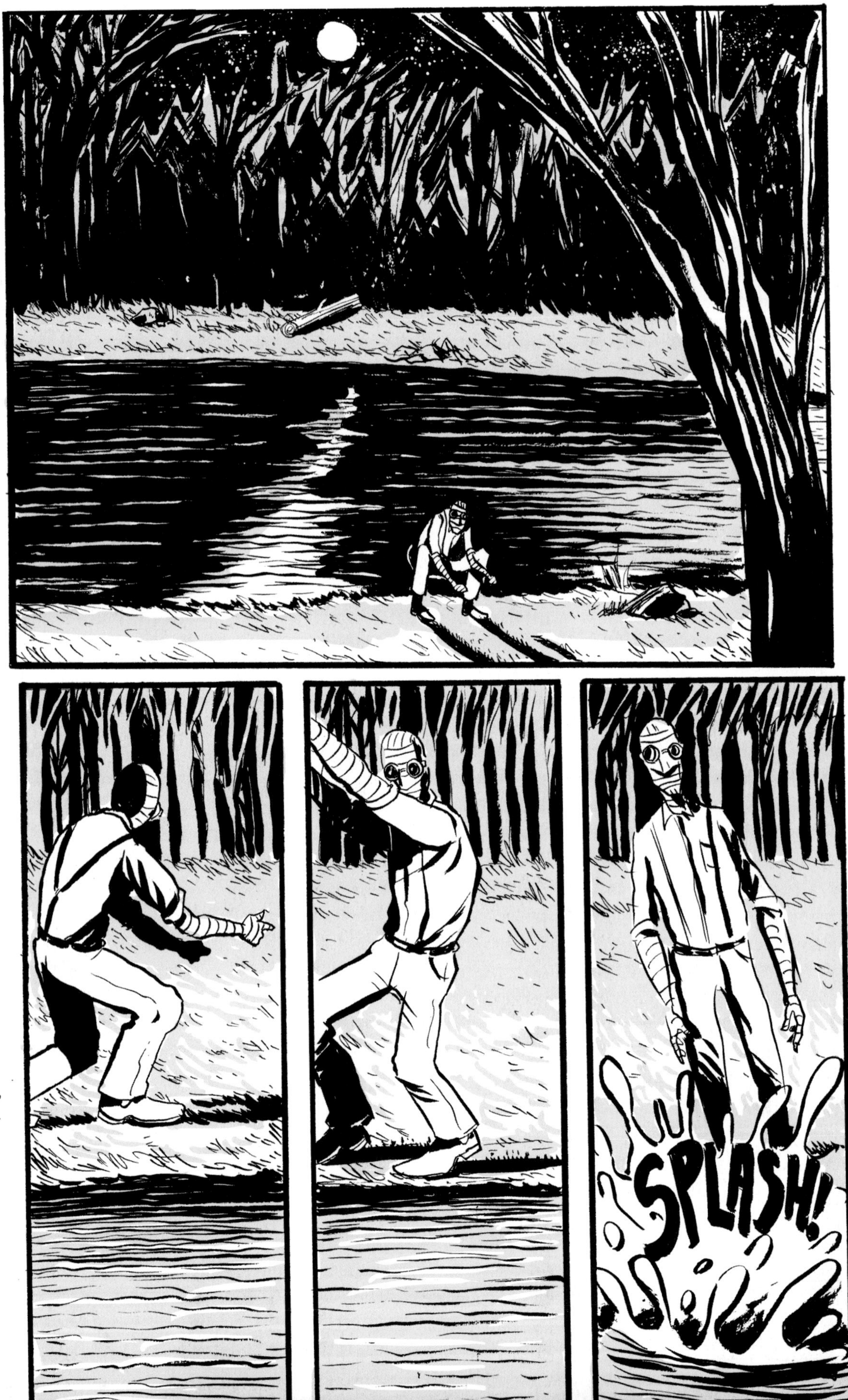
SPLASH!

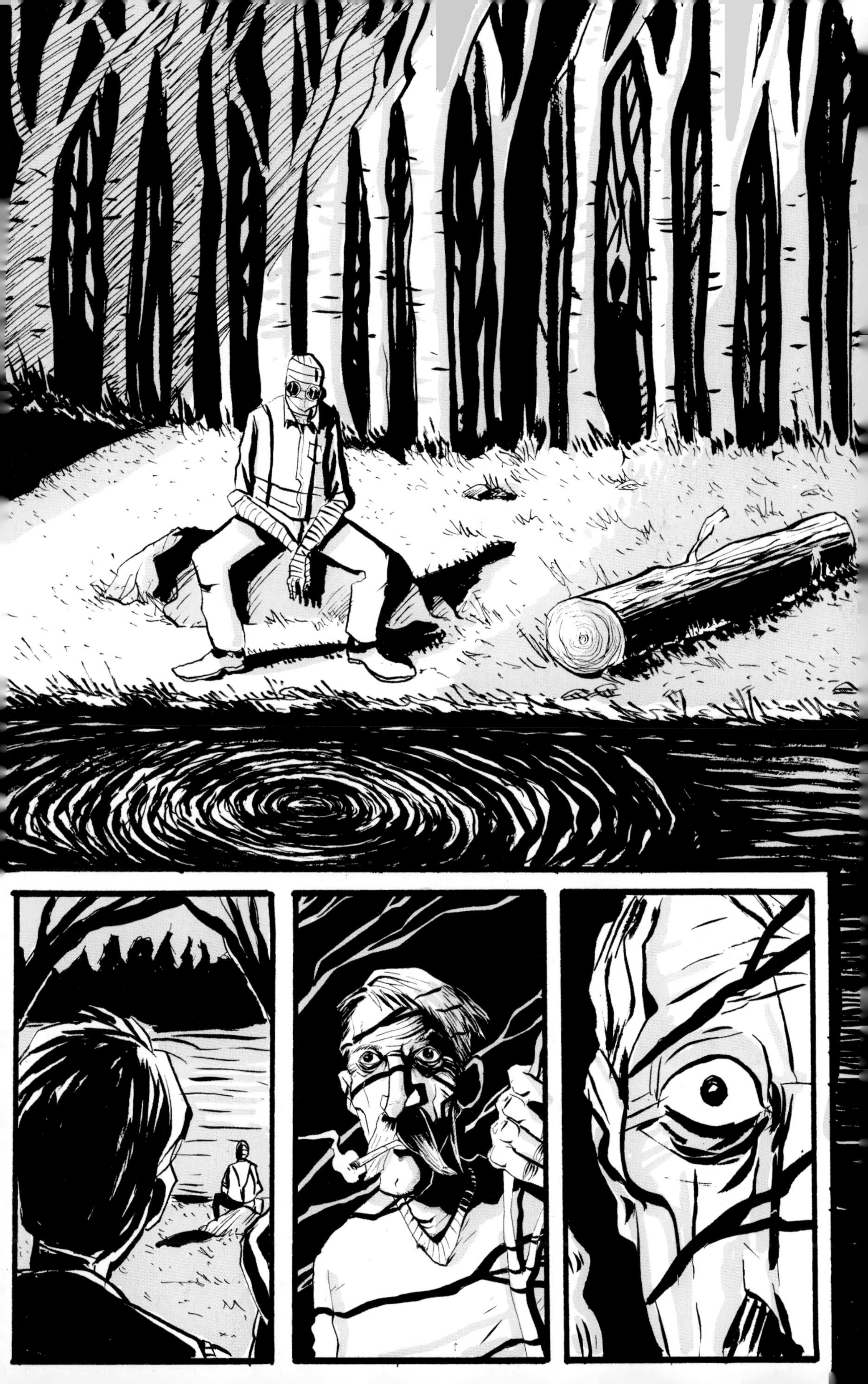

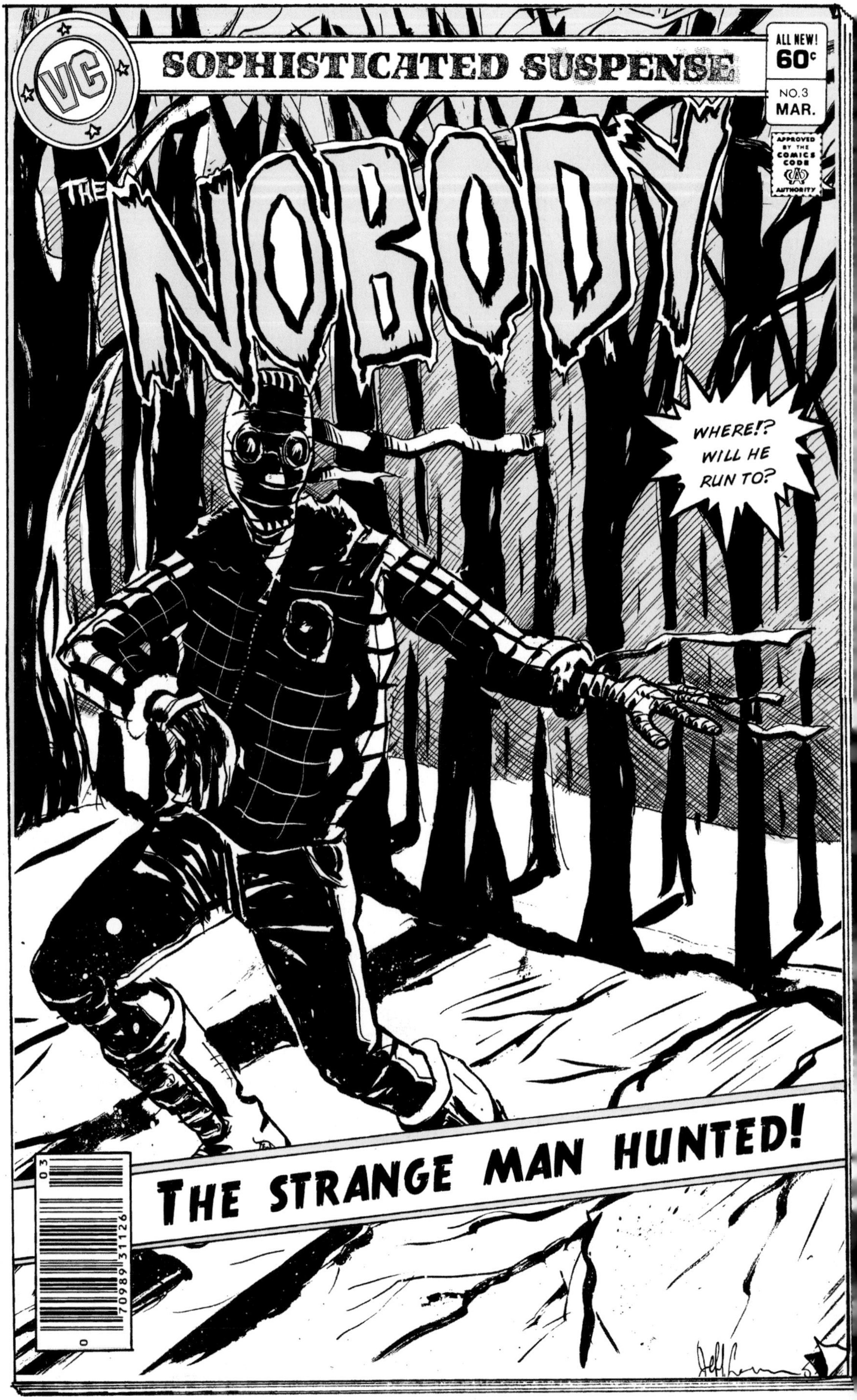
VC
SOPHISTICATED SUSPENSE
ALL NEW!
60¢
NO.3
MAR.
APPROVED BY THE COMICS CODE AUTHORITY
THE NOBODY
WHERE!? WILL HE RUN TO?
THE STRANGE MAN HUNTED!

WELCOME TO **LARGE MOUTH** "Home of the World's Biggest Bass!" Population 754

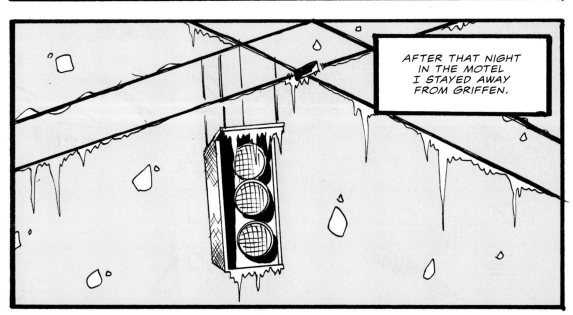

AFTER THAT NIGHT IN THE MOTEL I STAYED AWAY FROM GRIFFEN.

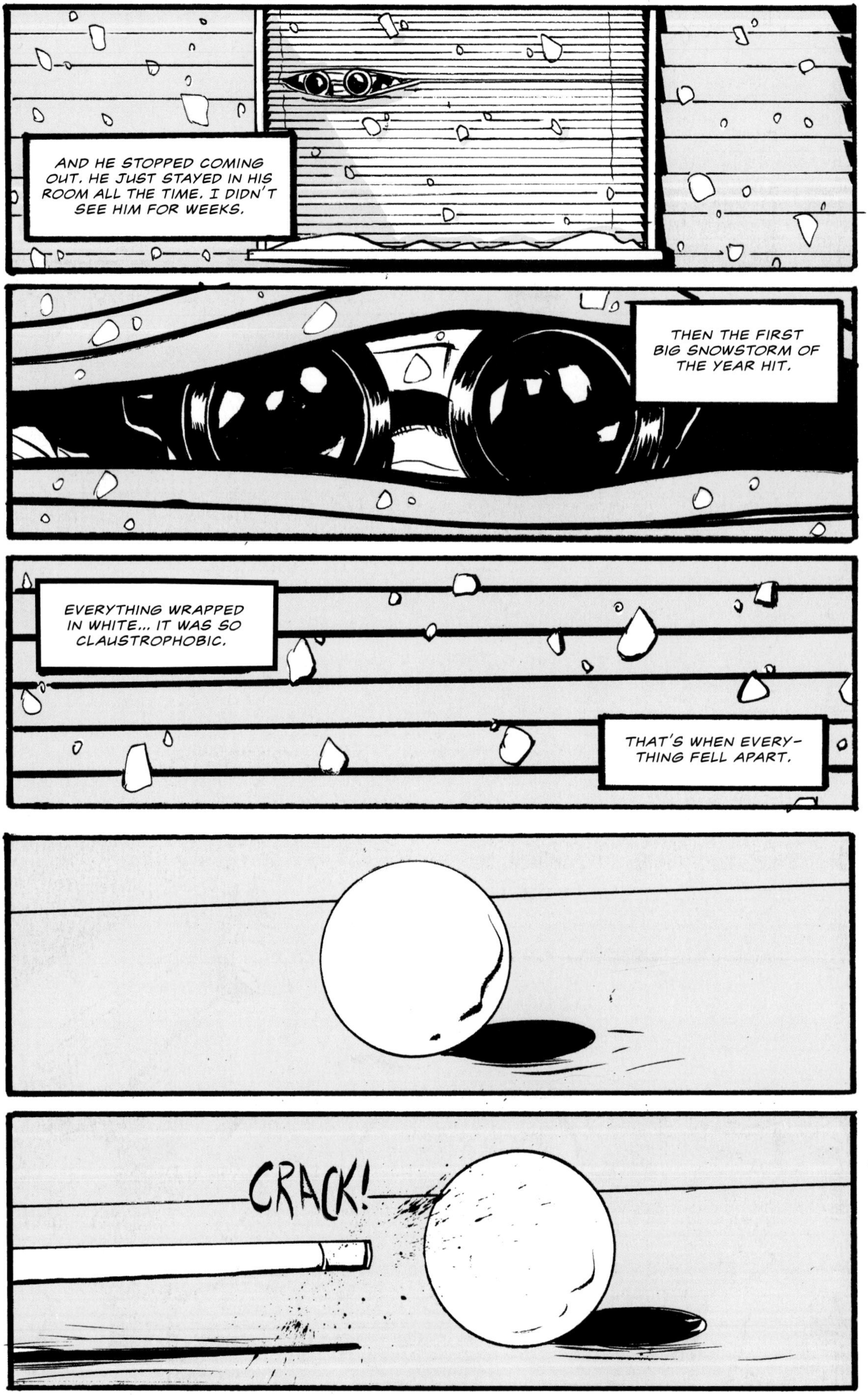
AND HE STOPPED COMING OUT. HE JUST STAYED IN HIS ROOM ALL THE TIME. I DIDN'T SEE HIM FOR WEEKS.
THEN THE FIRST BIG SNOWSTORM OF THE YEAR HIT.
EVERYTHING WRAPPED IN WHITE... IT WAS SO CLAUSTROPHOBIC.
THAT'S WHEN EVERY-THING FELL APART.
CRACK!

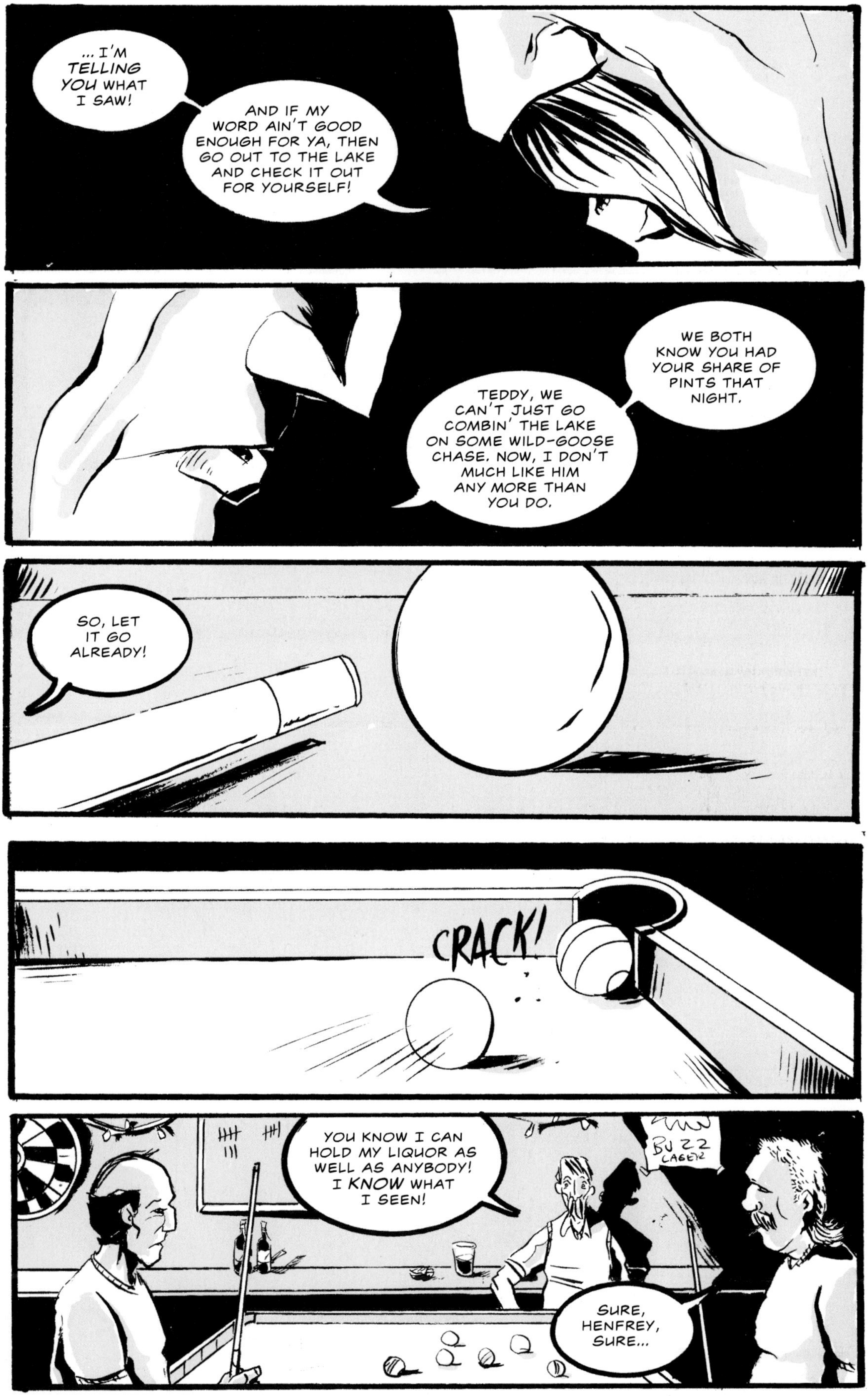
... I'M TELLING YOU WHAT I SAW!
AND IF MY WORD AIN'T GOOD ENOUGH FOR YA, THEN GO OUT TO THE LAKE AND CHECK IT OUT FOR YOURSELF!
TEDDY, WE CAN'T JUST GO COMBIN' THE LAKE ON SOME WILD-GOOSE CHASE. NOW, I DON'T MUCH LIKE HIM ANY MORE THAN YOU DO.
WE BOTH KNOW YOU HAD YOUR SHARE OF PINTS THAT NIGHT.
SO, LET IT GO ALREADY!
CRACK!
YOU KNOW I CAN HOLD MY LIQUOR AS WELL AS ANYBODY! I KNOW WHAT I SEEN!
SURE, HENFREY, SURE...

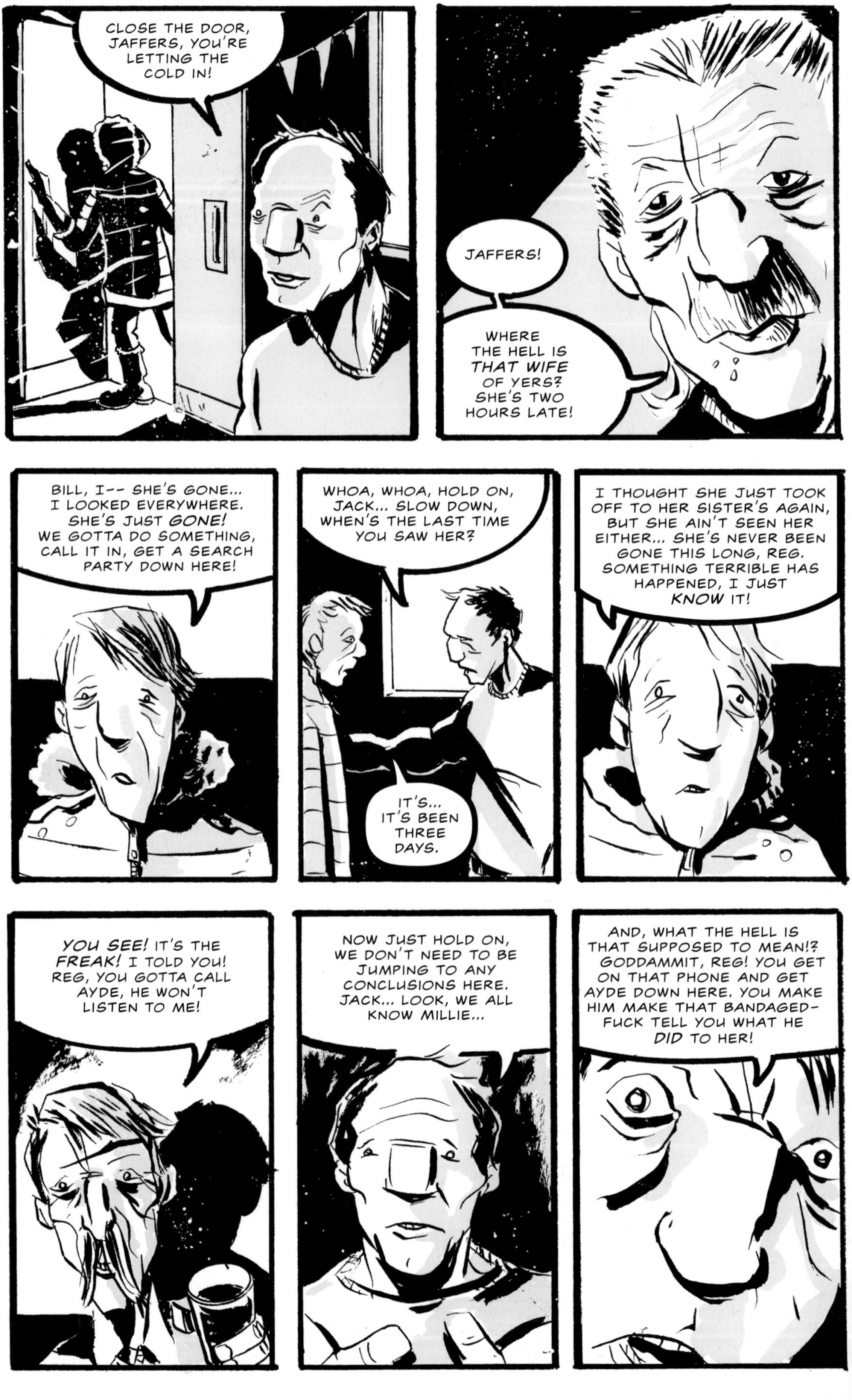
CLOSE THE DOOR, JAFFERS, YOU'RE LETTING THE COLD IN!
JAFFERS!
WHERE THE HELL IS *THAT WIFE* OF YERS? SHE'S TWO HOURS LATE!
BILL, I-- SHE'S GONE... I LOOKED EVERYWHERE. SHE'S JUST *GONE!* WE GOTTA DO SOMETHING, CALL IT IN, GET A SEARCH PARTY DOWN HERE!
WHOA, WHOA, HOLD ON, JACK... SLOW DOWN, WHEN'S THE LAST TIME YOU SAW HER?
IT'S... IT'S BEEN THREE DAYS.
I THOUGHT SHE JUST TOOK OFF TO HER SISTER'S AGAIN, BUT SHE AIN'T SEEN HER EITHER... SHE'S NEVER BEEN GONE THIS LONG, REG. SOMETHING TERRIBLE HAS HAPPENED, I JUST *KNOW* IT!
YOU SEE! IT'S THE *FREAK!* I TOLD YOU! REG, YOU GOTTA CALL AYDE, HE WON'T LISTEN TO ME!
NOW JUST HOLD ON, WE DON'T NEED TO BE JUMPING TO ANY CONCLUSIONS HERE. JACK... LOOK, WE ALL KNOW MILLIE...
AND, WHAT THE HELL IS THAT SUPPOSED TO MEAN!? GODDAMMIT, REG! YOU GET ON THAT PHONE AND GET AYDE DOWN HERE. YOU MAKE HIM MAKE THAT BANDAGED-FUCK TELL YOU WHAT HE *DID* TO HER!

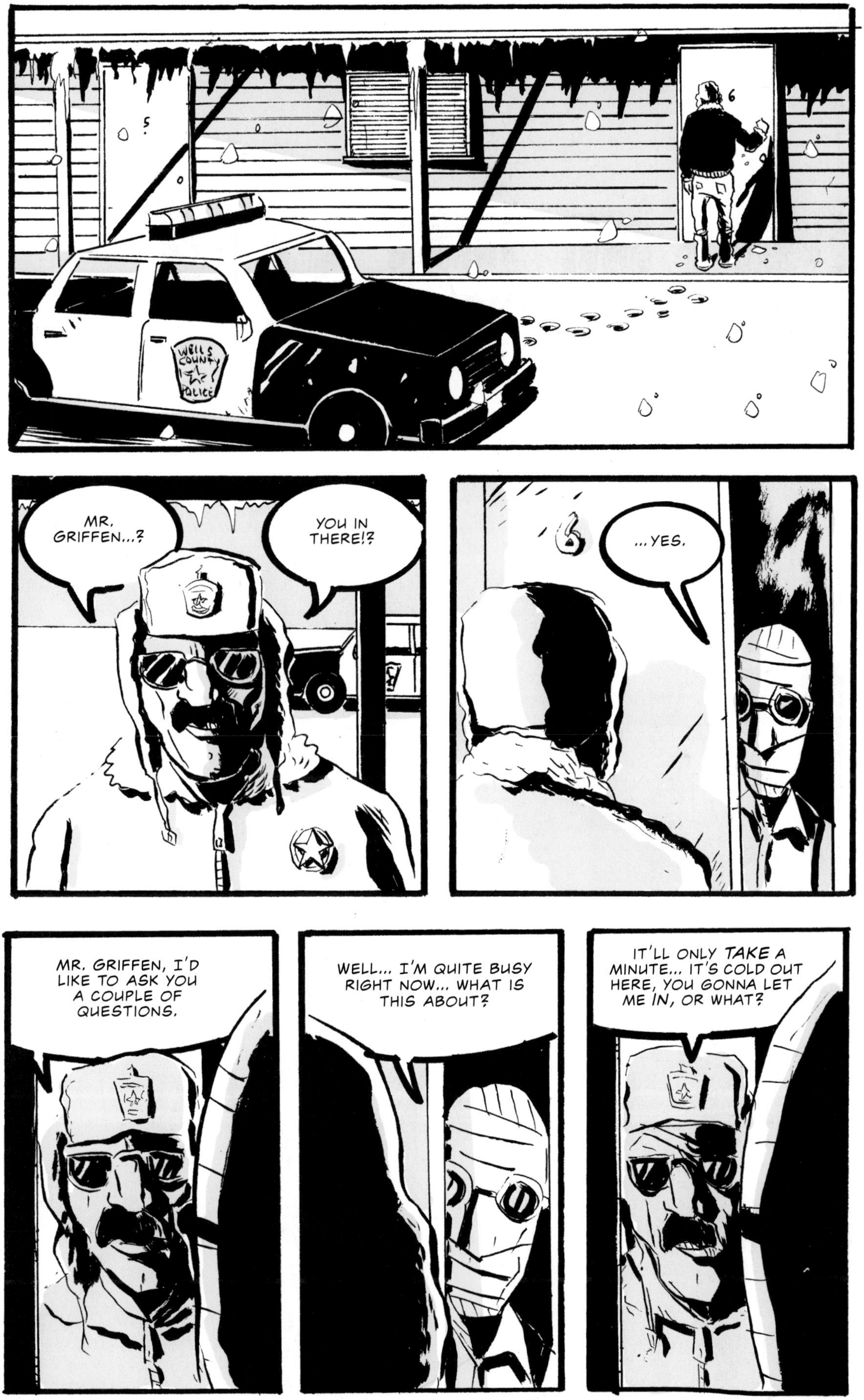
WELLS COUNTY POLICE
MR. GRIFFEN...?
YOU IN THERE!?
...YES.
MR. GRIFFEN, I'D LIKE TO ASK YOU A COUPLE OF QUESTIONS.
WELL... I'M QUITE BUSY RIGHT NOW... WHAT IS THIS ABOUT?
IT'LL ONLY *TAKE* A MINUTE... IT'S COLD OUT HERE, YOU GONNA LET ME *IN*, OR WHAT?

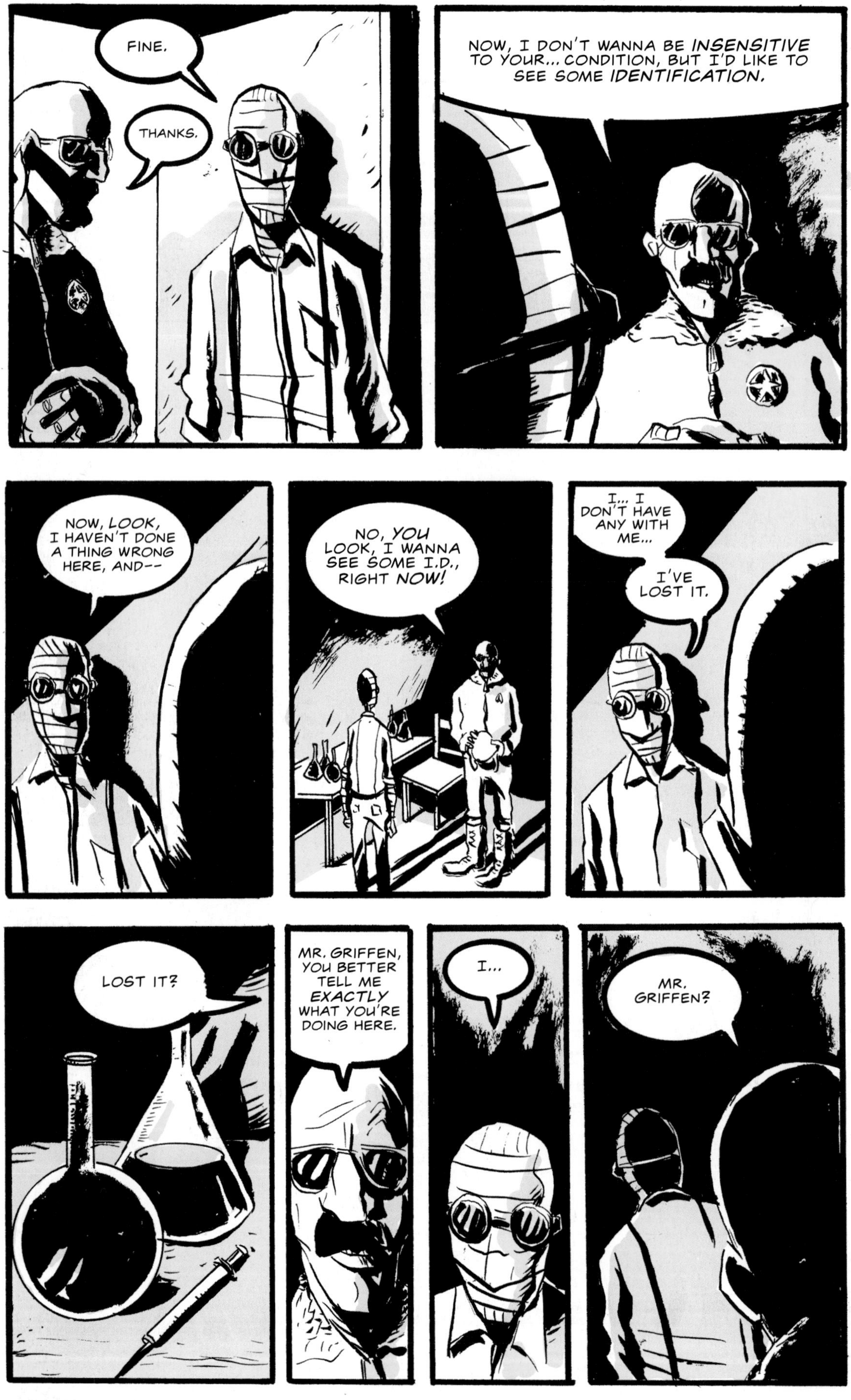
FINE.
THANKS.
NOW, I DON'T WANNA BE INSENSITIVE TO YOUR... CONDITION, BUT I'D LIKE TO SEE SOME IDENTIFICATION.
NOW, LOOK, I HAVEN'T DONE A THING WRONG HERE, AND--
NO, YOU LOOK, I WANNA SEE SOME I.D., RIGHT NOW!
I... I DON'T HAVE ANY WITH ME...
I'VE LOST IT.
LOST IT?
MR. GRIFFEN, YOU BETTER TELL ME EXACTLY WHAT YOU'RE DOING HERE.
I...
MR. GRIFFEN?

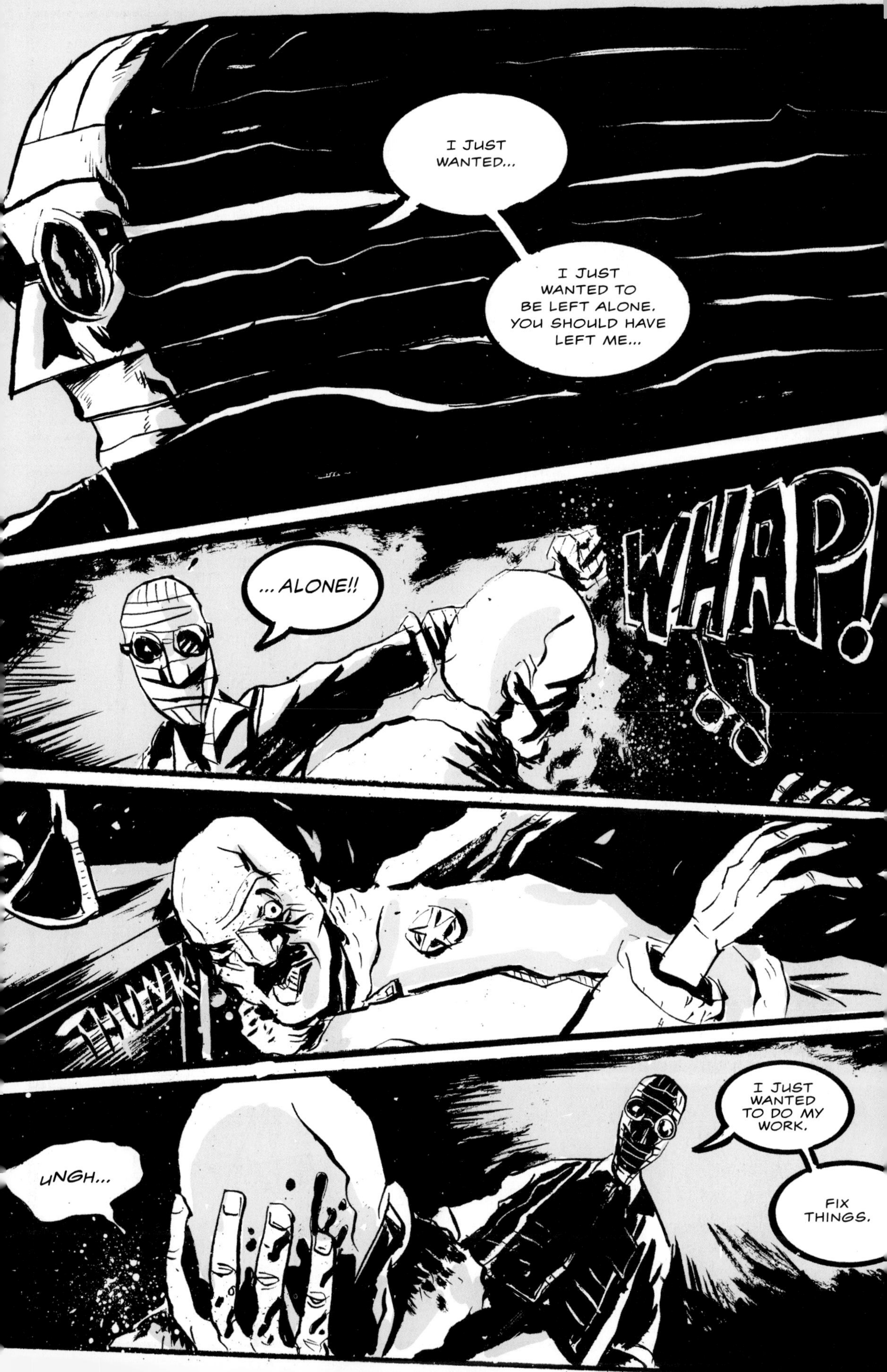

I JUST WANTED...
I JUST WANTED TO BE LEFT ALONE. YOU SHOULD HAVE LEFT ME...
...ALONE!!
WHAP!
THONK!
UNGH...
I JUST WANTED TO DO MY WORK.
FIX THINGS.

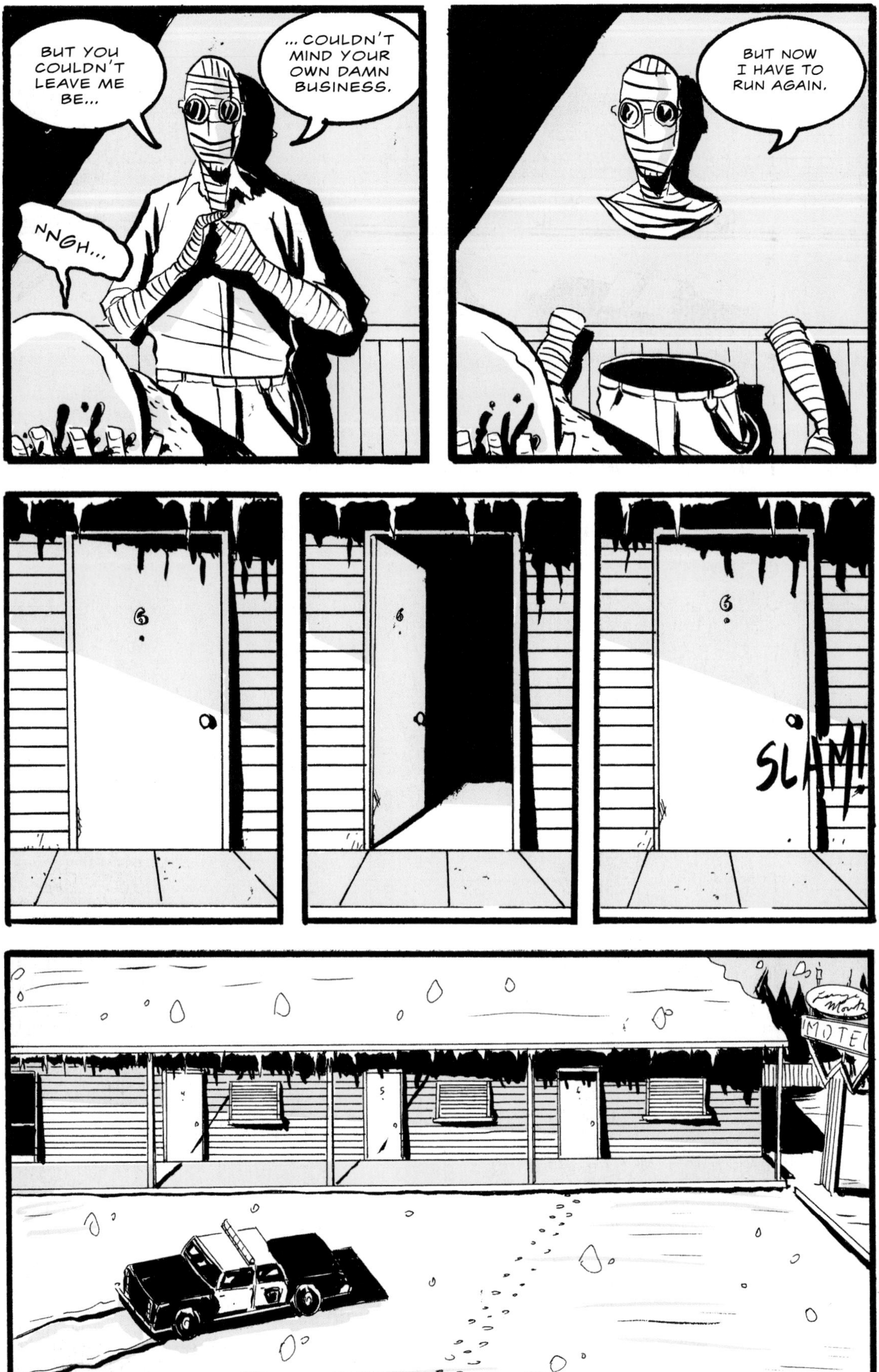
BUT YOU COULDN'T LEAVE ME BE...
...COULDN'T MIND YOUR OWN DAMN BUSINESS.
NNGH...
BUT NOW I HAVE TO RUN AGAIN.
SLAM!

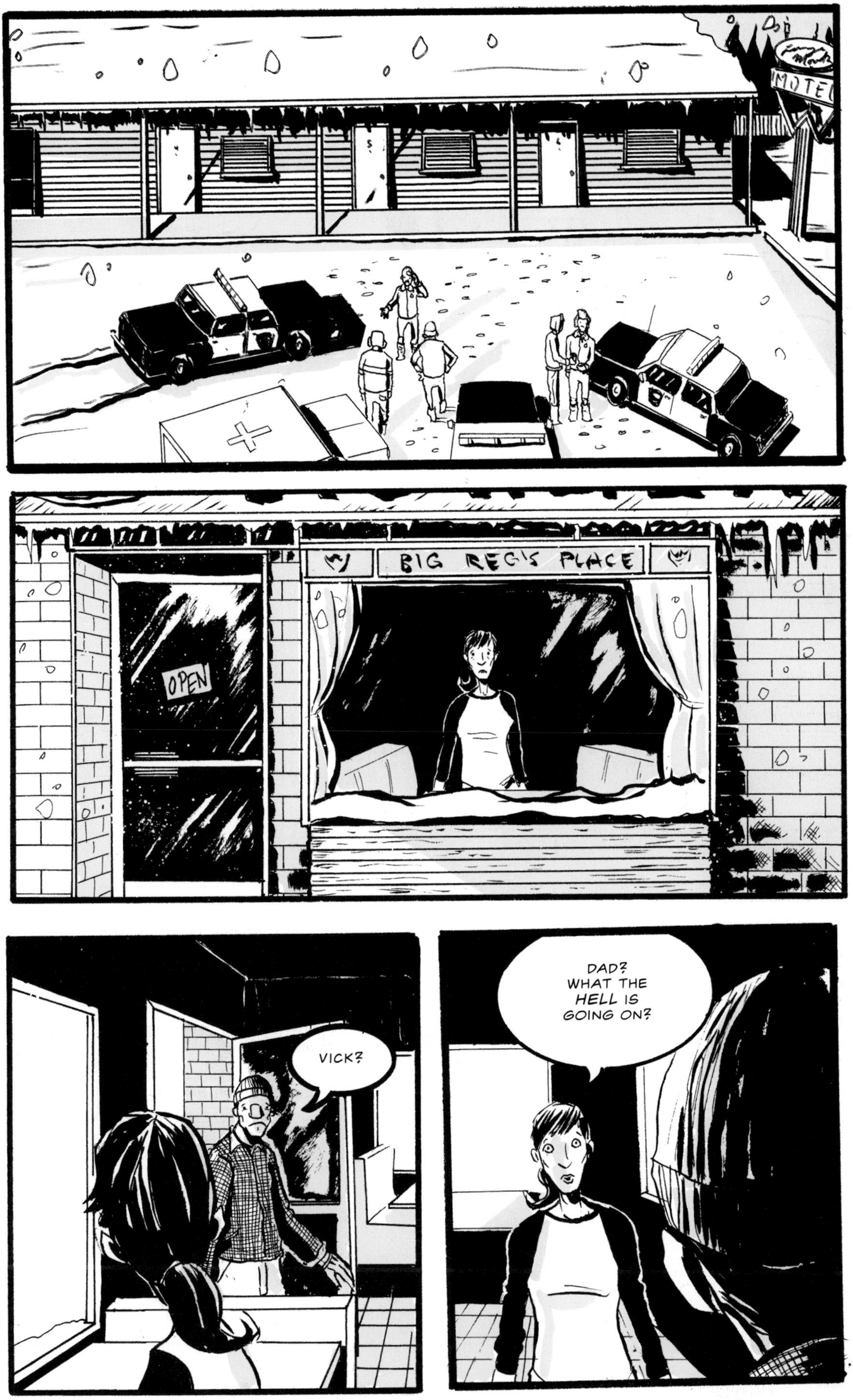
MOTEL
BIG REG'S PLACE
OPEN
VICK?
DAD? WHAT THE HELL IS GOING ON?

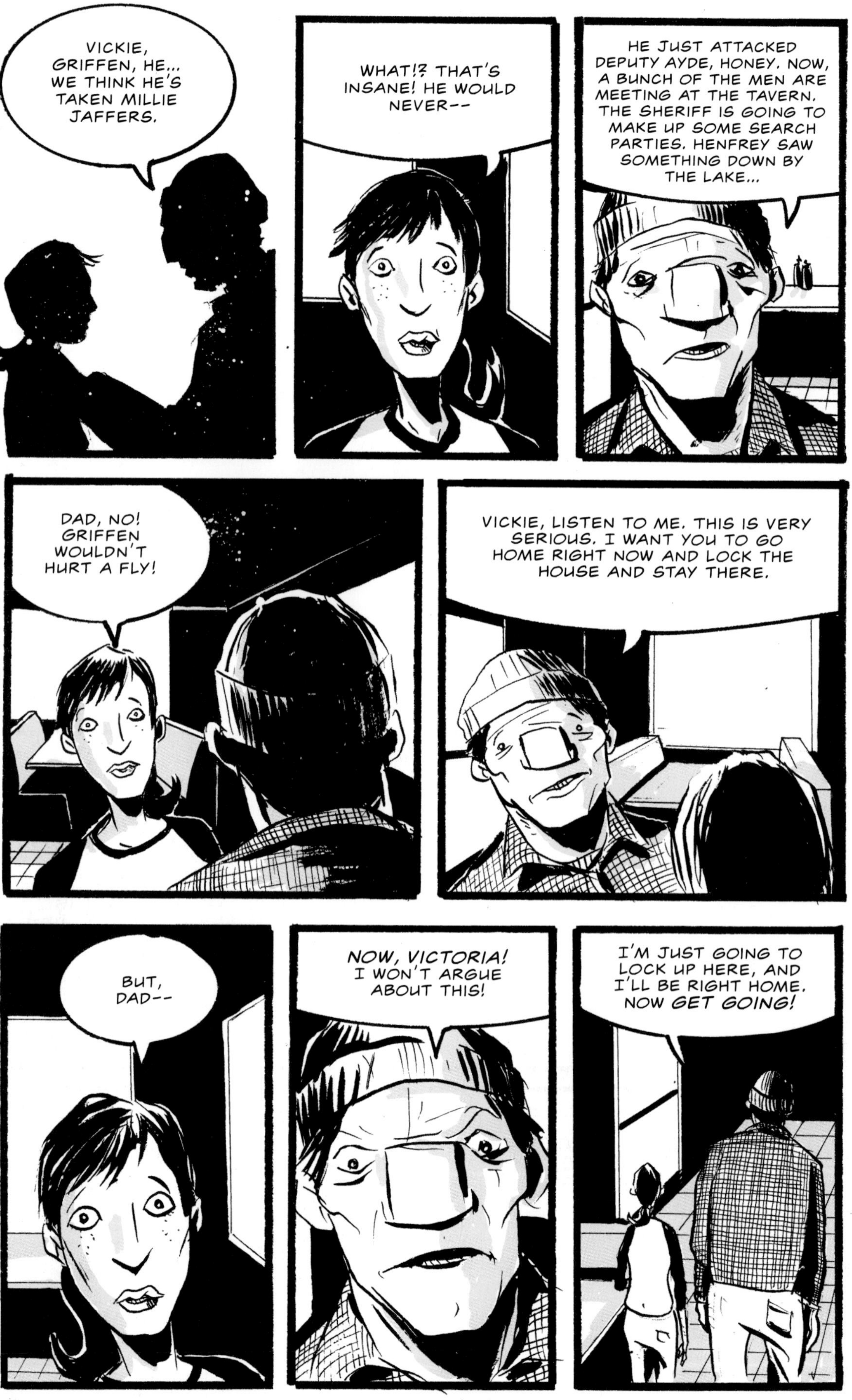
VICKIE, GRIFFEN, HE... WE THINK HE'S TAKEN MILLIE JAFFERS.
WHAT!? THAT'S INSANE! HE WOULD NEVER--
HE JUST ATTACKED DEPUTY AYDE, HONEY. NOW, A BUNCH OF THE MEN ARE MEETING AT THE TAVERN. THE SHERIFF IS GOING TO MAKE UP SOME SEARCH PARTIES. HENFREY SAW SOMETHING DOWN BY THE LAKE...
DAD, NO! GRIFFEN WOULDN'T HURT A FLY!
VICKIE, LISTEN TO ME. THIS IS VERY SERIOUS. I WANT YOU TO GO HOME RIGHT NOW AND LOCK THE HOUSE AND STAY THERE.
BUT, DAD--
NOW, VICTORIA! I WON'T ARGUE ABOUT THIS!
I'M JUST GOING TO LOCK UP HERE, AND I'LL BE RIGHT HOME. NOW GET GOING!

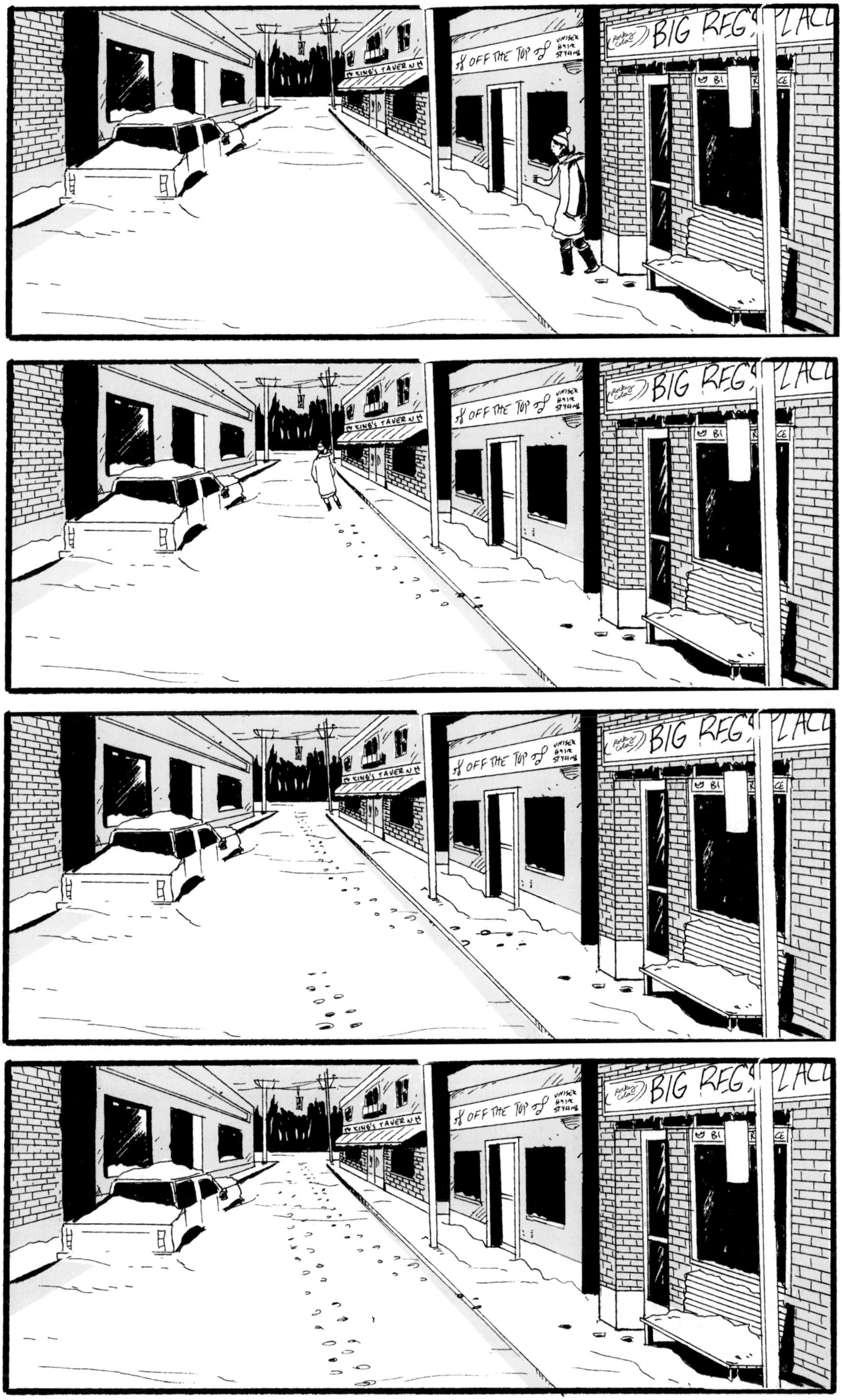
OFF THE TOP
UNISEX HAIR STYLING
KING'S TAVERN
Rocky Cola
BIG REG'S

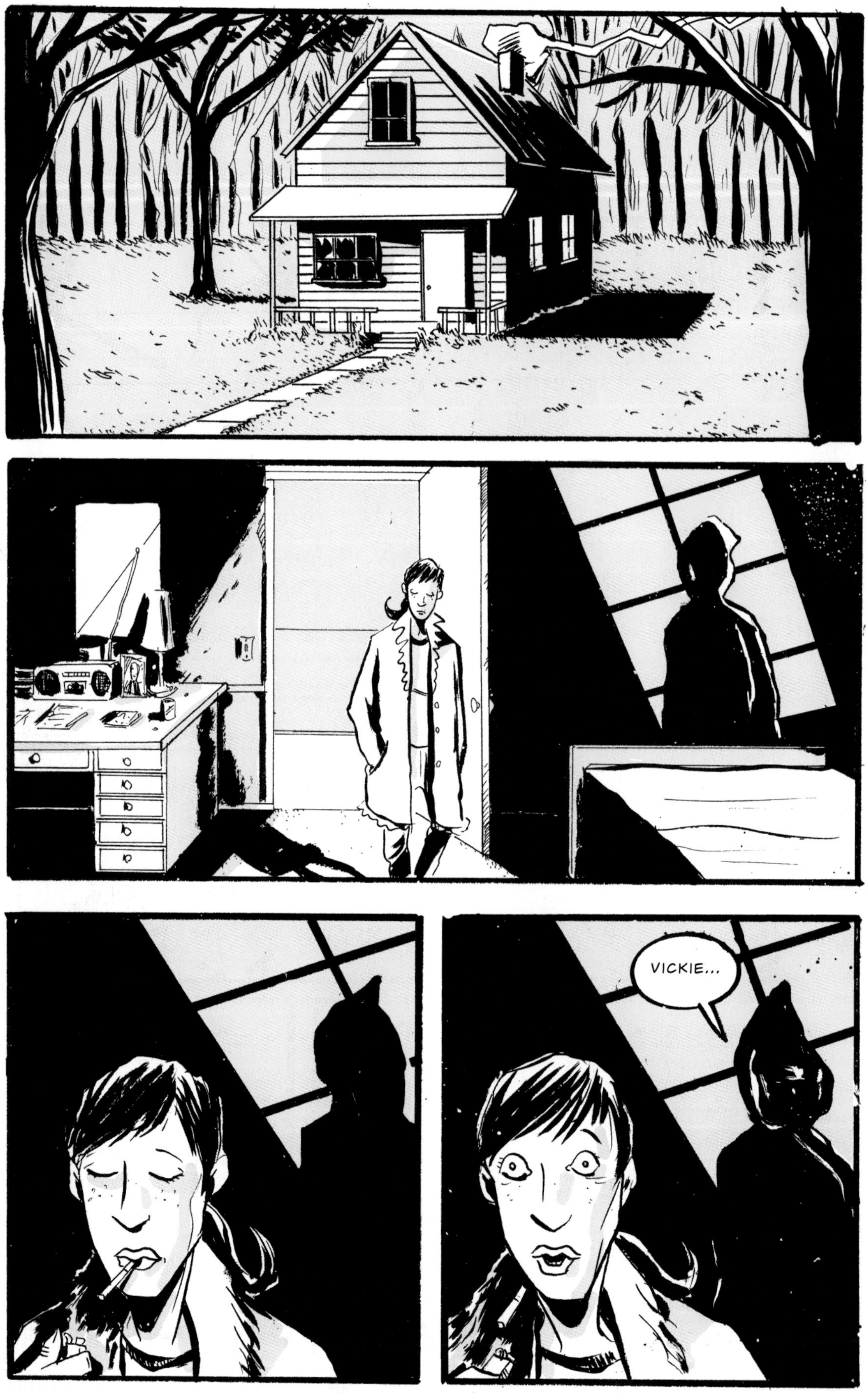
VICKIE...

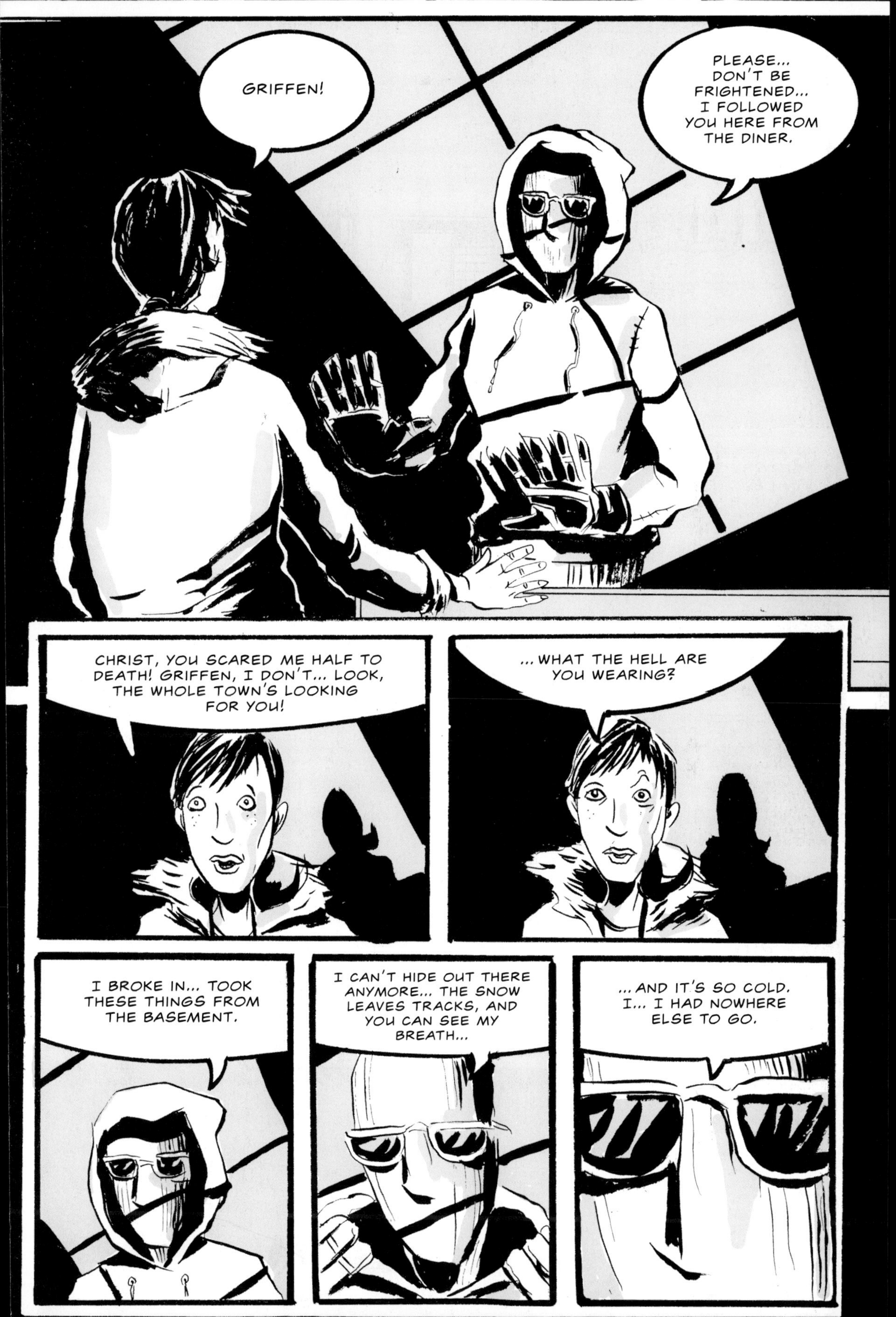
GRIFFEN!
PLEASE... DON'T BE FRIGHTENED... I FOLLOWED YOU HERE FROM THE DINER.
CHRIST, YOU SCARED ME HALF TO DEATH! GRIFFEN, I DON'T... LOOK, THE WHOLE TOWN'S LOOKING FOR YOU!
...WHAT THE HELL ARE YOU WEARING?
I BROKE IN... TOOK THESE THINGS FROM THE BASEMENT.
I CAN'T HIDE OUT THERE ANYMORE... THE SNOW LEAVES TRACKS, AND YOU CAN SEE MY BREATH...
...AND IT'S SO COLD. I... I HAD NOWHERE ELSE TO GO.

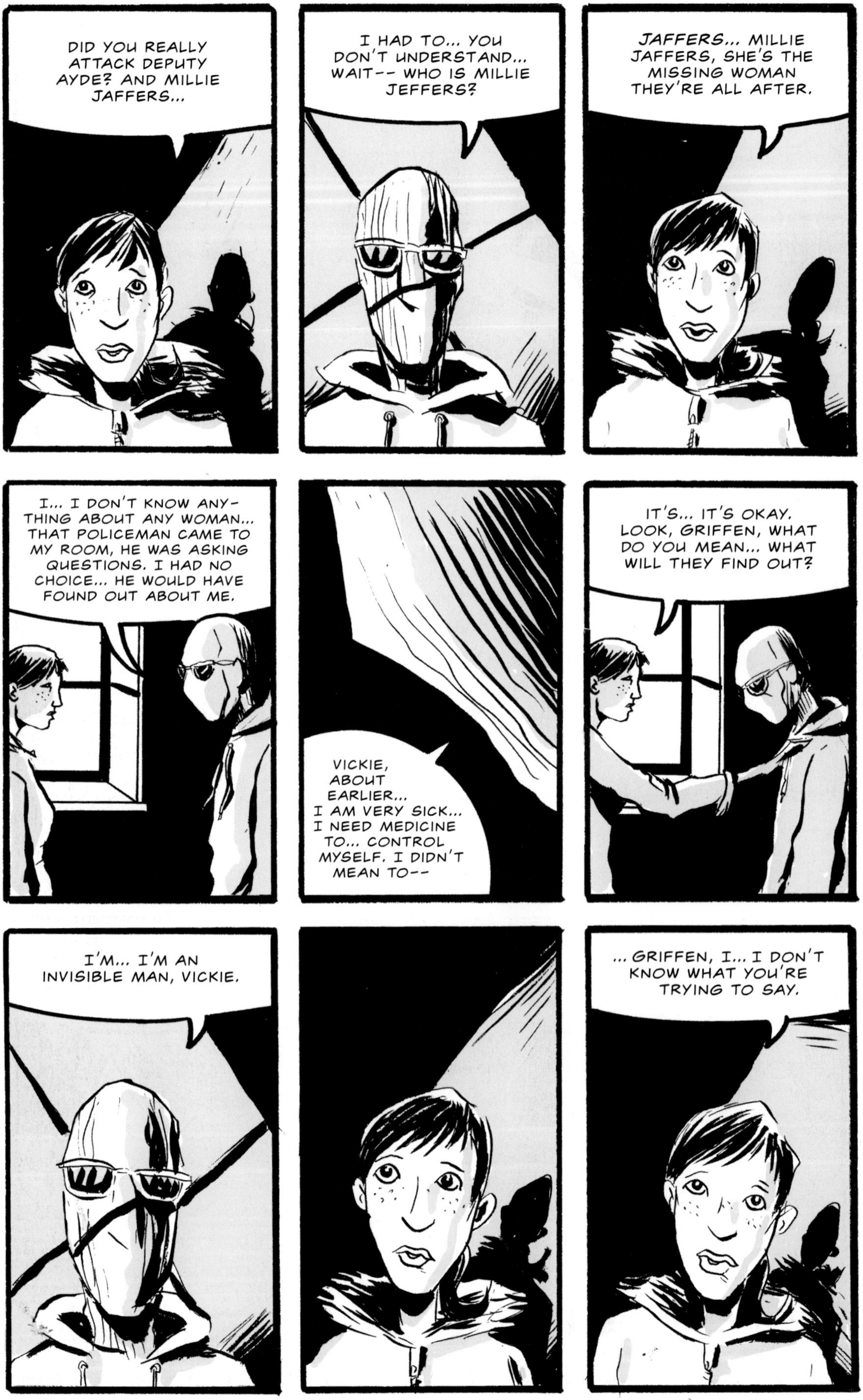
DID YOU REALLY ATTACK DEPUTY AYDE? AND MILLIE JAFFERS...
I HAD TO... YOU DON'T UNDERSTAND... WAIT-- WHO IS MILLIE JEFFERS?
JAFFERS... MILLIE JAFFERS, SHE'S THE MISSING WOMAN THEY'RE ALL AFTER.
I... I DON'T KNOW ANY-THING ABOUT ANY WOMAN... THAT POLICEMAN CAME TO MY ROOM, HE WAS ASKING QUESTIONS. I HAD NO CHOICE... HE WOULD HAVE FOUND OUT ABOUT ME.
VICKIE, ABOUT EARLIER... I AM VERY SICK... I NEED MEDICINE TO... CONTROL MYSELF. I DIDN'T MEAN TO--
IT'S... IT'S OKAY. LOOK, GRIFFEN, WHAT DO YOU MEAN... WHAT WILL THEY FIND OUT?
I'M... I'M AN INVISIBLE MAN, VICKIE.
... GRIFFEN, I... I DON'T KNOW WHAT YOU'RE TRYING TO SAY.

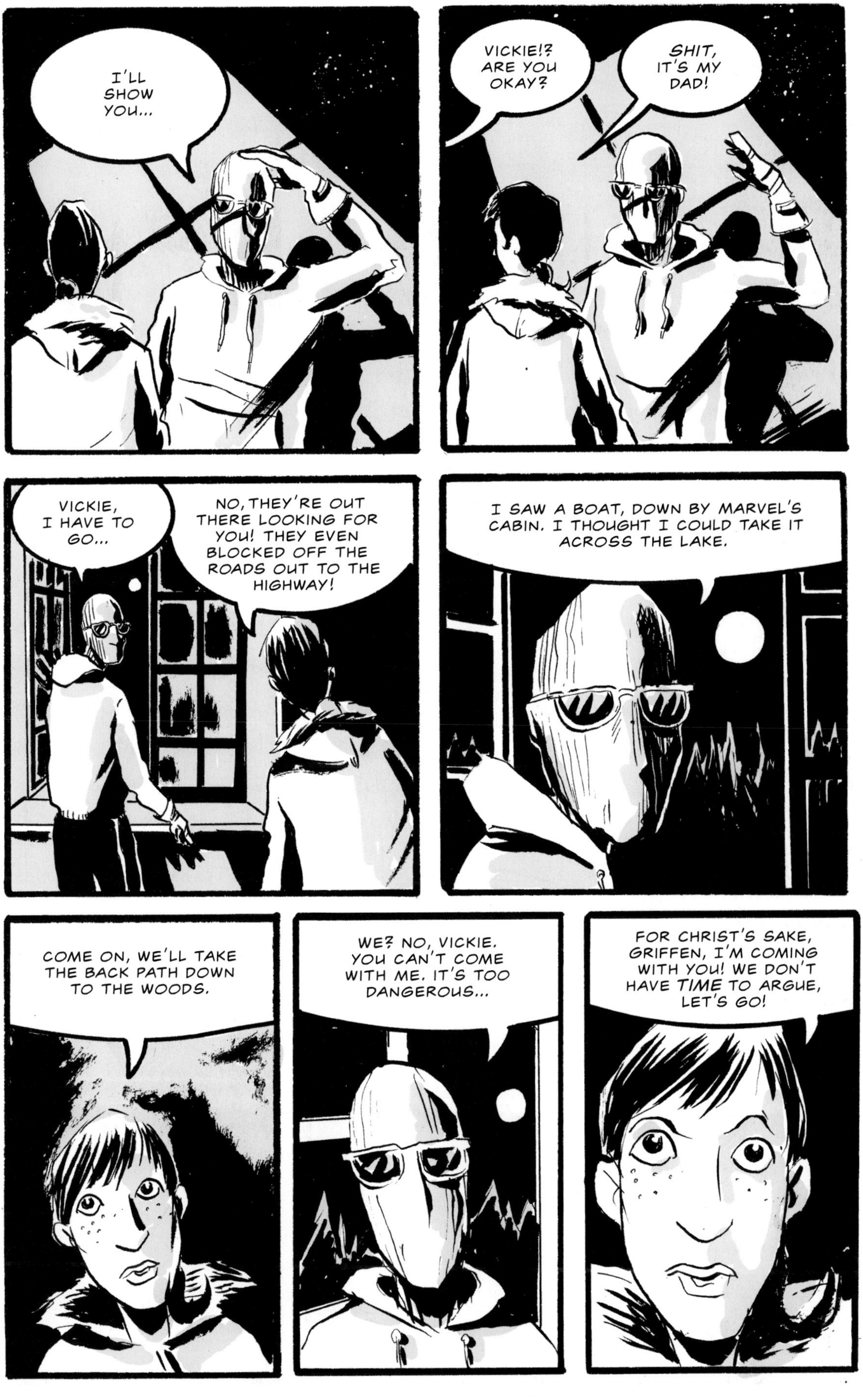
I'LL SHOW YOU...
VICKIE!? ARE YOU OKAY?
SHIT, IT'S MY DAD!
VICKIE, I HAVE TO GO...
NO, THEY'RE OUT THERE LOOKING FOR YOU! THEY EVEN BLOCKED OFF THE ROADS OUT TO THE HIGHWAY!
I SAW A BOAT, DOWN BY MARVEL'S CABIN. I THOUGHT I COULD TAKE IT ACROSS THE LAKE.
COME ON, WE'LL TAKE THE BACK PATH DOWN TO THE WOODS.
WE? NO, VICKIE. YOU CAN'T COME WITH ME. IT'S TOO DANGEROUS...
FOR CHRIST'S SAKE, GRIFFEN, I'M COMING WITH YOU! WE DON'T HAVE TIME TO ARGUE, LET'S GO!

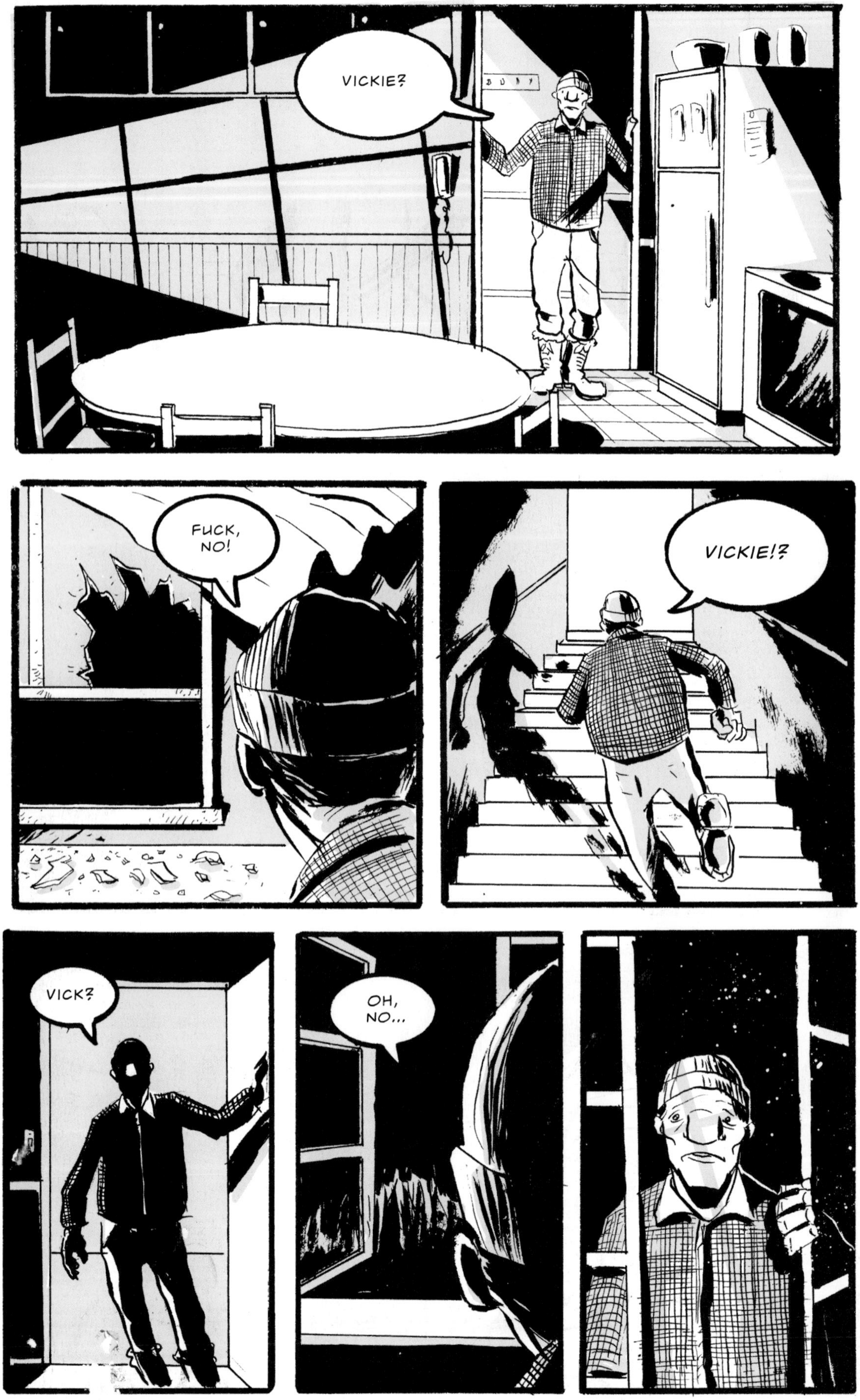
VICKIE?
FUCK, NO!
VICKIE!?
VICK?
OH, NO...

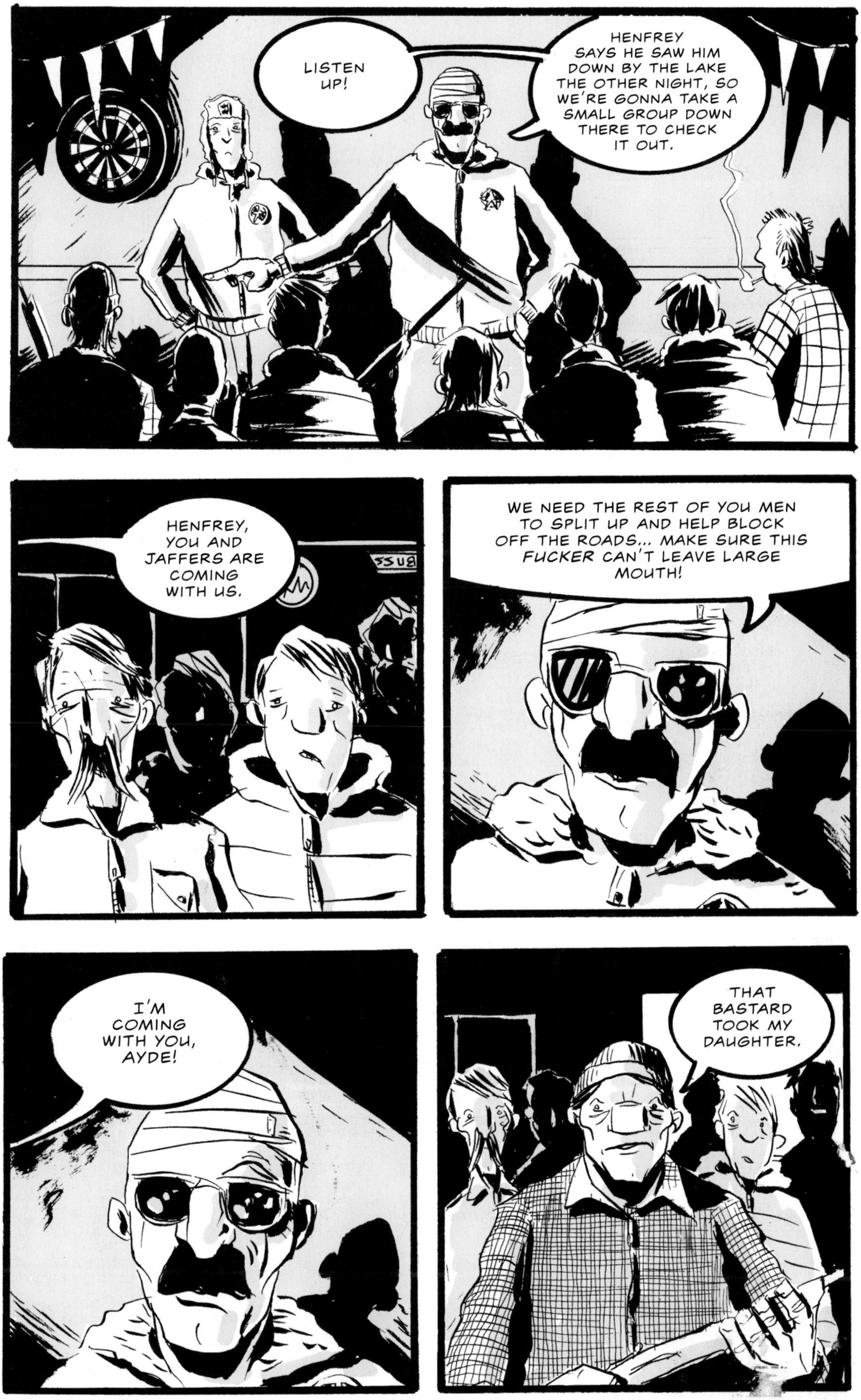
LISTEN UP!
HENFREY SAYS HE SAW HIM DOWN BY THE LAKE THE OTHER NIGHT, SO WE'RE GONNA TAKE A SMALL GROUP DOWN THERE TO CHECK IT OUT.
HENFREY, YOU AND JAFFERS ARE COMING WITH US.
WE NEED THE REST OF YOU MEN TO SPLIT UP AND HELP BLOCK OFF THE ROADS... MAKE SURE THIS *FUCKER* CAN'T LEAVE LARGE MOUTH!
I'M COMING WITH YOU, AYDE!
THAT BASTARD TOOK MY DAUGHTER.

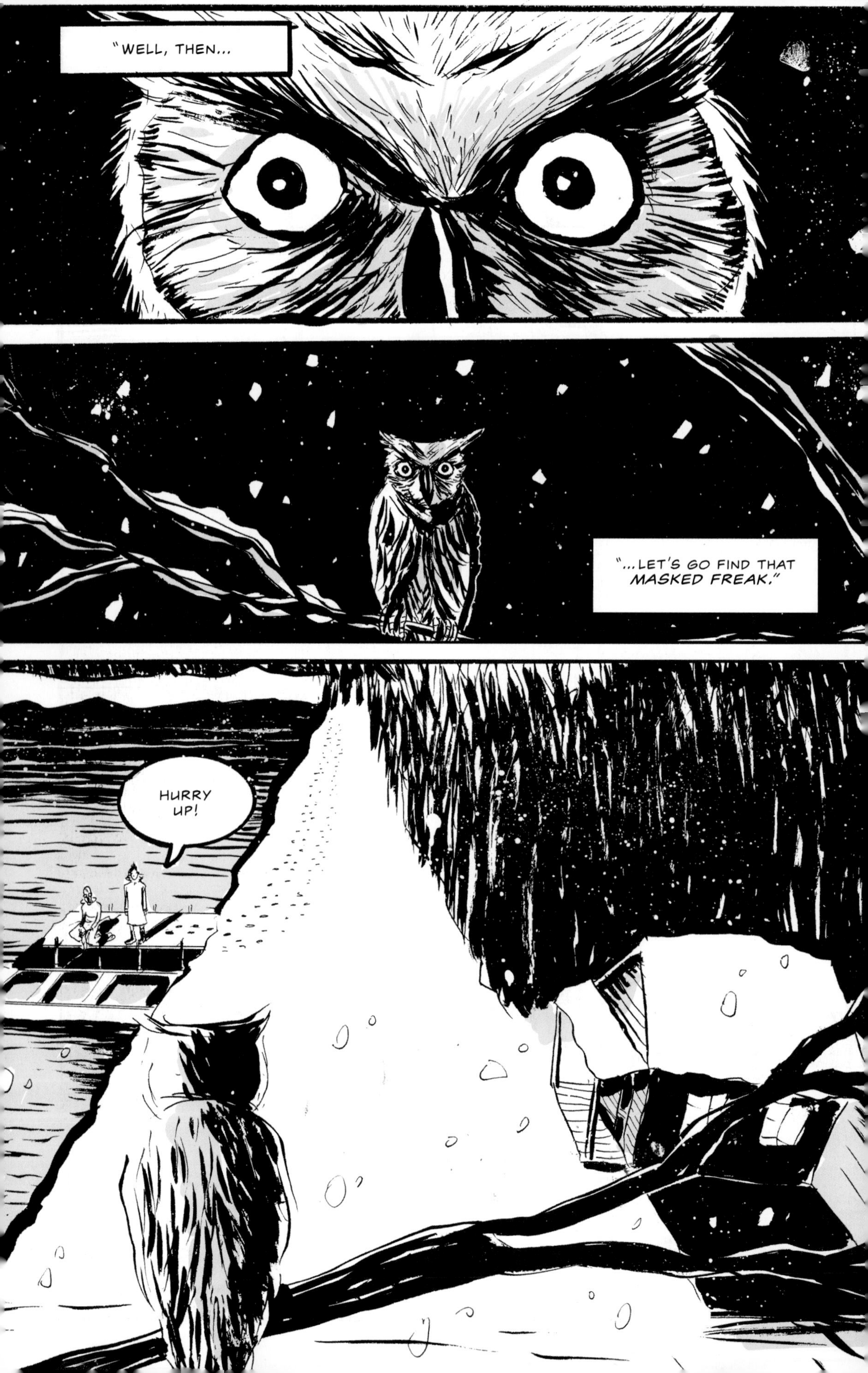
"WELL, THEN...
"...LET'S GO FIND THAT MASKED FREAK."
HURRY UP!

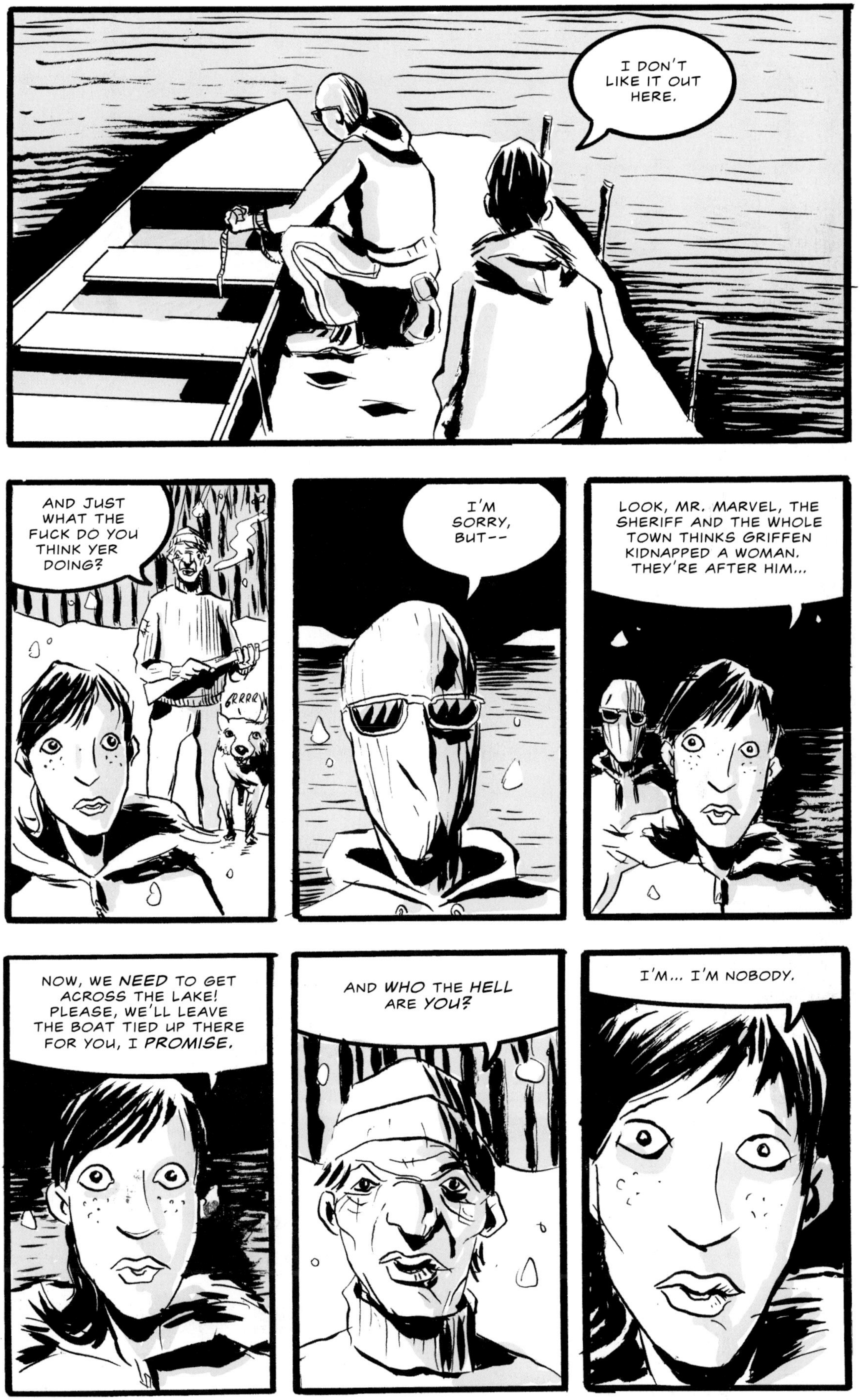
I DON'T LIKE IT OUT HERE.
AND JUST WHAT THE FUCK DO YOU THINK YER DOING?
GRRRR
I'M SORRY, BUT--
LOOK, MR. MARVEL, THE SHERIFF AND THE WHOLE TOWN THINKS GRIFFEN KIDNAPPED A WOMAN. THEY'RE AFTER HIM...
NOW, WE NEED TO GET ACROSS THE LAKE! PLEASE, WE'LL LEAVE THE BOAT TIED UP THERE FOR YOU, I PROMISE.
AND WHO THE HELL ARE YOU?
I'M... I'M NOBODY.

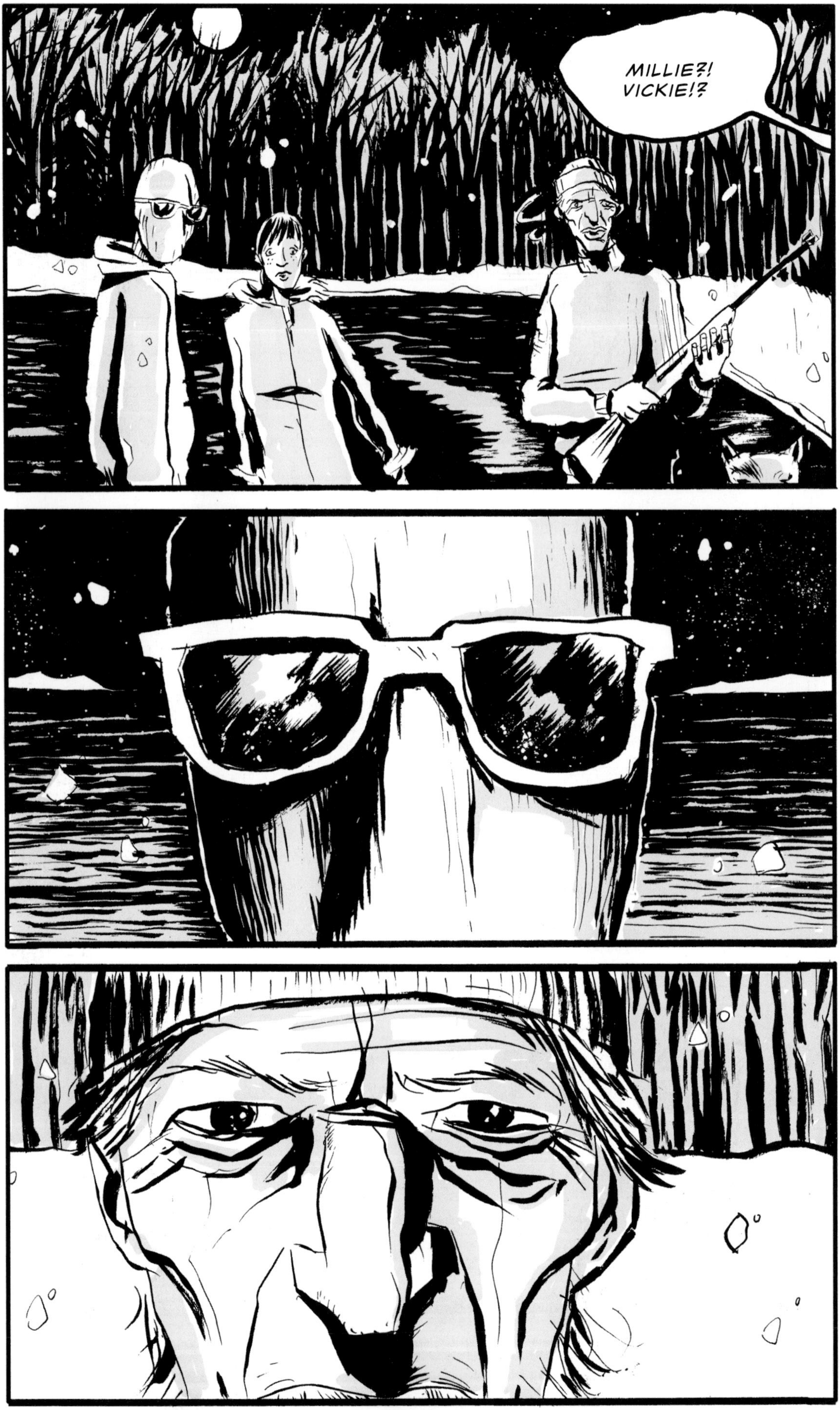
MILLIE?! VICKIE!?

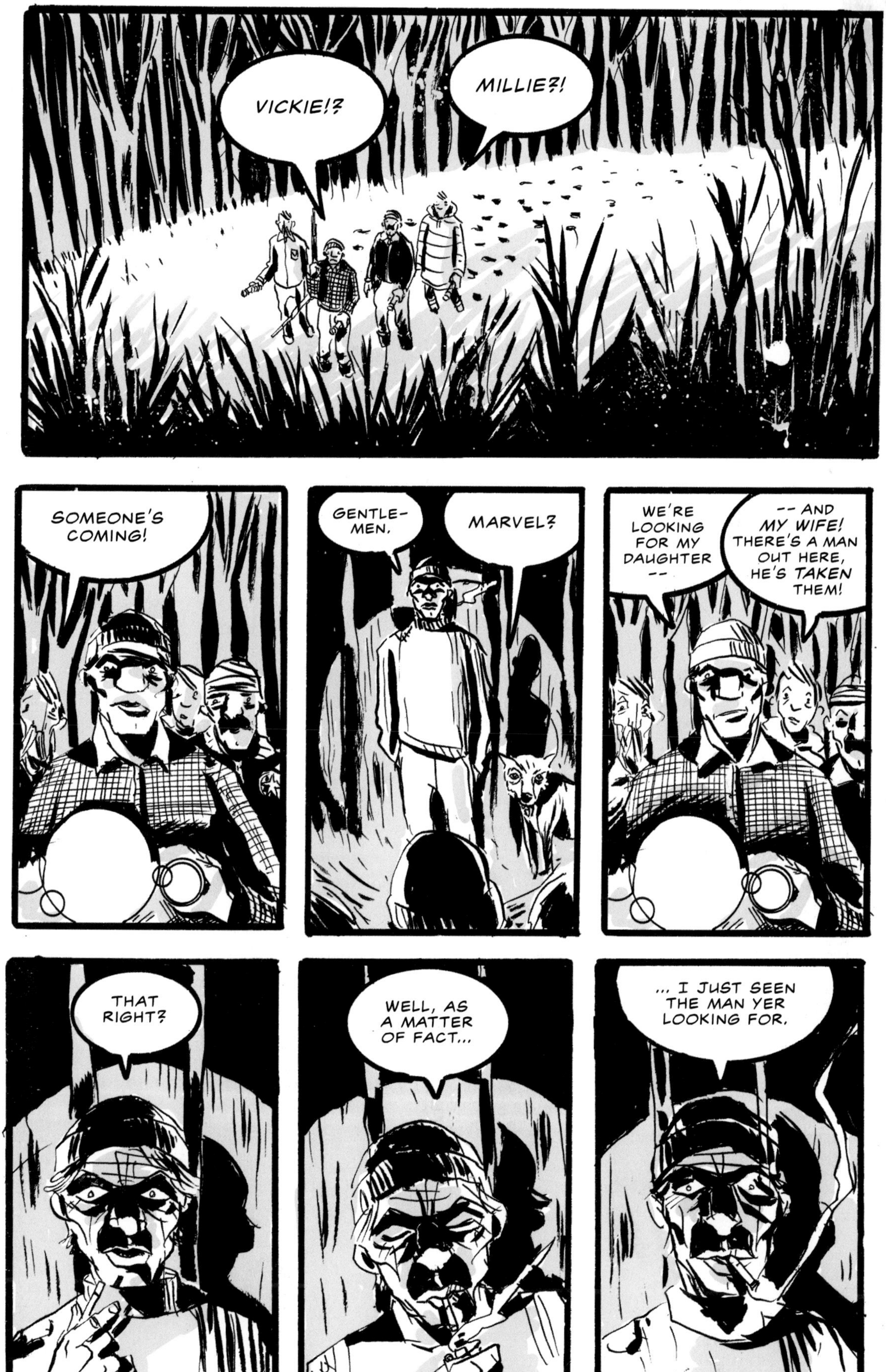
VICKIE!?
MILLIE?!
SOMEONE'S COMING!
GENTLE-MEN.
MARVEL?
WE'RE LOOKING FOR MY DAUGHTER --
-- AND MY WIFE! THERE'S A MAN OUT HERE, HE'S TAKEN THEM!
THAT RIGHT?
WELL, AS A MATTER OF FACT...
... I JUST SEEN THE MAN YER LOOKING FOR.

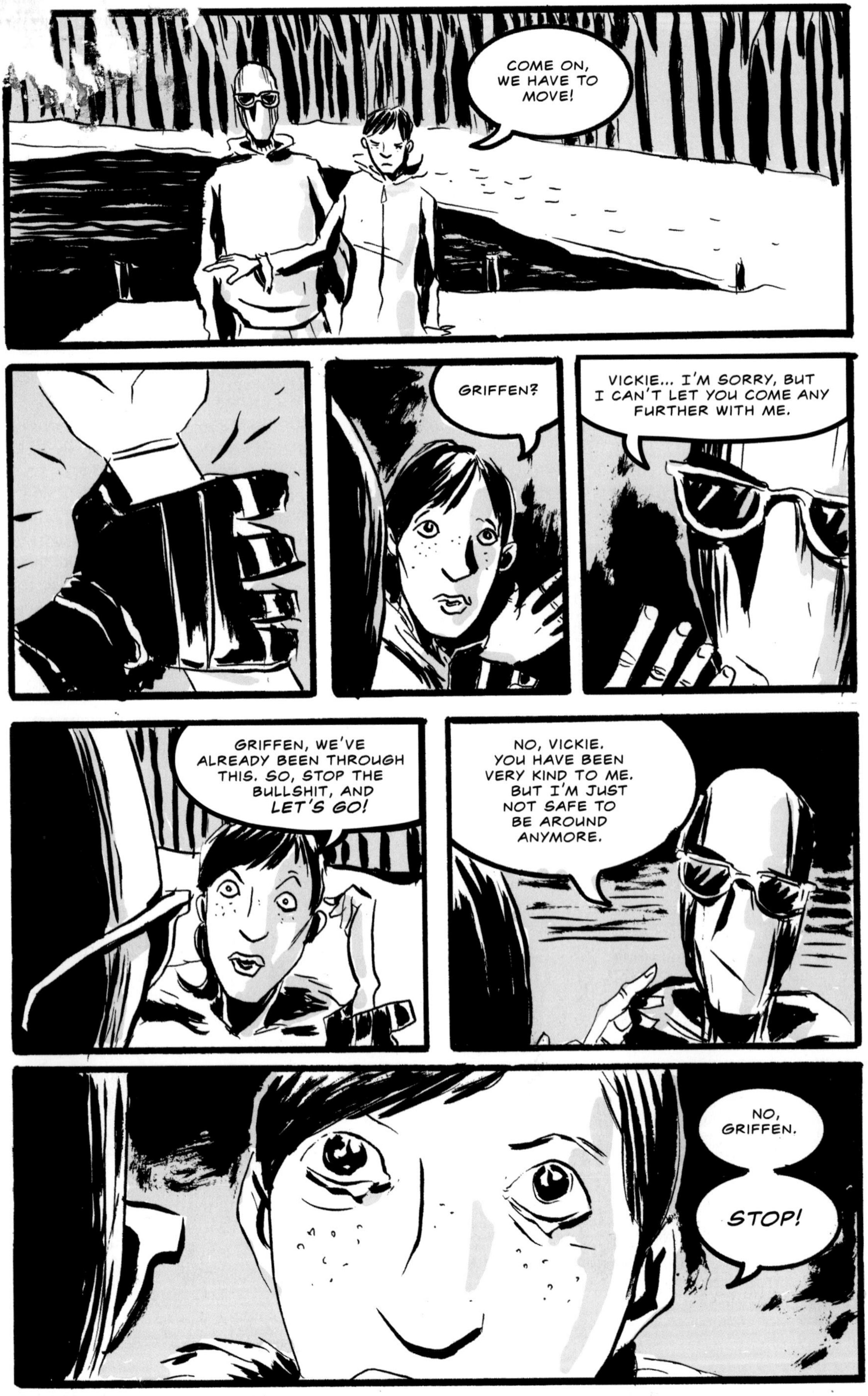
COME ON, WE HAVE TO MOVE!
GRIFFEN?
VICKIE... I'M SORRY, BUT I CAN'T LET YOU COME ANY FURTHER WITH ME.
GRIFFEN, WE'VE ALREADY BEEN THROUGH THIS. SO, STOP THE BULLSHIT, AND LET'S GO!
NO, VICKIE. YOU HAVE BEEN VERY KIND TO ME. BUT I'M JUST NOT SAFE TO BE AROUND ANYMORE.
NO, GRIFFEN.
STOP!

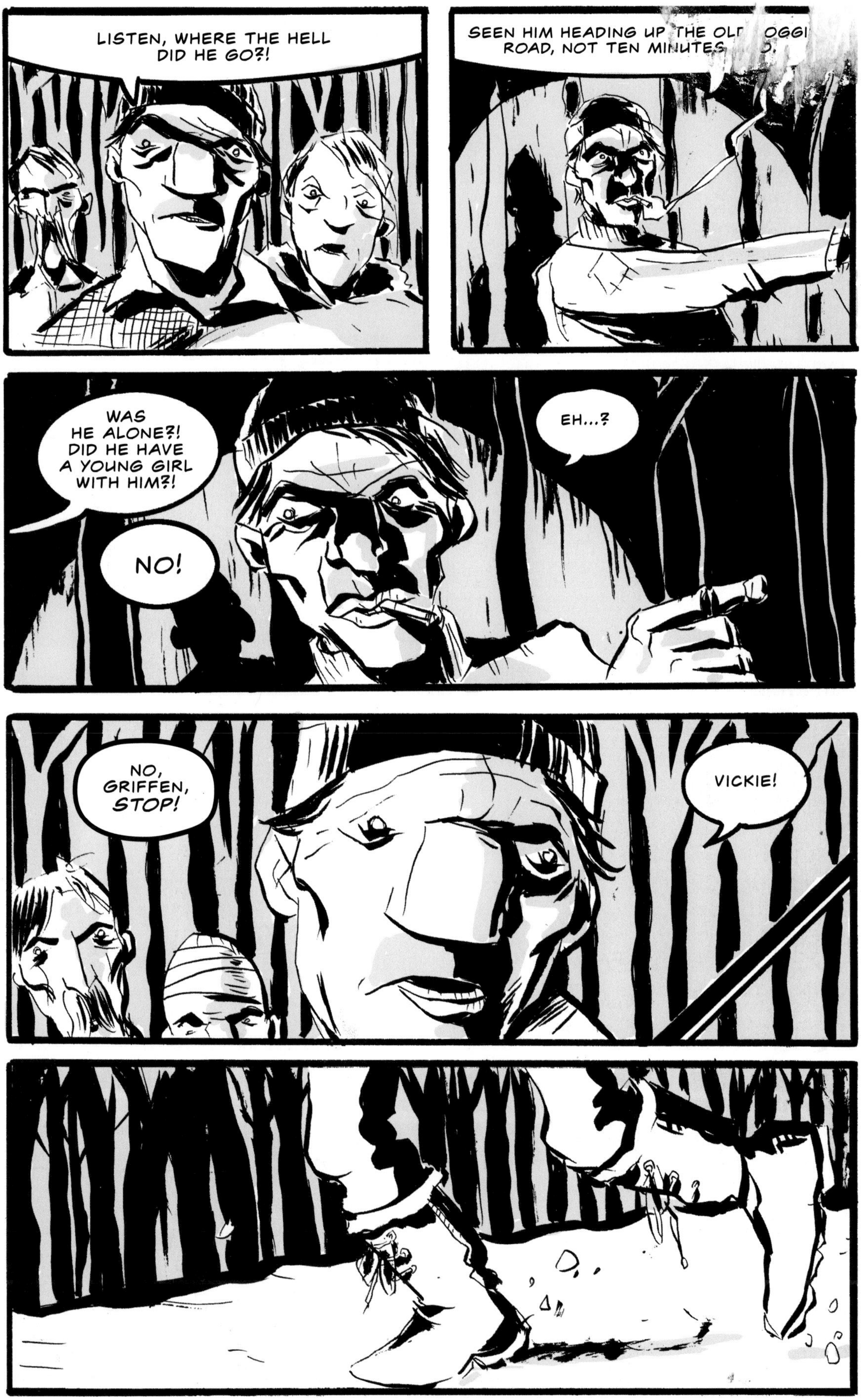
LISTEN, WHERE THE HELL DID HE GO?!
SEEN HIM HEADING UP THE
ROAD, NOT TEN MINUTES
WAS HE ALONE?! DID HE HAVE A YOUNG GIRL WITH HIM?!
EH...?
NO!
NO, GRIFFEN, STOP!
VICKIE!

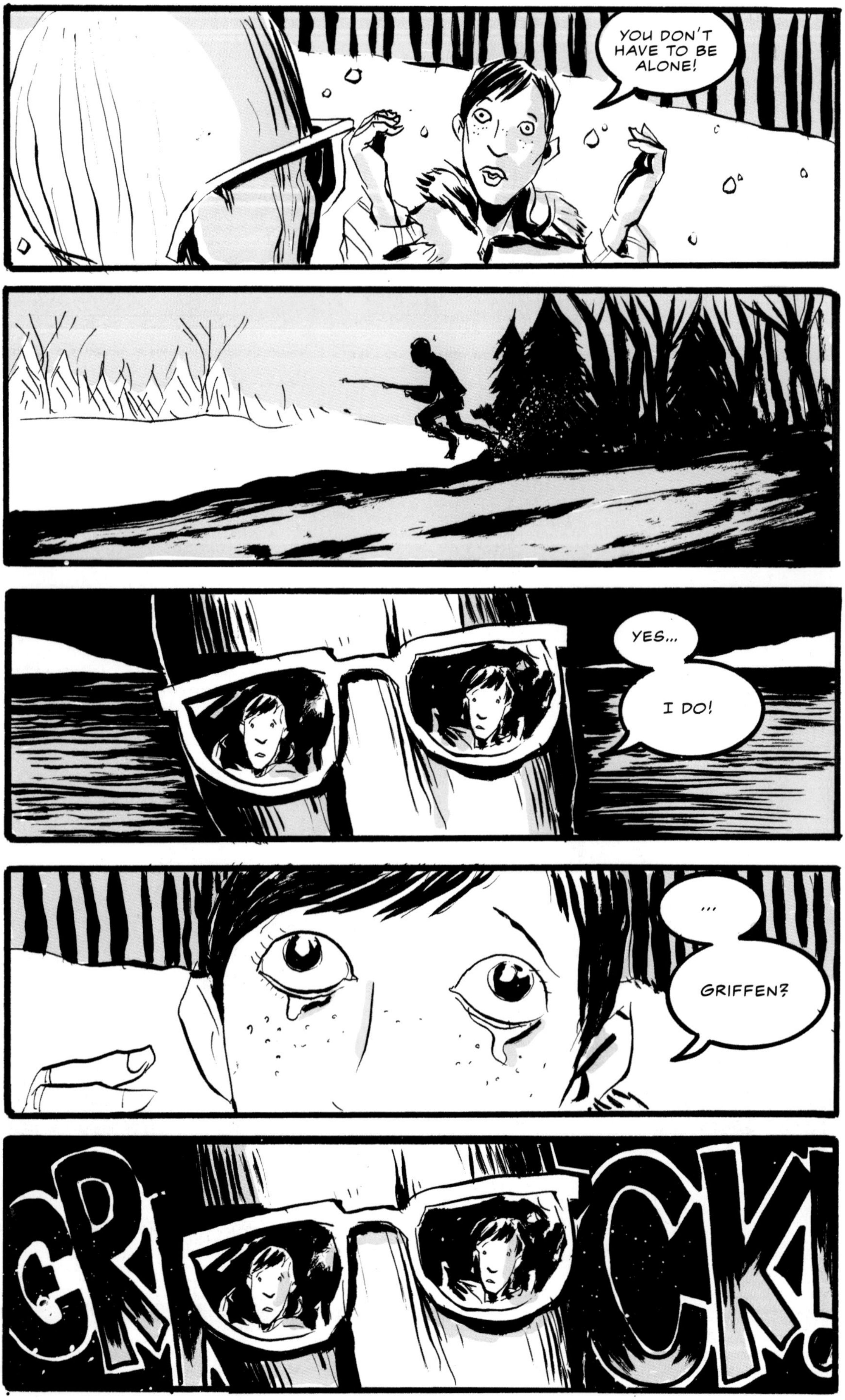
YOU DON'T HAVE TO BE ALONE!
YES...
I DO!
...
GRIFFEN?
CRACK!

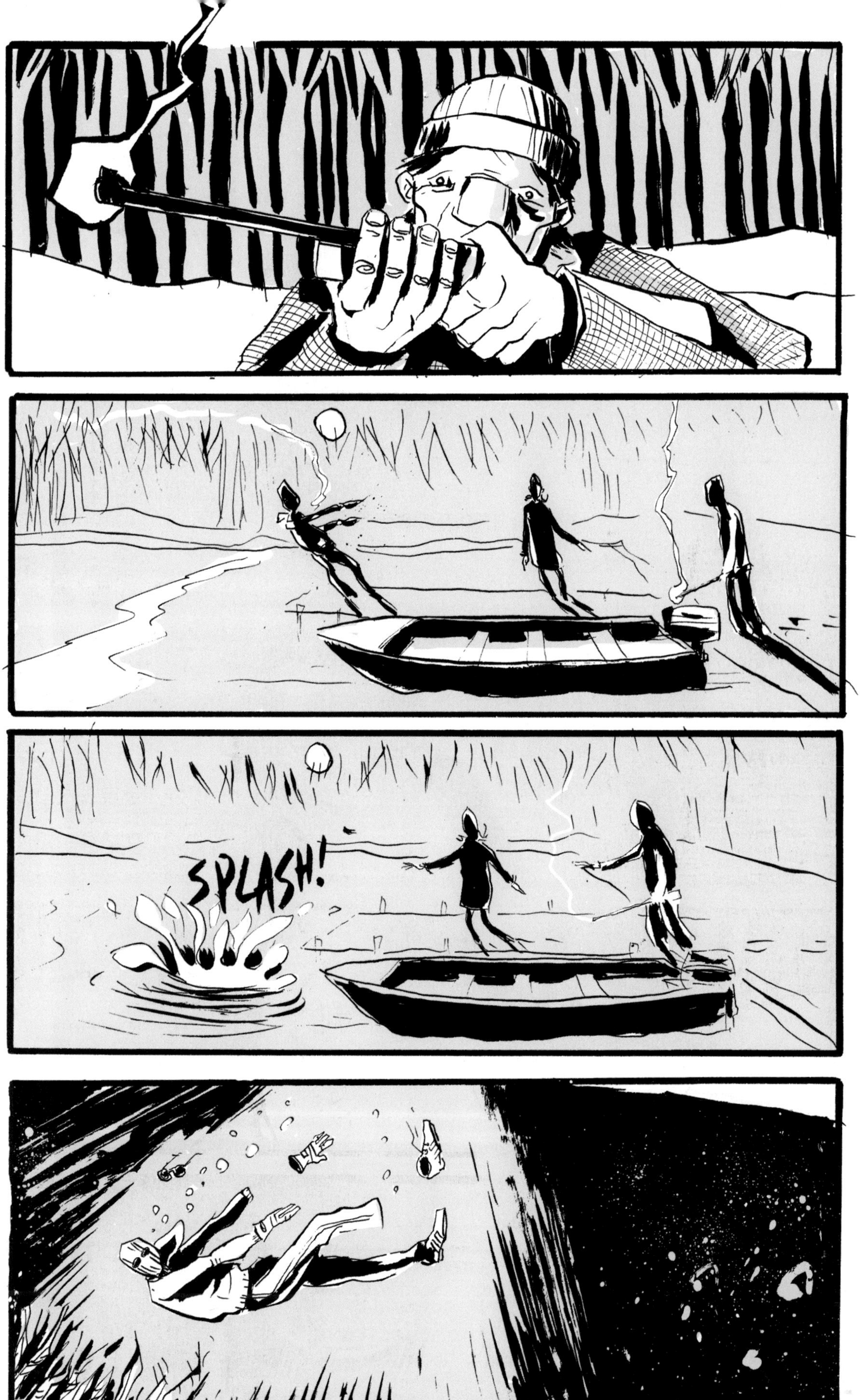
SPLASH!

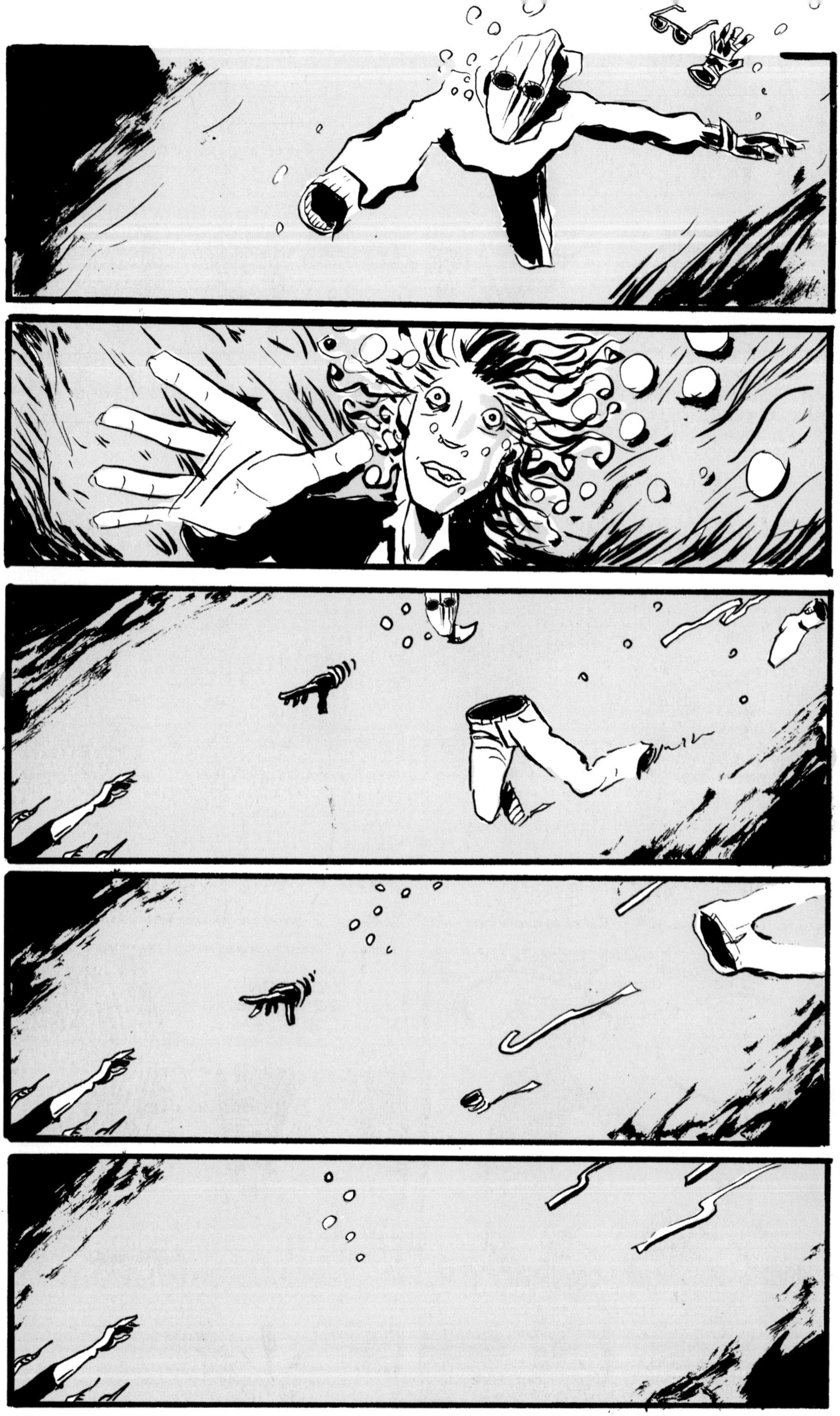

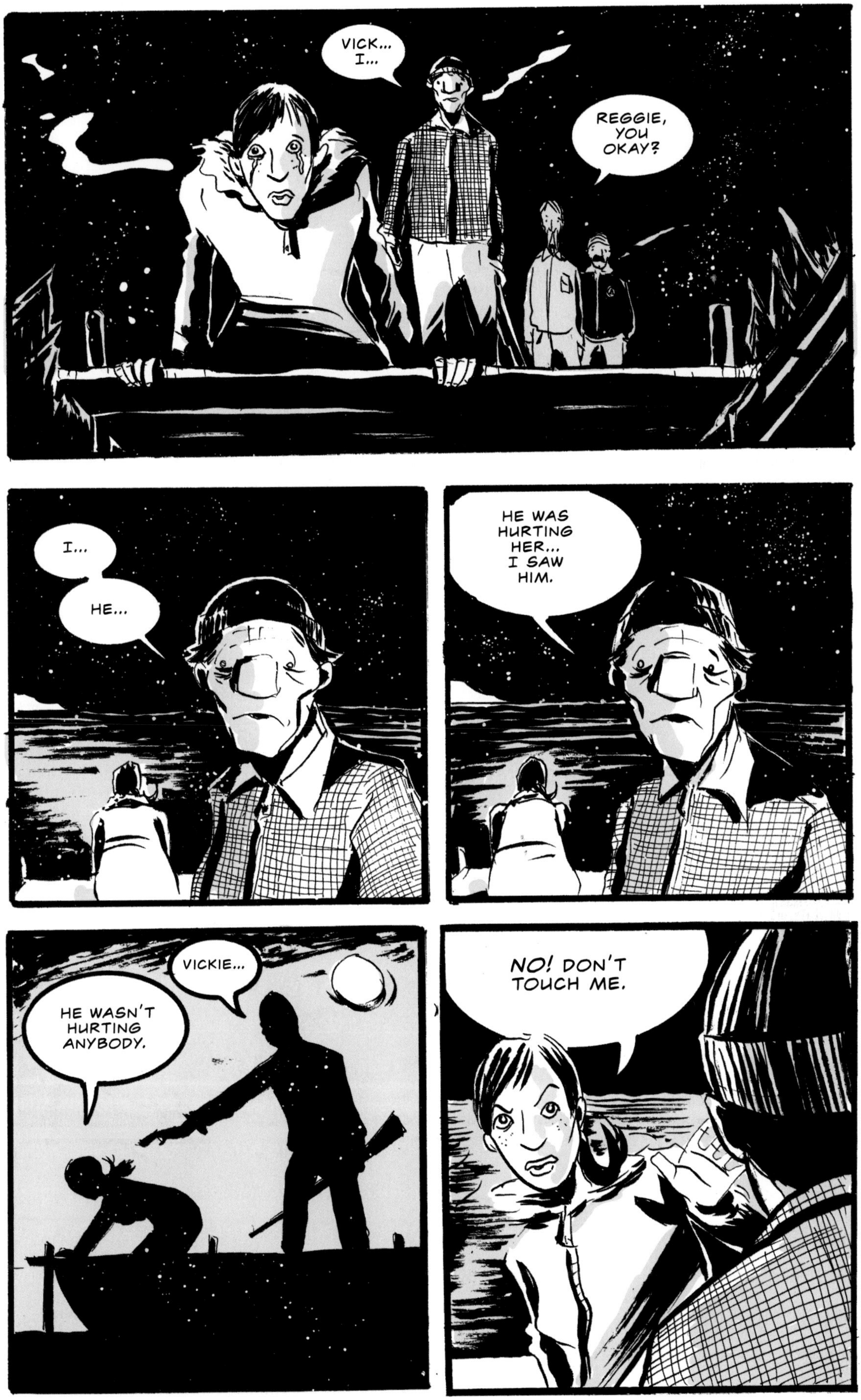
VICK...
I...
REGGIE, YOU OKAY?
I...
HE...
HE WAS HURTING HER... I SAW HIM.
VICKIE...
HE WASN'T HURTING ANYBODY.
NO! DON'T TOUCH ME.

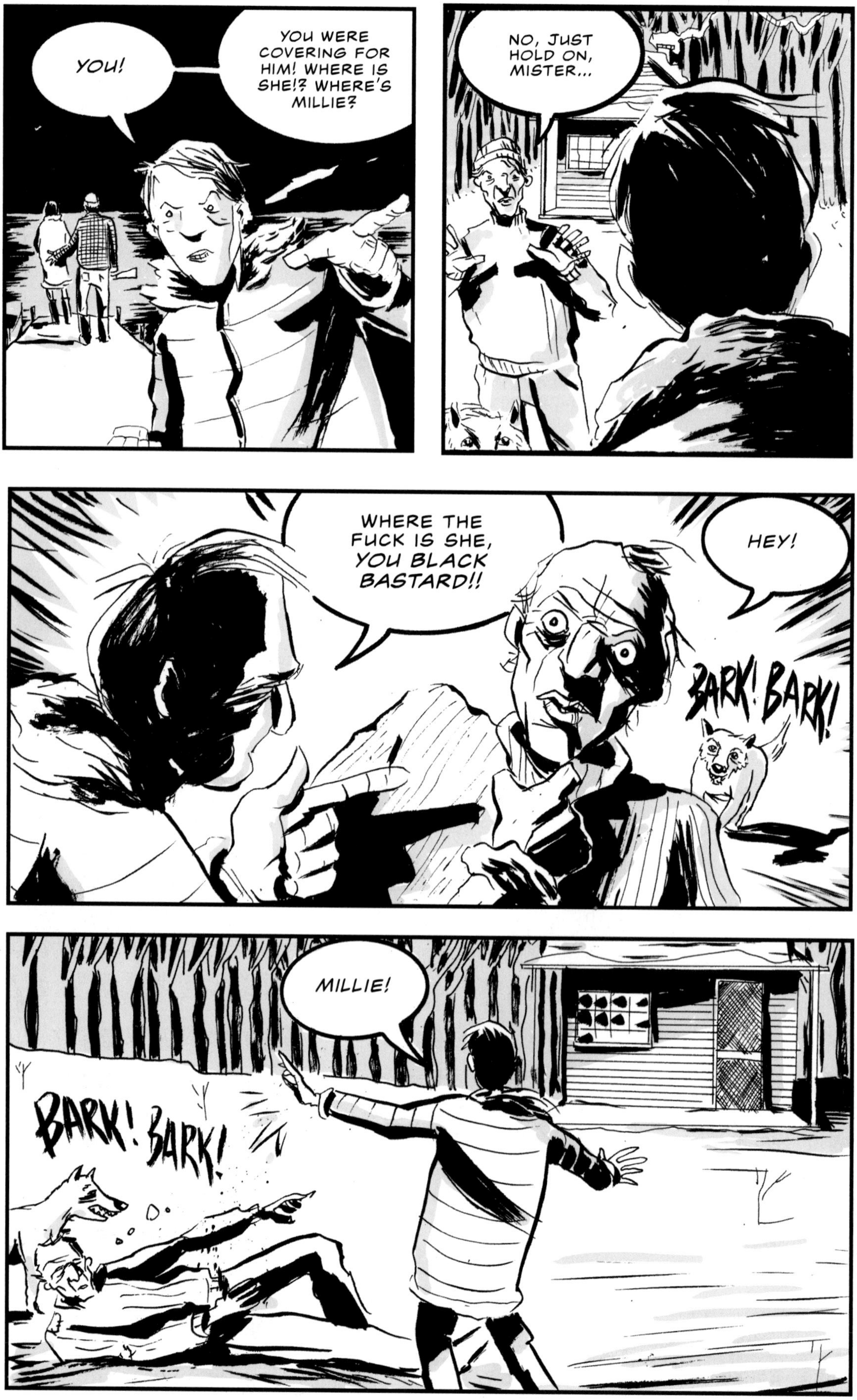
YOU!
YOU WERE COVERING FOR HIM! WHERE IS SHE!? WHERE'S MILLIE?
NO, JUST HOLD ON, MISTER...
WHERE THE FUCK IS SHE, YOU BLACK BASTARD!!
HEY!
BARK! BARK!
MILLIE!
BARK! BARK!

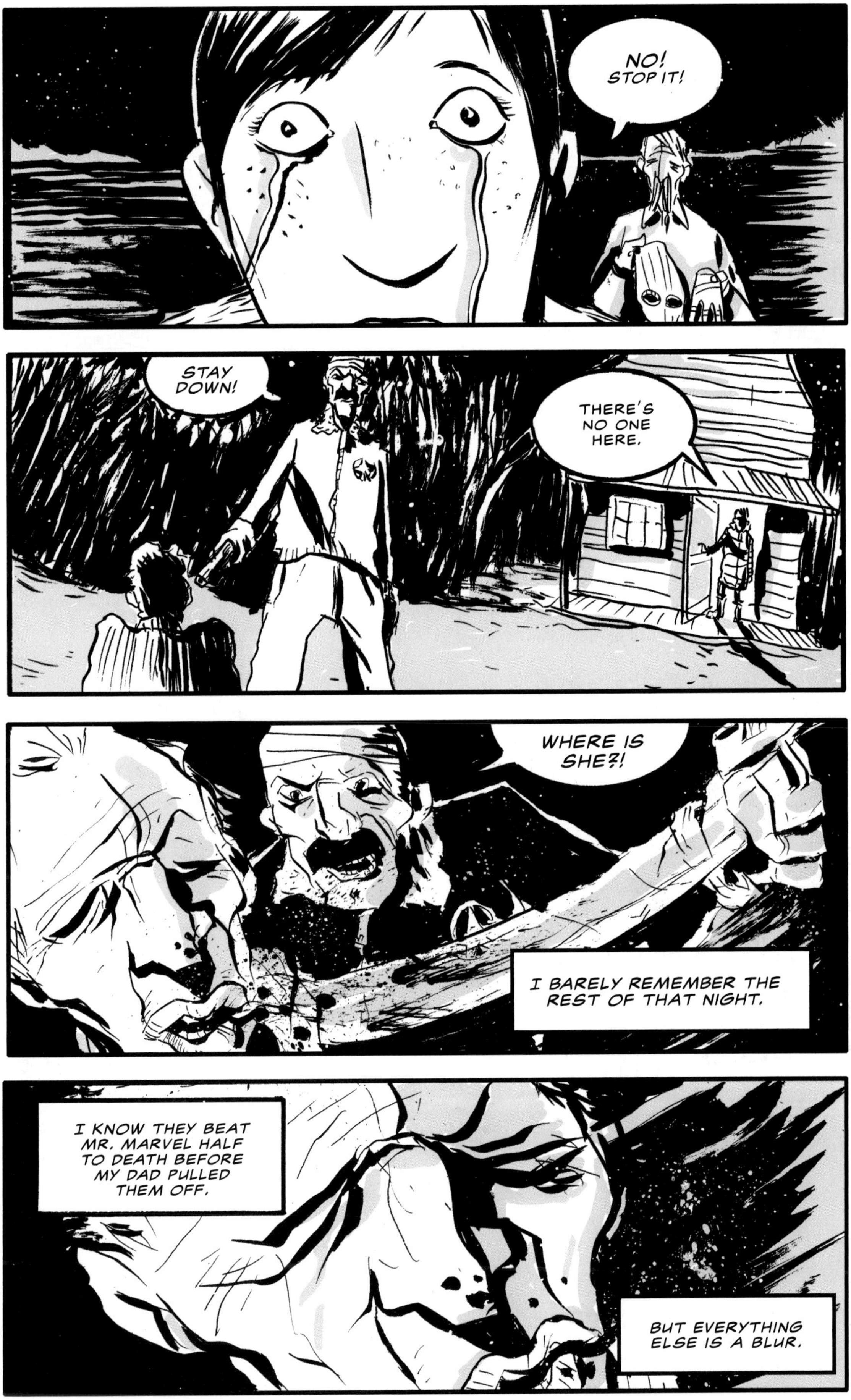
NO! STOP IT!
STAY DOWN!
THERE'S NO ONE HERE.
WHERE IS SHE?!
I BARELY REMEMBER THE REST OF THAT NIGHT.
I KNOW THEY BEAT MR. MARVEL HALF TO DEATH BEFORE MY DAD PULLED THEM OFF.
BUT EVERYTHING ELSE IS A BLUR.

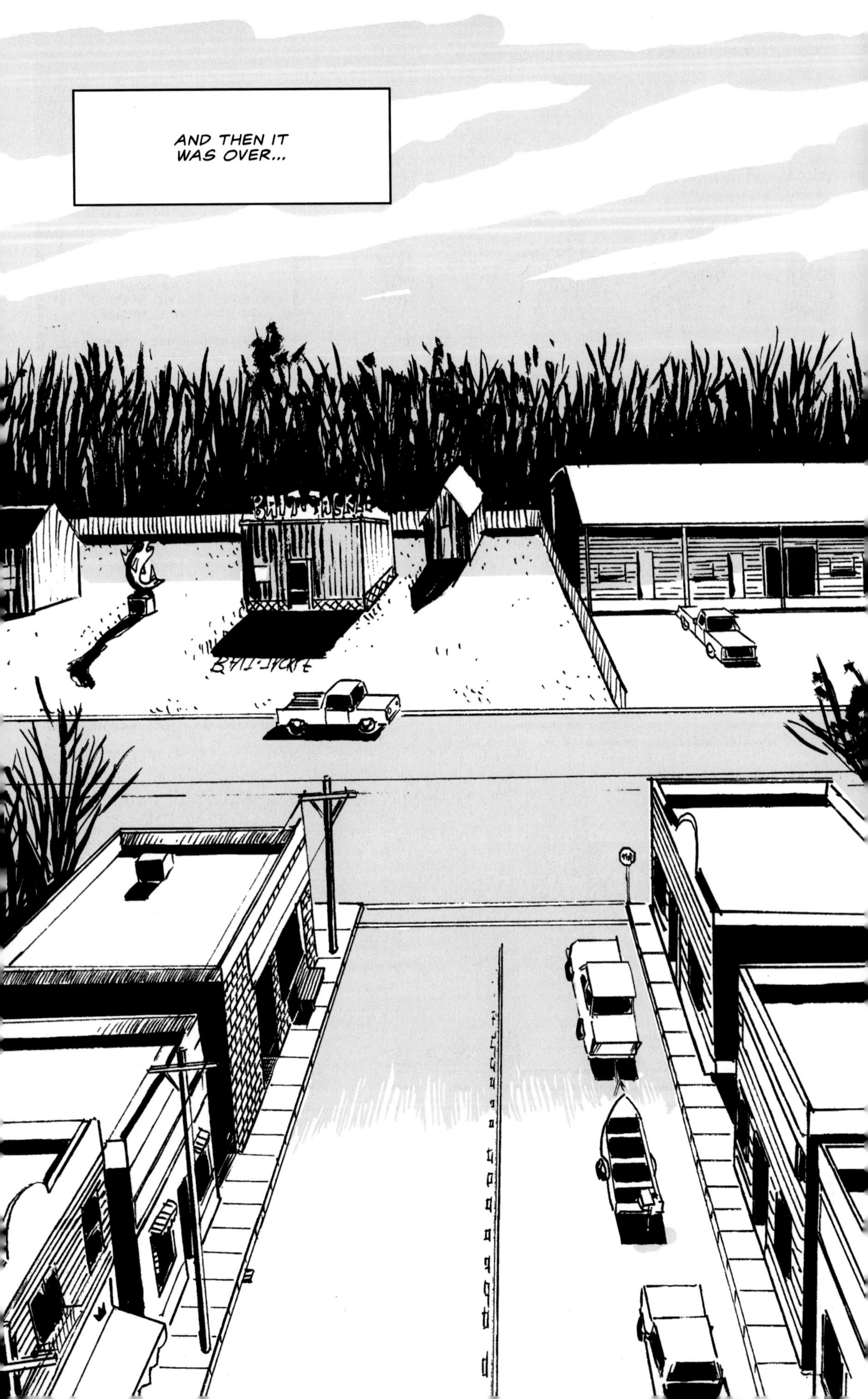
AND THEN IT WAS OVER...

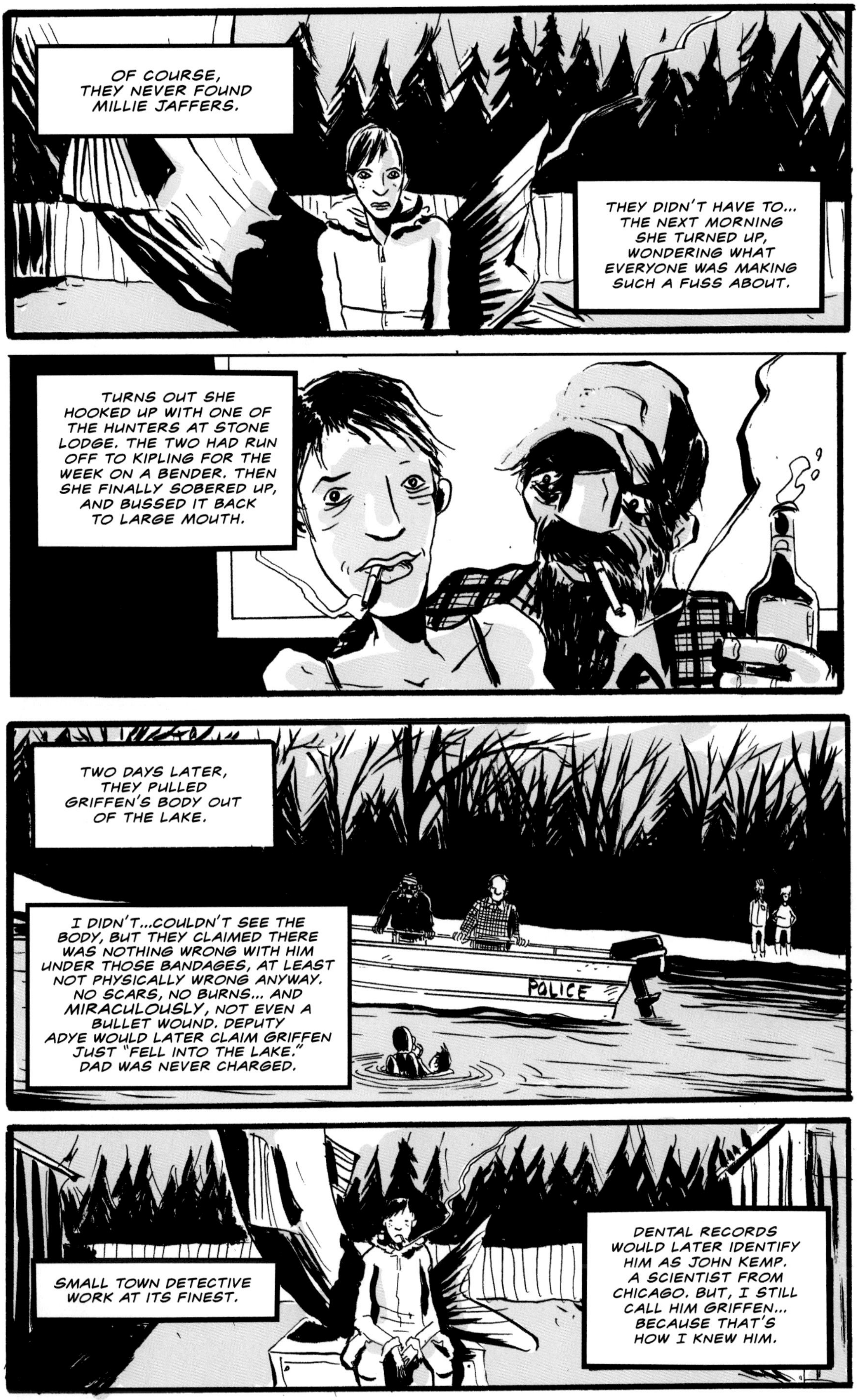

OF COURSE, THEY NEVER FOUND MILLIE JAFFERS.
THEY DIDN'T HAVE TO... THE NEXT MORNING SHE TURNED UP, WONDERING WHAT EVERYONE WAS MAKING SUCH A FUSS ABOUT.
TURNS OUT SHE HOOKED UP WITH ONE OF THE HUNTERS AT STONE LODGE. THE TWO HAD RUN OFF TO KIPLING FOR THE WEEK ON A BENDER. THEN SHE FINALLY SOBERED UP, AND BUSSED IT BACK TO LARGE MOUTH.
TWO DAYS LATER, THEY PULLED GRIFFEN'S BODY OUT OF THE LAKE.
I DIDN'T...COULDN'T SEE THE BODY, BUT THEY CLAIMED THERE WAS NOTHING WRONG WITH HIM UNDER THOSE BANDAGES, AT LEAST NOT PHYSICALLY WRONG ANYWAY. NO SCARS, NO BURNS... AND MIRACULOUSLY, NOT EVEN A BULLET WOUND. DEPUTY ADYE WOULD LATER CLAIM GRIFFEN JUST "FELL INTO THE LAKE." DAD WAS NEVER CHARGED.
POLICE
SMALL TOWN DETECTIVE WORK AT ITS FINEST.
DENTAL RECORDS WOULD LATER IDENTIFY HIM AS JOHN KEMP. A SCIENTIST FROM CHICAGO. BUT, I STILL CALL HIM GRIFFEN... BECAUSE THAT'S HOW I KNEW HIM.

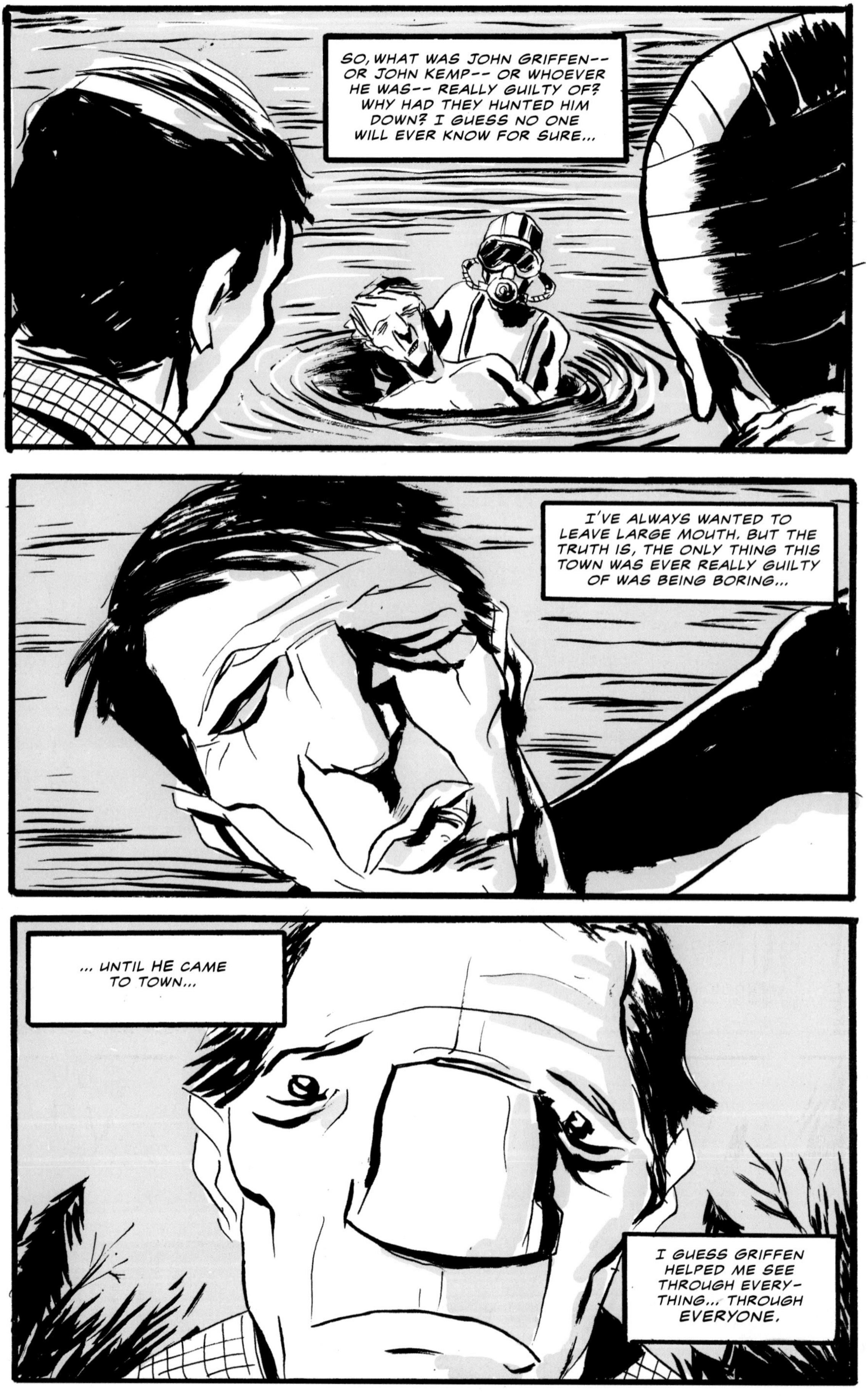
SO, WHAT WAS JOHN GRIFFEN-- OR JOHN KEMP-- OR WHOEVER HE WAS-- REALLY GUILTY OF? WHY HAD THEY HUNTED HIM DOWN? I GUESS NO ONE WILL EVER KNOW FOR SURE...
I'VE ALWAYS WANTED TO LEAVE LARGE MOUTH. BUT THE TRUTH IS, THE ONLY THING THIS TOWN WAS EVER REALLY GUILTY OF WAS BEING BORING...
... UNTIL HE CAME TO TOWN...
I GUESS GRIFFEN HELPED ME SEE THROUGH EVERY-THING... THROUGH EVERYONE.

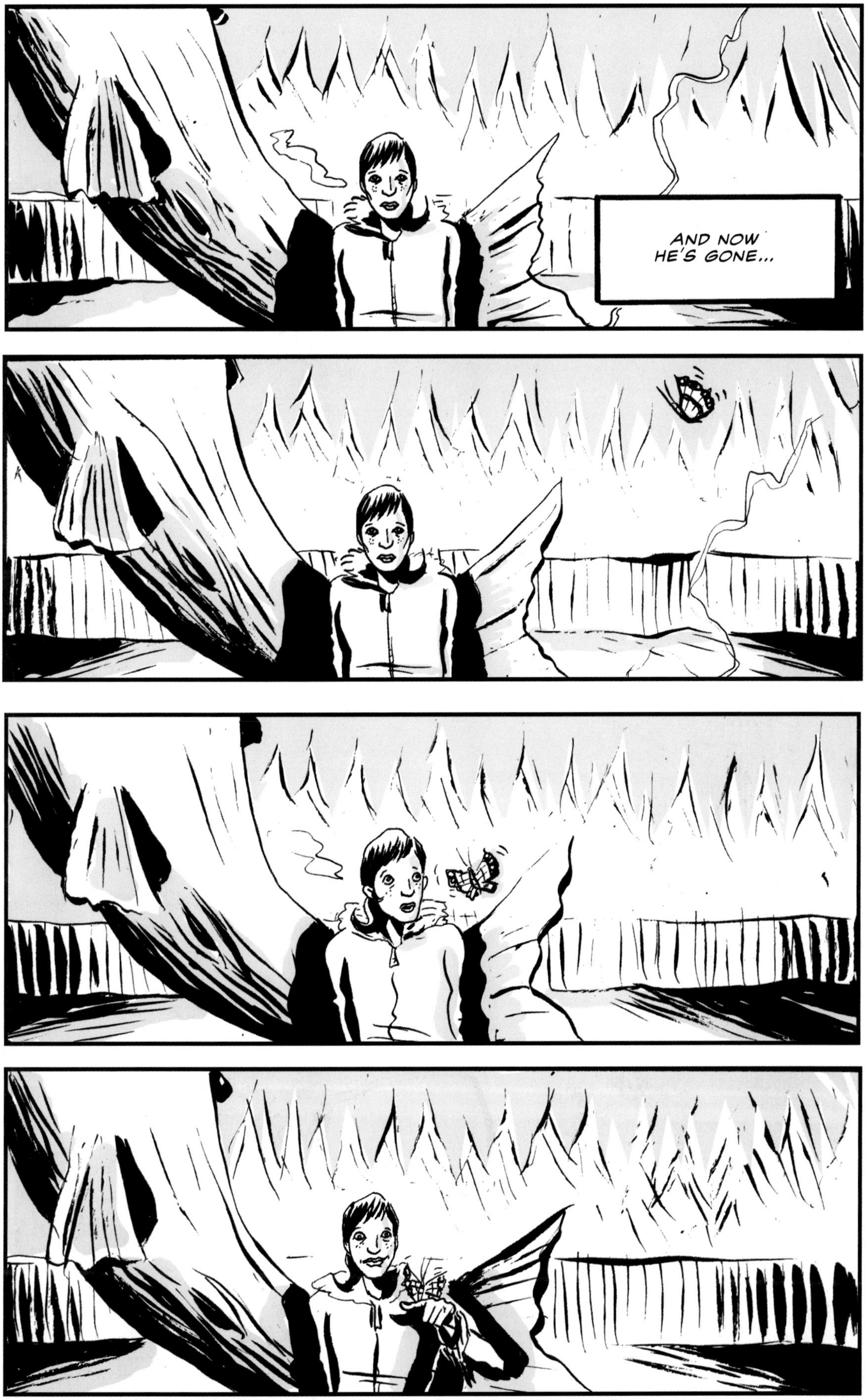
AND NOW HE'S GONE...

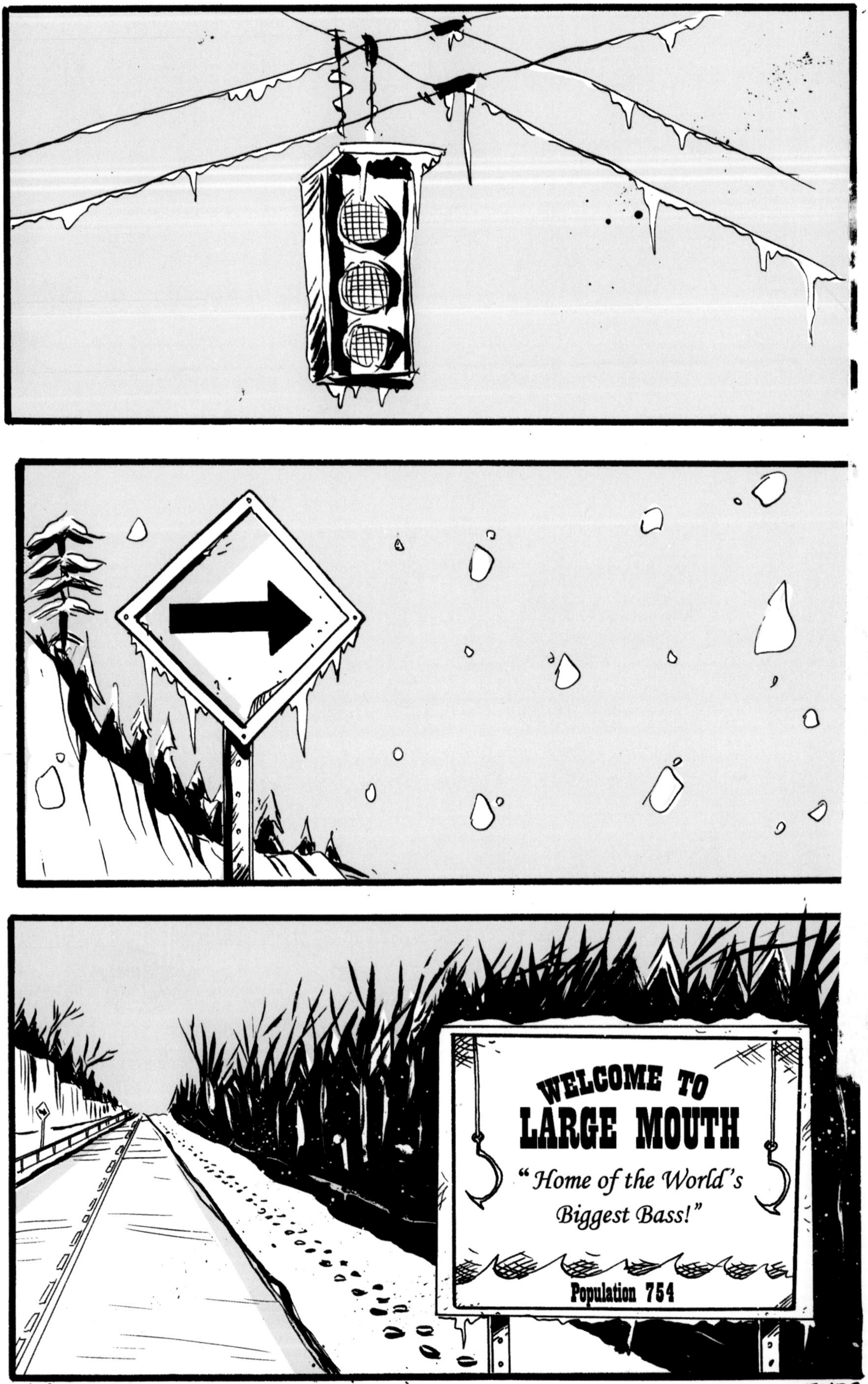
WELCOME TO
LARGE MOUTH
"Home of the World's
Biggest Bass!"
Population 754

END?

THE END

JEFF
LEMIRE

Born and raised in a tiny Canadian farming town, Jeff Lemire now lives and works in Toronto with his wife, son and three cats.

Lemire's previous graphic novels include the Eisner and Harvey Award-nominated *Essex County Trilogy*. In 2008 Jeff also won the prestigious Alex Award from the American Library Association, recognizing books with specific appeal for both adults and teens, as well as the Shuster and Doug Wright Awards recognizing the best in Canadian comics.

With *The Nobody*, Lemire is proud to add to DC/Vertigo's fine tradition of bandaged protagonists, from The Unknown Soldier to the Doom Patrol's Rebus.

Praise for Jeff Lemire's Essex County Trilogy

"Indy book of the year!"
— **Blair Butler, G4tv/ Attack of the Show**

"Truly inspired work... firmly establishes Lemire as one of the premier storytellers in the graphic arts "
— **The Oregonian**

"A great graphic novel ...
I had tears in my eyes when I was done."
— **USA Today**

"Is it too soon to say that Lemire is a major graphic novelist?"
— **Booklist**